# CONTEMPORARY AMERICAN CRAFT ART

# CONTEMPORARY AMERICAN CRAFT ART

## A COLLECTOR'S GUIDE

BARBARA MAYER

GIBBS M. SMITH, INC.
PEREGRINE SMITH BOOKS
SALT LAKE CITY

First edition

Printing: 91 90 89 88 87   5 4 3 2 1

Copyright © 1988 by Barbara Mayer

A Peregrine Smith Book, published by
Gibbs M. Smith, Inc., P.O. Box 667,
Layton, UT 84041

Design by J. Scott Knudsen

Printed and bound in the United States of America

Photo credits: front cover, back cover,
flaps

**Library of Congress Cataloging-in-
Publication Data**

Mayer, Barbara, 1938
    Contemporary American craft art.

    Includes index.
    1. Decorative arts—United States—
History—20th century—Collectors and
collecting. 2. Handicraft—United States—
History—20th century—Collectors and
collecting. I. Title.
NK808.M39   1988   745'.0973'075   87-12945
ISBN 0-87905-284-8

Front cover: *Leather Mask* by Dominique Caron
    *The Wedding: Lover's Quilt #1* by Faith Ringgold
    Border of *Sleeping: Lover's Quilt #2* by Faith Ringgold
Back cover: *Rose Doré Macchia Set with Antwerp Blue Lip Wraps* by Dale Chihuly,
        photo by Dick Busher
    *Frontier Vase* by Anne Kraus, photo by Vincent Lisanti
    Leg detail, table by Richard Scott Newman, photo by Northlight Studios
    *Choker #71* by Mary Lee Hu, photo by Richard Nicol
Back flap: Photo by John Voorhees

# DEDICATION

For
Blanche Carson
and
Gordon M. Mayer

# TABLE OF CONTENTS

# FOREWORD

Collecting can be a passion for many—even an obsession. For others it is a more conscious, controllable hobby—a chosen interest in owning a particular type of thing, the search for which affords a great deal of pleasure.

I'm not a collector, but an accumulator. My parents always said that I'd become a junkman because I was always dragging home someone else's castoffs, sure that a wooden chair or worn-out watering can still had value or could be made into something useful. But instead of becoming a junkman, I went to work at the Smithsonian Institution—sometimes called the "nation's attic." There, people's castoffs, as well as their valuable collections of art, do have value in telling a nation about its history and culture.

During the fifteen years I directed the Renwick Gallery, (the center for American craft art in the Smithsonian's complex of national museums), I got to know many collectors. Whether they collected Navajo rugs or contemporary glass sculpture, they taught me something about the collecting impulse. Some collectors end up giving their collections to museums. Others even collect with museums in mind.

I'm thinking right now of Edward "Bud" Jacobson, a Phoenix attorney who is also a cultural leader in his city. He has chosen the museums of Phoenix as the beneficiaries of his charitable efforts just as other civic-minded donors choose a hospital or university as a favorite charity. But Jacobson doesn't collect only money for museums, he collects objects. When he realized that the Heard Museum, with its wonderful American Indian collections, could use a collection of African art, he set about collecting it. He also collected French drawings for the Phoenix Museum of Art, and when I met him, he was learning all about turned wood bowls and collecting the best contemporary examples to give to a museum.

Though Jacobson is methodical in studying whatever he has decided to collect, his study is not without love of the objects he buys. That is essential to collecting and, in fact, governs why and how most collectors get involved. Few begin as rationally as Jacobson.

Robert and Jean Pfannebecker have one of the nation's most impressive private collections of contemporary American crafts. Unlike Jacobson's effort to buy at least one turned bowl by every American master, the Pfannebeckers have collected a number of objects by a few artists, starting when the artists were very young—some still in college. Bob Pfannebecker likes to spot new talent, and began to develop what museum people call "in-depth" collections of work by several artists. Though the Pfannebeckers responded initially to the talent of their young discoveries, their ongoing friendship with artists has increased the joy they take in collecting. Many collectors especially enjoy sharing through friendship the creative spirit with which the artists fill their work.

How does someone become a collector? Most collectors seem to begin by looking at things — by shopping, really. It may be a beautiful ceramic bowl at a craft fair that will be just right for that vacant spot on the mantel. Or it might be a glass candlestick that will complement the good china. But the shopper keeps on going to other stores, craft fairs or galleries, and there are always new, interesting or beautiful things for sale. If the buyer has money to indulge fantasy, more of those wonderful objects come home and are displayed proudly. It isn't a collection yet, but it soon will be one.

Many of the lenders of objects to Renwick Gallery exhibitions didn't think of themselves as collectors. They just liked ceramic bowls, or objects decorated with frogs or sculptural baskets. When they realized that there seemed to be an affinity among the objects they purchased, it dawned on them that they had become *collectors*.

Now this is serious business. When one acknowledges that he or she is a collector it is necessary to learn more about the kind of object that is collected, and to buy books and subscribe to magazines written for collectors. For some collectors, such as a friend who collects only teapots, a huge antique show is as much a lure as a contemporary craft gallery. It is the type of object — not the specific material or period — that interests him. For this collector, meeting and talking to antique dealers is as much fun as visiting potters in their studios. He enjoys seeing what each has that he might want to purchase. This is part of the social fun of collecting.

For other collectors there are clubs of like-minded folks, and for every organized kinds of collectors — such as those of dolls or contemporary crafts — there are national and international organizations, with conferences and newsletters. Their meetings might feature speakers on advanced levels of connoisseurship pertaining to the favored collectible, round-table discussions, cocktail parties and other social events to provide an informal exchange of information.

Serious collectors of contemporary crafts seem to be a fairly new phenomenon. People have collected antique crafts for years and some of them, like Henry Ford and Henry Francis duPont, established museums that resulted from their passion for early American crafts and other objects. Collectors of contemporary crafts can be as varied as those interested in antiques. In the field of ceramics alone, I know one collector who has only vessels and sculpture by Frans Wildenhain. He has hundreds of them in all shapes, sizes and glazes. Another has only bowls, bottles and tableware by American potters. Still another collects ceramic sculpture with human figures, usually with satirical imagery.

Just as individual collectors may look at crafts with a particular point of view, so do museums. Several museums may collect the same kind of object, but with quite different viewpoints. For example, Tiffany glass is often found in the decorative art collections of American art museums. But you can also find it in the design collection of the Museum of Modern Art, in the American Craft Museum collection exemplifying artistry in our nation's craft heritage, and in the Smithsonian's National Museum of American History in a gallery on the history and technology of glass.

Museum curators may be valuable allies to collectors because it is their responsibility to keep current in fields where they collect. However, it is also true that museum curators often have such broad responsibilities that they cannot keep up with everything, and must concentrate on a particular area. Collectors with a special devotion to a single medium or style of work may eclipse museum curators with their knowledge and connoisseurship; such individuals often are more diligent than museums in developing reference libraries of books, magazines and exhibitions catalogues. You may find that museums will be interested in a collection you have assembled with the educated taste this book may help you to develop. Just look at the museums bearing their founders' names—Freer, Walters and Terra, among others—and you will see where a collecting passion led. Other museums boast collections on a single subject or type of work given to them by dedicated collectors. The Goodman collection of American art pottery given to the Cooper-Hewitt Museum in New York; Joan Mannheimer's contemporary ceramic collection, a gift to the University of Iowa Museum of Art; and the Sperry collection of ceramics by Gertrud and Otto Natzler in the Los Angeles County Museum of Art come immediately to mind. Still other collectors enrich museums with single important objects, identifying themselves forever as discerning collectors who chose to share their love of art with others.

Don't ever think that you cannot develop the ability to select, and buy, art that a museum will want for its collection. In years of visiting private collections and looking at objects for exhibitions, I have seen many large collections. But I have also been taken by an artist to see a collector having only a single superb example of the artist's work—one so important it had to be included in a retrospective exhibition. Few collectors can afford, as Joseph Hirshhorn and Patrick Lannan did, to buy an artist's entire show and select favorite pieces later. But anyone with the interest and patience to look, think and evaluate before buying a single object can make a significant purchase.

It amazes me that only a few years ago prints, then photographs, were recognized as significant art to be collected. Then the prices escalated. Generally speaking, objects in the crafts media—basically clay, glass, fiber, metal and wood—remain undervalued. I believe that will change, too.

Can craft be art? Of course! Anything that humans produce with skill and creative ingenuity can be art, whether a building, a table or a spoon. Objects that are made for use are often categorized as "decorative art" by museums, but that doesn't denigrate the quality of the designer-maker's artistry. In fact, I personally believe that a beautiful and original object that fulfills functional requirements deserves admiration beyond that given to an object that only has to *look* wonderful.

Much of what American craftspeople are designing and making today compares favorably with the best historical examples. They are producing the heirlooms of tomorrow—refined or stunningly original in design, and meticulously made. And, unlike much of the best painting, drawing and printmaking, these craft objects are still affordable to beginning collectors. I hope that after reading this book you will look anew at American crafts (if you're not already collecting in this field), and enjoy the pleasure of owning a piece of today. Remember, Chippendale chairs were once modern, too.

Lloyd E. Herman

# ACKNOWLEDGEMENTS

Writing this book has introduced me to the worlds of artists, collectors, museum and gallery professionals and some of the critics and scholars who keep track of and interpret the activities of all the others. I met invariable kindness in each of these worlds and acknowledge with pleasure that many individuals along the way helped make this book better than it would otherwise have been.

Every writer should be lucky enough to have an editor like Laura Tringali. Her suggestions unfailingly improved the manuscript and her contributions substantially increased lucidity. I will always remember with great pleasure her editorial care and personal qualities of humor and enthusiasm.

Nothing seemed to be impossible for Madge Baird, editorial director at Gibbs M. Smith, Inc., a publishing house whose actions speak louder than words for the fact that they care deeply about books. I also thank Frank J. Cook, director of publicity, for his cooperative guidance and interest in having this book reach a wide audience.

My agent, Henry Dunow of Curtis Brown Associates, is a staunch ally and has been untiring in his efforts on behalf of this book.

I want to thank the American Craft Council's helpful librarians, the South Salem (N.Y.) Library staff for numerous kindnesses and the Westchester Library System and its interlibrary loan service.

Many individuals have a place in my heart and memory for the help they gave me, but for a work which took more than four years to prepare, it would be impossible to mention all by name. Apologizing in advance for undoubtedly leaving out some names, I would like to mention a few of those who helped me.

Among those who read some or all of the manuscript and offered helpful suggestions were Axel Horn, Daniel Jacobs, Derek Mason, Tom Patti, Joanne Polster, Carol Sedestrom and Rosanne Somerson. I am grateful to Lloyd Herman for correcting some errors of fact that would otherwise have remained undetected.

I also thank Louise Allrich, Jamie Bennett, Ruth Braunstein, Karen Chambers, Garth Clark, Lia Cook, Julie Schafler Dale, Robert Ebendorf, David Ellsworth, Michael and Douglas Heller, Bebe Johnson, Jack Lenor Larsen, Lili Lihn, Mark Lindquist, Vanessa Lynn, Shirley Mathews, Eleanor Moty, Sylvia Netzer, Lee Nordness, Robert Pfannebecker, Elaine Potter, Narcissus Quagliata, Mary Roehm, Mary Ann Scherr,

Robert Sedestrom, Ruth Snyderman, Paul Stankard, Blair Tate, James Wallace, Anne Wilson and Richard Zakin. Each of these individuals went beyond simple courtesy to respond to my questions and to offer elucidation or special help.

Among collectors (other than those already named) who were kind enough to share with me their point of view were the following individuals: Anne and Ronald Abramson, Helen Bershad, Michael and Kathryn Brillson, Karen Johnson Boyd, Judy Coady, Jane Corman, Andrew Heineman, Ruth Julian, Sue and Malcolm Knapp, the late Sy Kamens, Gail and Harold Kurtz, Andrew and Virginia Lewis, Vincent Lim, Nancy McNeil, Elmerina and Paul Parkman, Chris Peterson, the late Barbara Rockefeller, Warren Rubin and Bernice Wollman, Esther Saks, Dorothy and George Saxe, Judith Schwartz, Jean and Hilbert Sosin and Robert Tooey.

I acknowledge gratefully the galleries and artists who provided photographs. Readers who wish to know more about these artists should contact the gallery listed. If there is no gallery, consult the resources section in chapter 3 for leads.

Every effort has been made to identify and credit photographers for the photos they took. If there have been inadvertent omissions, they will be corrected in future editions upon notification.

Robert Eben-
dorf's bead
invites the
viewer to touch
and caress it.
*Silver Bead*,
1985, 2 inches in
diameter. (Photo
by Bob
Hansson.)

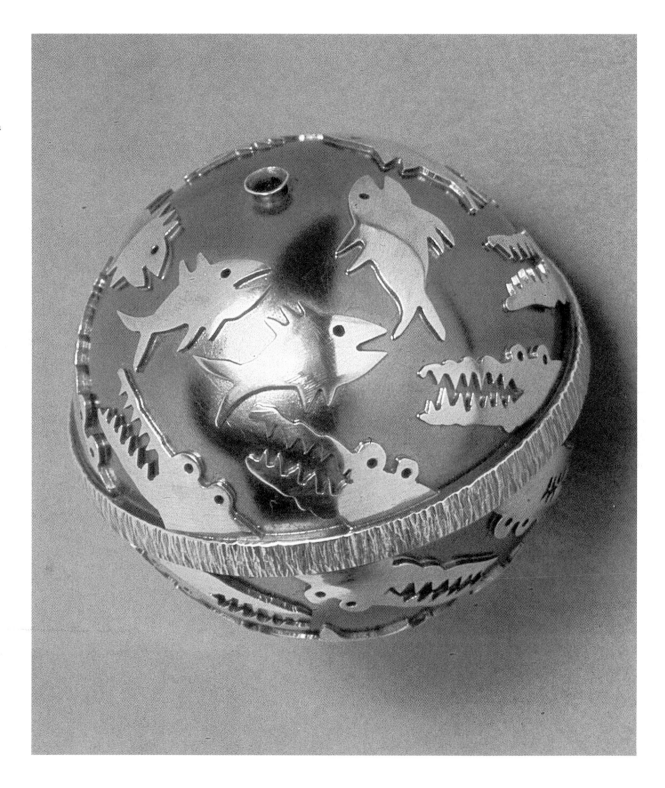

# INTRODUCTION

I first became aware of crafts as a special category of products one sunny day in June in the mid 1970s. In the course of my duties as a reporter, I attended the annual craft fair in Rhinebeck, N.Y., sponsored by the American Craft Council. I had visited the Dutchess County Fair Grounds in the past to attend annual county fairs each August. But this time, instead of prize bulls, sheep, chickens and 4-H exhibits, the rustic barns and livestock pens held some of the liveliest and most wonderful objects for display, living and personal adornment that I had ever seen. Furthermore, these fascinating items cost no more than the mass-produced variety normally found in stores—some even cost less.

As I walked around the sprawling grounds and talked to craftsmen and their customers, I was struck by the unusually joyous atmosphere. It seemed enough for many exhibitors that viewers appreciated and understood their work, while those who were buying acted as if they were receiving a gift, instead of parting with hard-earned money.

I went back to my office imbued with the desire to tell everybody about this wonderful new world I had discovered where creativity and car-ing were part of every single object for sale. At the time, of course, it didn't occur to me that I had just come face to face with an extraordinary cultural phenomenon—the American Studio Craft movement—or that eventually I would devote four years of my life to writing about it.

After that first craft fair, I attended many others and visited the growing number of shops and galleries specializing in studio crafts. When I began this book I had a great deal of enthusiasm, but little knowledge of the shape of the contemporary craft movement. My idea was to describe the many kinds of crafts available, to give some guidelines about buying, using and enjoying them and to tell the story of the development of contemporary craft.

As is so often the case, fools rush in where angels (and experienced travelers) fear to tread. Eventually I learned that my simple goal was akin to sitting on top of one mountain and deciding to take a stroll over to the neighboring peak. It turned out to be a much longer and more complicated trip than I had anticipated.

The biggest challenge was finding information. As you will read, handicraft has been an important part of our culture, but it has been so taken for granted that nobody has written much

Tom Loeser's trays transform with imagination and color the conventional idea of a tray. *3 Trays*, 1987. Painted ash and walnut, largest 28 inches. (Photo by Andrew Dean Powell.)

about it. The story of the development of crafts is buried in primary sources such as defunct publications and first-person accounts. Some information is found in books that are really about something else. The rich material from the 1930s to the 1960s exists mainly in the memories of the participants, who proved to be among my best sources. In retrospect, finding and interviewing these people were among the most exhilarating parts of the research.

As I read and talked to collectors and craftsmen, I found a more interesting story than the one I originally set out to tell. I saw that divisions were occurring. Some craftsmen are channeling their energies into producing multiples, either as small manufacturers or by designing for others, while other practitioners have set their sights on an artist's life, pursuing their muse wherever it takes them. Those who buy crafts also have a variety of motives, which can range from selecting a distinctive, good-quality functional item like a teapot or chair, to choosing a work of art that will have heirloom status.

I soon discovered that the differing goals of craftsmen have created a dialogue (which sometimes sounds like an argument) among various factions, as each strives to express its point of view. The word craft has many different possi-

Displaying and using Karen Karnes' subtly colored covered vessel would enrich a collector's daily life. *Stoneware Vessel*, 1982. Wood-fired stoneware, 13 × 14 inches. (Photo by Joshua Schreier.)

ble interpretations, and whenever I said I was working on a book about American crafts, it was always necessary to add several sentences of clarification. Most people guessed I was writing about crafts as a hobby and would tell readers how to make things. Some thought of the folk crafts of the past. A number were a little surprised to learn that the craftsmen I would be writing about are individuals whose education and interests classify them as artists.

But is their work art? You have only to ask this question to cast an immediate pall on any group of craft enthusiasts. To treat crafts as art requires a willingness to go beyond traditional narrow definitions of art and craft, but it is a leap well worth taking and one that is being validated by growing public acceptance. Many craft objects elicit an immediate intuitive response from viewers. They are powerful, moving and evocative and therefore embody the highest aesthetic achievements of fine art. Yet they retain the celebration of the object that is inherent in any craft work.

I have no wish to participate in intellectual slugging matches, exchanging definitions like punches. But I have noticed that the material of which it is made is often the subject of many art objects in craft media. The choice of materials

Nance O'Banion's mixed media work employs vibrant color and a tangle of wire to convey a personal vision of home. *Hot House*, 1987. Bamboo, paint and wire, 14 × 15 × 13 inches. (Photo by Jacques Cressaty, courtesy of The Allrich Gallery, San Francisco.)

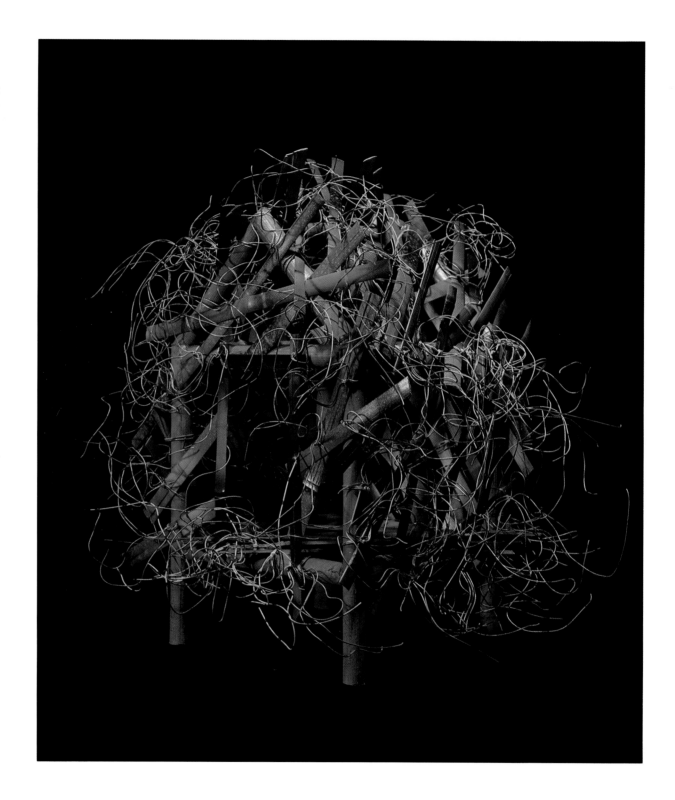

In Michael Glancy's hands, the techniques of sandblasting and electroforming glass have produced an evocative art object. *Magna Eclipsed,* 1986, 8 inches tall. (Photo courtesy Heller Gallery, New York.)

and the way those materials are handled are as much a part of a piece's identity as the conceptual ideas it contains. As well as being an end in itself, the mastery of materials and processes provides contemporary craftsmen with a vocabulary for communicating their artistic vision. It seems to me that this synthesis of pure craft and fine art leads to craft art. This term is preferable as a description to the term decorative art, to which the ceramic, glass, fiber, wood and metal arts traditionally have been confined.

In 1946, which is the date usually advanced as the beginning of the contemporary American Studio Craft movement, there was disdain in intellectual circles for interdisciplinary studies, American culture and the selection of craft media by artists. All appeared to be garments stitched together of fragments. Intellectually, the orthodox areas of study such as history, social science, literature and art were considered to be more worthwhile. Our polyglot culture appeared to be ill-placed to compete with that of ancient Europe. And craft media appeared to bear too close a relationship to domestic and industrial usefulness to contain artful statements.

Today, interdisciplinary studies and Ameri-

Though abstract, Ferne Jacobs' fiberwork invites the viewer to speculate on the nature of the human figure. *Red Figure Column*, 1986. Coiled, twined thread, 19 inches tall.

can cultural icons are so dominant that many say the pendulum has swung too far. American art, music, clothing, food, heroes, films and television are glorified all over the world. Craft art is approaching acceptance.

The lesson in this progression of attitudes is that values change. Objects are part of the value system of the culture in which they were created, but they also stand outside it if they survive. They are almost certain to have a different meaning to future societies. As the arts are handed down, we reassess their value for our own time. Since objects have a survival value, collecting them has merit even beyond the immediate pleasure they offer. Crafts collectors are participating in the richness of contemporary life, but they are also preserving art that might otherwise be lost for future consideration.

If craft art collecting seems different from collecting painting and sculpture, it is not surprising. Unlike these arts whose best examples are usually found at high prices primarily in New York and a few other large cities, craft art is not necessarily a big-city phenomenon. Academia and art institutions outside the major urban areas have provided the most hospitable setting for the pursuit of craft art. As a result, both craft artists and the galleries and museums where the best work can be seen are dispersed. Collectors may travel across the country in search of objects of merit.

Craft art has heretofore not been so noisy as other art forms. But the depth of its roots and the breadth of interest in making and looking at it have created a strong plant that has flourished regardless of critical attention, or lack of it. In the meantime, collectors are providing their money, time and energy to preserve and care for the art in their keeping. Through their commit-

Peter Vandenberge's ceramic sculpture is profoundly humanistic. *The Bird Watcher*, 1981. Stoneware, 35 × 17½ × 15½ inches. (Photo by Malcolm Varon, collection of Daniel Jacobs.)

Through the use of unconventional materials, in this piece Marjorie Schick expands on the concept of what jewelry is. *Bracelet,* 1985. Painted wood and rubber, 4¾ × 5 × 3 inches. (Photo by Joel Degen, courtesy Helen Drutt Gallery, Philadelphia.)

ment, others will enjoy the rich treasure that is found in today's craft art.

Besides illustrating the great variety and imaginative quality of today's work, this book offers some suggestions about how to pursue that commitment. By its end, you will have had access to formal knowledge of craft art, as it might be conveyed in a course, and also to the practical tips, pointers and even gossip that collectors can supply. You will have read about how to buy from a gallery and commission work from artists, how to recognize and evaluate aesthetic and tech-

nical quality, how to build and improve a collection, how to shop and pay for, insure, conserve and display the craft art in your home.

I hope the book's impact will also be to advance the acceptance of craft art by showing it and by placing it in its historic context. As I see it, reframing the "is it art" question is the next order of business for craft art. But while aestheticians and art historians are delving into these arcane realms and analyzing the essence of craft art, the rest of us can simply enjoy it.

Craft artists find subjects in daily life, as Terrie Mangat's quilt illustrates. *Covington Slickers: Rainy Days in Cincinnati*, 1981, 76 × 84 inches.

This haunting ceramic work by Jack Earl is at the same time a celebration of the American experience and an exploration of the darker side of the myth. *Ohio Chair,* 1979. Ceramic, 6 × 3½ × 3½ inches. (Photo by Bernard Handzel, courtesy Theo Portnoy Gallery, New York, collection of Daniel Jacobs.)

Though it is part of the ceramic tradition in glazing technique, Robert M. Winokur's salt-glaze stoneware vase is spiritually a work of the present. *With Wings: Priapus Variations,* 1986. Salt-glaze stoneware, wood-ash glaze, 20½ inches tall.

CHAPTER ONE
# A NEW TYPE OF ART, A NEW TYPE OF COLLECTOR

Even those having only a nodding acquaintance with modern art are likely to have heard of the 1913 exhibition at the New York Armory, when European Post–Impressionist works were shown publicly in the United States for the first time. The paintings and sculptures by artists such as Pablo Picasso, Marcel Duchamp and André Derain enraged some in the art establishment and were ridiculed by many among the large public who went to see them. But there is a clear moral and a happy ending to the tale.

The exhibition *did* stir tremendous opposition, but a result of the controversy was that many saw the work, struggled to understand it and a countermovement supporting the new art was organized. Eventually even some of the most hostile critics accepted the upstart. Soon thereafter, the former revolutionary became respectable, successful, loved by all and very rich.

This art-world Horatio Alger tale is being repeated today in the American craft revolution, which has as great a potential for changing the established order.

Crystal balls work better when applied to the past. It is easy to see that the Armory exhibition which occurred more than seven decades ago was a turning point in the acceptance of modern art. Although so far craft art has had no comparable symbolic event, with time it will be possible to identify the epochal occurrences responsible for changing the course of its history. But for now, craft art appears to be in an ambiguous position and skirmishes won in one arena are simply reopened elsewhere. To some embattled artists working in craft media, change is too slow in coming. They and their supporters insist their work should be evaluated and judged purely as art, for it makes aesthetic statements, contains conceptual and intellectual ideas, challenges and reorders perceptions and expands the viewer's vision. The creators of this work therefore claim full identity as artists.

Among collectors who hold this point of view is Daniel Jacobs. "I have never understood what discussions of craft are all about. I have always felt that I collect art, art in any medium. To me the expression of a creative person is art and what form it takes is not important; nor is the means by which it is expressed. I respond to the work itself," he said recently.

These ideas are still being challenged by some

Michael Lucero's ceramic work illustrates that art knows no material boundaries. *Pink Nude,* 1984. Ceramic, 19 × 25 × 21 inches. (Courtesy Charles Cowles Gallery, New York, collection of Daniel Jacobs.)

members of the art establishment. Craft art is thus denied entry into some of the most prestigious museums, or at best treated as a poor relation. Rarely are funds made available for its purchase or exhibition. Following this pattern of discrimination, the most established art galleries may choose not to represent individuals working in craft media. Publications may refuse to review craft art exhibitions and the work may not figure in many master's and doctoral theses.

The most common reasons advanced for rejection include lack of time and funds. Museum curators and art critics point to their overloaded calendars, to the impossibility of keeping up with burgeoning numbers of painting and sculpture exhibitions and artists. Only the rare museum has resources to add a new curatorial department to a typically overburdened roster. Furthermore, the craft tradition of usefulness does not encourage the self-conscious practices of the curator and art critic. Even today, the first definition of craft is dexterity. An attribute that distinctly characterizes a craftsman is the deep and overriding respect for technical skill, which must be acquired before venturing into creative expression.

Yet handicraft, so far as we know, has always furnished artful as well as practical objects. Archeological investigations show that the slipping and burnishing of pottery, for example, were developed to make pots more aesthetically pleasing. It is speculated that objects of use, such as the hammer and the mace, the bowl and the beaker, eventually became ritualized as objects of art. Through use in daily life, examples of these objects were endowed with spiritual meaning.[1] Buried with King Tutankhamen, for example, were miniature iron tools, household furnishings and jewelry.

The English designer and philosopher William Morris is among those who have traced the intellectual schism of craft and fine art to the Renaissance, when a distinction began to be made between useful forms and those having no purpose other than to please the senses. Painters and sculptors then and later sought to separate themselves from the restraints of guild systems and to ally themselves with literature and the liberal arts. Maintaining these distinctions led to an economic advantage for painters who sought princely patronage.[2]

By the 18th century, craft skills revealing

Harvey K. Littleton's sculpture clearly relates to art, not to drinking glasses. *Red/Blue Sliced Descending Form*, 1984. Glass, 12½ × 10¼ × 5½ inches. (Photo by Jon Littleton, courtesy Heller Gallery, New York.)

to social equality with his patrons, while Chippendale did not.[3] Reynolds' writings served to justify his practices as a painter and practitioner of fine art. Chippendale composed a directory to provide practical guidance to his fellow craftsmen. Reynolds' title indicates that his status was more elevated than Chippendale's. Yet their clients were members of the same families. Today, as tacit admission of the spuriousness of the distinctions between craft and art, the works of both men are in the same museums.

Art historian Penelope Hunter-Stiebel traces a prejudice against decorative arts to the 19th century, when the great art collections became bureaucratized and professionals took over their management, divorcing collecting from sensuous enjoyment. Three-dimensional objects that can be handled and caressed are to many collectors more satisfying than paintings. But curators were too busy carving up territories and specialties; they had minimal interest in caressing what they didn't own, said the former Metropolitan Museum curator.

From her vantage point, that simple adjective *craft* is a stumbling block to acceptance. Craft art shares this descriptive word with rural crafts, folk crafts and functional crafts—brooms and mugs and storage jars. Today's craft art bears about the same relationship to this kind of work as Rembrandt's paintings do to the output of Sunday painters. "It creates confusion that both share the name of craft. The Harvey Littletons of this world are not concerned with making a set of drinking glasses," Hunter-Stiebel points out.

But although many people are disturbed by the descriptive adjective *craft*, it is a perfectly acceptable term that recognizes the historic framework of current work and calls attention to its objectness.

dexterity and virtuosity were established as one class of behavior and art making as another. Even though skill at laying down paint and creating sculptural forms was appreciated, it was the intellectual or spiritual content of art that most impressed viewers.

Comparing the careers of Thomas Chippendale and Sir Joshua Reynolds, art historian Edward Lucie-Smith notes that Reynolds aspired

Taking the long view, craft art is making steady, if slow, progress, says Hunter-Stiebel. "It took 40 years for Art Deco to be accepted as art. Craftsmen *are* gaining recognition, especially from collectors and others who love their work, even if not from many curators." She is correct, of course. More Americans and international collectors are devoting ever larger amounts of money to buy increasingly more costly craft art objects. The collectors' willingness to buy the work is encouraging more galleries to take on craft artists and more museums to show and collect their work, especially as collectors encourage this with gifts and financial support. In a survey for the National Endowment for the Arts in 1983, over 90 percent of 259 participating museums said they had a craft art exhibition within the last ten years.[4]

In 1985, a number of major museums reported craft accessions. They included the Brooklyn Museum in New York, The Nelson-Atkins Museum of Art in Kansas City, Mo., the High Museum of Art in Atlanta and the Oakland Museum in California. The Brooklyn Museum, for example, updated a 2,000-piece collection of early American ceramics with the purchase of contemporary works by Rudy Autio, Wayne Higby, Ken Ferguson, Beatrice Wood, Christina Bertoni, Rick Dillingham and Maija Grotell.[5]

Examples of some important recent museum exhibitions of craft art include the Whitney Museum's presentation of Viola Frey's ceramic figures and Claire Zeisler's fiber works, and Boston's Museum of Fine Arts' ceramics exhibition, all in 1984; Jack Lenor Larsen's fabrics at the Louvre in 1984; and in 1986 a show of Dale Chihuly's glass sculpture at the Musée des Arts Décoratifs in Paris. When the new 20th-century

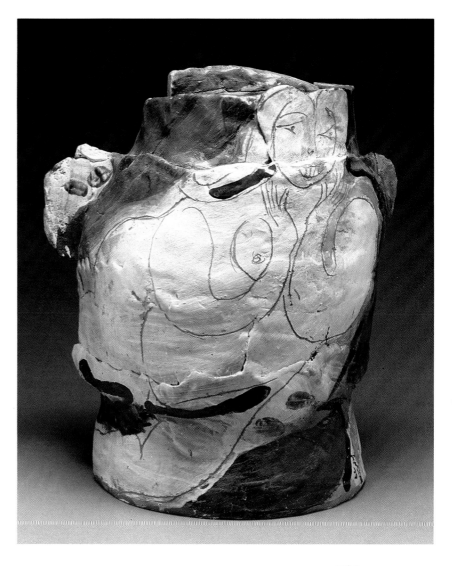

wing opened at the Metropolitan Museum of Art in 1987, a permanent installation of craft art (albeit along with industrial design) was included.

Major historic exhibitions of craft art were held in 1986 and 1987. They include the Metropolitan's investigation of the Aesthetic Period of the late 19th century and early 20th century, the Brooklyn Museum's look at machine forms in art during the early to mid-20th century

This expressionist work by Rudy Autio has roots in 20th-century art. *Smiling Lady*, 1979. Ceramic, 23 × 19 × 13 inches. (Photo by Eric Shambroom, collection of Daniel Jacobs.)

The strange and fascinating breaks and glaze patches on Rick Dillingham's pot (1985) suggest timeless endurance. Dillingham's ceramic work has recently been acquired by the Brooklyn (N.Y.) Museum. (Photo by Herbert Lotz, courtesy Nina Freudenheim Gallery, Buffalo, N.Y.)

and, in 1987, the Museum of Fine Arts' (Boston) comprehensive look at the Arts and Crafts movement in the late 19th and early 20th centuries. Also in 1987, the Everson Museum of Art in Syracuse, N.Y., revived its regular ceramics exhibitions known as the Ceramic National.

Other examples of the growing acceptance of craft art can be gleaned from newspaper and magazine listings of crafts exhibitions, which are now more likely than in the past to be located in the art sections than in the women's pages and style sections, and occasional reviews of those exhibitions. Secondary markets are also slowly developing as dealers are asked to locate early examples of artists' work to fill in collections. In auction listings and antiques publications, early to mid-20th century ceramics, furniture and glass are ever more frequently included.

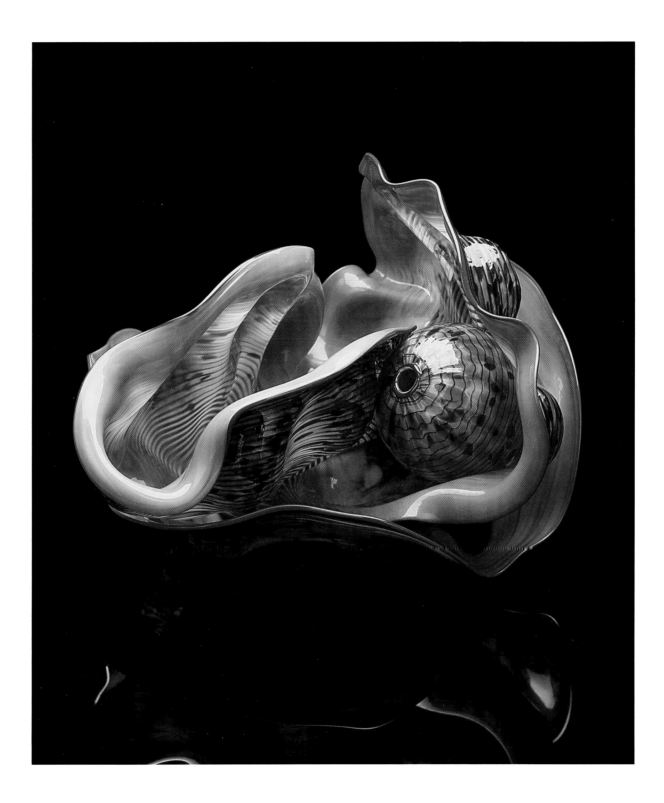

Sheer physical beauty exerts a powerful appeal, as this bio-morphic blown glass form by Dale Chihuly illustrates. *Rose Doré Macchia Set with Antwerp Blue Lips,* 1986, 7 × 6 × 10 inches. (Photo by Dick Busher.)

Craft artists often employ the teapot form in nonfunctional objects, as does Philip Cornelius in this work. *Independence Pass*, 1985. Porcelain, 12 × 9½ inches. (Photo courtesy Garth Clark Gallery, Los Angeles / New York.)

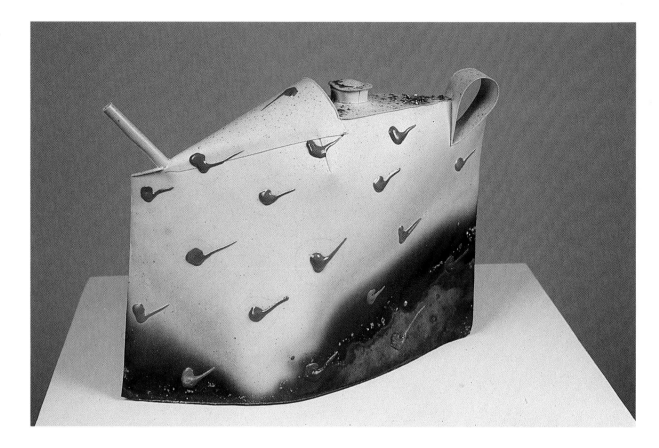

The seeming contradiction between the perception of lack of interest and the very real activity can be resolved by noting that despite many individual examples of acceptance, craft art collecting is still in the pioneering stages and attitudes toward it tend to zigzag back and forth from the old (it is a lesser category of work) to the new (it deserves to be treated as art). For example, when the American Craft Museum reopened in a new museum space in October of 1986, the *New York Times* accorded the opening considerable attention. They sent an arts writer to cover the inaugural exhibition, and then ran the review in the newspaper's Thursday Home section. On the other hand, another story about the museum opening appeared in the Sunday Arts & Leisure section under the headline, "But Is It Art? The Always Tenuous Relationship of Craft to Art."[6]

This indecision represents a very real dilemma for some people who wonder if a teapot or a plate can also be art. Are nonfunctional objects resembling teapots and plates art? Do objects made by those who call themselves craftsmen and who sell to stores qualify as art? If it is not in all the museums, do we dare put it on a pedestal? These questions and similar ones continue to preoccupy individuals inclined to discuss them. But a growing self-confidence is evident as articles appear in the journals urging an end to such speculation and an assertion of a right to equality.

Commentators point out that in this country from colonial times on, the dividing line

Finding beauty in materials others call trash is a characteristic many craft artists share. This turned wood vessel by Mark Lindquist is made of rotted wood. *Unsung Bowl Ascending*, 1982. Spalted maple, 18 × 16 inches. (Photo by Paul Avis, collection of Mrs. E. J. Kahn.)

Precious materials worked with consummate skill are frequently chosen by craft artists, as this piece by Mary Lee Hu illustrates. *Choker #71*, 1987, 18 and 22K gold. (Photo by Richard Nicol.)

between art and craft has never been rigid and crafts provided a means of entry into art. For example, both Benjamin West and John Singleton Copley started as craftsmen and went on to paint pictures. Today, craftsmen may become artists and decide not to paint pictures, but to continue exploring reality in craft media.

And yet it is a fact that craft art is incredibly diffuse, defeating clear categorization. Media are intensely varied. Craft artists have pressed into service every type of clay and fiber, plastics, rubber and spare parts.

Woodworkers may work with rare veneers, rotten pieces of decayed wood or boards salvaged from old pieces of furniture. Jewelers may produce gold or silver pieces embellished with gemstones or fashion a necklace out of safety pins or cellophane. Glass workers create with hot glass and a blowpipe or they pour melted glass into molds or they melt glass sheets and bend them into new configurations. Some choose plate glass or colored glass, etching or painting it. Ceramists may form earthenware or porcelain or stoneware by hand, in molds or on the wheel. One craft artist fires his clay pieces at a local hobby shop.

Nor does philosophy necessarily unite today's craft artists. Historically, the goals and values of the contemporary craft movement arose in the 19th century, from a deep fear that the Industrial Revolution and mass production would allow machines to dominate and change human beings for the worse. In his groundbreaking book published in 1944, *Language of Vision*, art theorist Gyorgy Kepes recounts the concern expressed by English philosopher Thomas Carlyle, social theorist and art critic John Ruskin and later William Morris with "the devastating consequences of . . . machine production to creative activity and thus to the life of man." Kepes summarizes the 19th-century predicament:[7]

> *The increasing mechanization of production, with all its compulsion of uniformity, rapidly led to the disappearance of real craftsmanship based upon respect for the truth of material, tool, and maker. . . . This disregard of the inherent qualities of tools and materials became a dangerous epidemic in every field of human endeavor. From the making of the simplest, every-day object to the widest dimensions of expression, a false attitude was dominant. Not only did it stamp out all rhythmic pleasure in the making, the enjoyment of the work, but it also eclipsed the understanding of the materials and tools.*

From the vantage point of the 1980s, it seems clear that dire predictions of the imminent loss of creative power to machinery have not been proven accurate. We live in desperate times, but

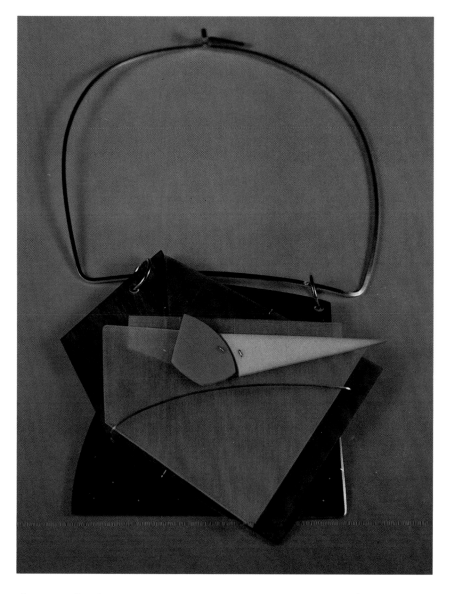

the growth of the number of artists, art collectors, art amateurs and museums suggests that a machine culture does not necessarily stifle human creativity. Many contemporary craft artists in fact rely on machine techniques, bearing witness through their work to the concerns of the society in which they produce. A few examples are the use of electroforming pioneered by jewelers

**Alice H. Klein's *Starlight* (1986) necklace combines acrylic and plastic laminate with sterling. Mixing the precious and nonprecious is a theme in craft art.**

Stanley Lechtzin
pioneered the use
of electroforming
to create jewelry
that, though
large, is light
enough to wear.
*Cameo Corsage
#83D*, 1979.
Cast acrylic, elec-
troformed silver,
gilt and pearls,
6¼ × 3¾ × 3
inches.

such as Stanley Lechtzin in the 1960s and Vernon Reed's use of microchips for moving images in jewelry. Glassmaker Linda MacNeil employs industrial grinders to make sculpture and Susanna Lewis creates wearable art on knitting machines.

These are early efforts, however, and integrating the positive aspects of machine production with humanism remains an important, largely unrealized task. Craft artists, because of their firm grounding in technical skills, may be best placed to undertake this task. In the face of a social dilemma posed by a culture that depends on machines to produce material possessions and a high level of physical comfort, and that appears to depreciate the capacity of the single individual working alone, craftsmen have chosen to reassert control through mastery—in Kepes' words, by "searching for renewed contact with the pulsation of the dynamic forces of nature's processes."

Another important ingredient contributing to the diversity of today's craft art movement is the range of credentials of the craft artists themselves. Some have graduate degrees and teaching positions. Some are self-taught. Some were the contemporary equivalent of wandering minstrels only 20 years ago. Today, they have galleries and groupies. Some refuse to be known as artists and insist on calling themselves craftsmen; others with the same training answer only to the name of artist and may refuse to be in an exhibition modified by the adjective *craft*.

Considering some of the contradictions and complexities, Lee Hall, former president of the Rhode Island School of Design, which has harbored and graduated a number of craft artists, described the current situation by noting that "a new breed of object grows now in a juncture between art and craft. While akin to both craft

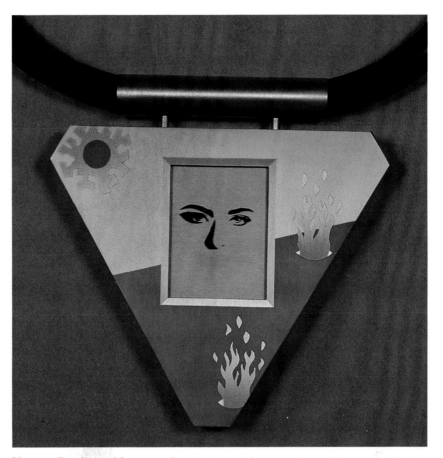

Vernon Reed's necklace reveals moving random numbers. Viewers hold the microcomputer-generated patterns in memory to see the whole image. *Visage Mnemonique,* 1987. Titanium, acrylic, rubber and electroplated brass, 3½ inches.

and art, these objects refuse to serve purposes traditionally associated with craft and simultaneously refuse to yield their meaning when subjected to strictly defined ideas about art . . . They tell me that my unchallenged mode of looking has lost its effectiveness. I see vessels that will not hold anything. I see fabrics that will not submit to use as a covering for the body or adornment for furniture. The new objects step forth out of the skilled workmanship commonly associated with craft. Whether they exist as decoration or as sym-

Knitting machines make highly detailed images possible in fiberworks, as in this piece by Susanna Lewis. *Flight Path Poncho*, 1980. Machine-knit wool yarn, 54 inches wide. (Photo courtesy Julie: Artisans' Gallery, New York.)

bols, it is the power of their presence that links them to art and obscures their relationship to the tradition of craft."[8]

Hall's statement is certainly true, yet one cannot discount history. Explaining the importance to him of his material's traditions, metalsmith Jamie Bennett said that "my work is about the tradition of the material in which I work in the same way that a poem about a rose is really about poetry, not about the rose. The rose is simply a convenient material for voicing the poet's feelings about poetry."

Growing out of the functional tradition, one

of the most important attributes of craft art is its accessibility to everyone. A cup, for example, can be counted on to trigger memories, historic and metaphorical associations—the morning cup of coffee, the family's cups and saucers and the times they were used, the fascinating inconsistencies of a cup made of fur.

It is no accident that the growth in the number of craft artists and their audience coincided with changes in the traditional art world and, according to Lucie-Smith, reflects a human need that was not being met by art. Today craft art satisfies "the hunger for physical virtuosity in the

Industrial grinding tools have been employed by Linda Mac-Neil in this multi-media work. *Tri Form Construction,* 1985. Glass, polished granite and gold-plated brass, 12 inches square. (Photo by Susi Cushner.)

Irvin Tepper's *I'm Happy . . . If You're Happy* porcelain cup made in 1986 invites the viewer to ponder the cup as a metaphor. (Photo courtesy Vanderwoude Tananbaum Gallery, New York.)

handling of materials."[9]

Functional crafts are easy to understand since they relate to use. As one continues to explore a medium, either as appreciator or artist, more abstract forms often become familiar and interesting. But it is possible to enter the process at any point, from the pleasure of wielding a handmade pocketknife to admiration for its design; from enjoyment of the use of a cup to appreciation of its color, pattern and shape. One can have a complex relationship to objects of use and can come to a recognition of art through use.

Craft artists object to an attitude they perceive in the art establishment, which implies that objects coming from a tradition of use are unfit to carry additional meanings. But reflection will easily prove that any material or form can be imbued with philosophical value. However, in seeming despair some craft artists have requested that the craft tradition be eliminated from consideration of their work. This is probably an error, for traditions have an awesome power to stimulate, and a subtle but still meaningful play between past and present can imbue an artist's work with power. Typically, craft artists are proud of their traditions and this pride coupled with undeniable talent gives the strength to pursue success on their own terms and to fashion a new chapter in art.

Are craft artists doing uniquely important work and healing the uneasy rift that has existed since at least the Renaissance? Are they creating a new synthesis in which craft is taken as a matter of course and art is the result when a strong personal vision illuminates the created object? Four years of reading and looking at objects and talking to artists indicate to me that some individuals are well on the way to accomplishing this extraordinary mission.

I f the artists are breaking new ground, so are the collectors of craft art. The American soil grows collectors. Stamps, coins, plates, figurines, miniatures, dolls, baseball cards, political memorabilia: The list is almost endless. Early collectors such as J. Pierpont Morgan, Isabella Stewart Gardner and the Havemeyers were among the American elite; their personal collections have filled America's great museums. These men and women were possessed by the art they assembled and later gave the nation.[10]

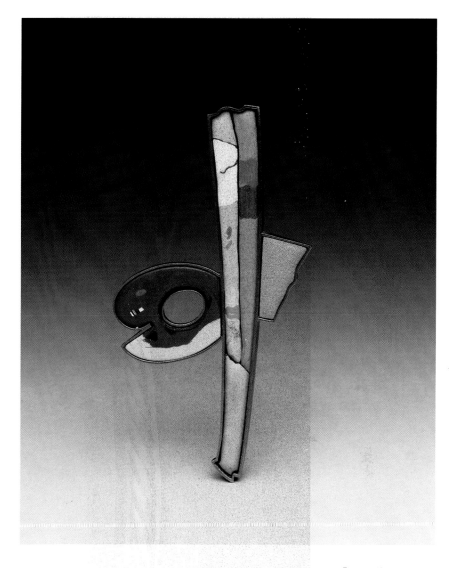

Some of today's craft art collectors are also possessed by a desire to make a contribution to art and to safeguard important artifacts of our era. But there are important differences between them and the art patrons of the past whose collections were often assembled according to the advice of art gurus. For example, today's craft art acquisitors are typically of the middle class and, in art, self-educated. Some started with a single,

Jamie Bennett's enameled brooch combines form, texture and color to create surface interest. *Coloratura,* 1985, 4¼ inches tall. (Photo by Andrew Dean Powell, private collection.)

We can know the past only through a distorted mirror, this work by Lee Schuette and Linda Schiwall-Gallo suggests. *Wobbly Marble Mirror*, 1986. Gilded wood, glass and marbles, reverse glass painting. (Photo courtesy Alexander F. Milliken, Inc. New York.)

Miriam Schapiro's collage is a bittersweet look at the role of homemaking women and their crafts in American life. *Wonderland,* 1983. Acrylic and fabric on canvas, 90 × 144 inches. (Photo courtesy Bernice Steinbaum Gallery, New York.)

humble acquisition—perhaps a coffee mug or piece of jewelry. Then enthusiasm and knowledge grew, changing buying habits, and almost by accident some collectors discovered they were building valuable collections of craft art. Such individuals usually were not raised in a family tradition of art collecting and thus had no concept of the correct way to form a collection. Their emergence as collectors has encouraged a friendly, egalitarian ambience. Within the world of craft art itself—artists, gallery owners and museum curators—is a camaraderie that transcends class. Recently, with the ascending value of many objects, a veneer of sophistication has been applied, but craft art continues to be accessible to everyone.

The craft artists, too, contribute to this atmosphere; many reject traditional art world snobberies. By working in craft media, they have chosen a course they know is not likely to lead to financial success or popular acclaim. The willingness of many craft artists to break with tradition also engenders energy and enthusiasm, both of which are palpable to collectors. "We didn't sit down and say 'let's collect crafts,' but it was the most exciting area of art when we started buying in 1973," recalls Sue Knapp, a New York collector. The content of her remark was echoed in various ways by many collectors.

Others have proffered different reasons why contemporary craft art attracts them: the women's movement, for example. Miriam Schapiro, whose acrylic and fabric collages are composed of motifs found in patchwork quilts, is one of the growing number of artists who incorporate crafts techniques and make no distinction

Anne Kraus' porcelain vase melds the style of the past with the content of the present. The written narrative on the vase tells of a couple who part—the man goes away. On the vessel's back, the woman wonders "if you would be proud of me today." *Frontier Vase*, 1986, 11¼ inches tall. (Photos by Vincent Lisanti, courtesy Garth Clark Gallery, Los Angeles/New York, collection of Daniel Jacobs.)

Physical virtuosity is a characteristic of craft art. This example shows a leg detail on an extension table in figured cherry, maple, ebony and ormolu by Richard Scott Newman. (Photo by Northlight Studios, courtesy Pritam & Eames, Easthampton, N.Y.)

between painting, sculpture and craft media. Schapiro said recently that "women have been responsible for the decorative arts across cultures and throughout history. In all cultures where blankets were made, pots thrown and tapestries woven, this was woman's work."[11]

A new interest in their own history has encouraged women artists to use these traditions in their work, she said. Perhaps the same impulse to honor the work of women through the ages has motivated some collectors to seek out particular crafts.

Throughout the past, leaders of church and state have acquired masterful art objects. But in our own time the amassing of contemporary objects by individuals for their own art collections is probably not much older than a quarter-century. Not surprisingly, since craft art appeared first in academia, several academics are usually mentioned as among the earliest collectors. For example, Professor Fred Marer, at UCLA, and his wife, Mary, began collecting ceramics in Los Angeles during the late 1950s and Professor R. Joseph Monsen, at the University of Washington, began in the mid-1960s to collect contemporary ceramics.

Robert Pfannebecker, a lawyer who started to collect in 1961, is another pioneer. His collection grew large enough to require two additional structures to house some of the overflow. Daniel Jacobs, a partner in a design firm, bought his first ceramics in 1979. His collection of more than 800 ceramic objects has been described as the best of its kind in the country. George and Dorothy Saxe began buying glass in 1980. Today their glass collection is important enough to have been exhibited at the Oakland Museum.

Often collectors can provide little reason for their first purchases. In hindsight they are seen as acts of love and leaps of faith, gratification of a little-understood desire to own the work. Jacobs happened to attend an exhibition of British contemporary ceramics at a New York art gallery. Shortly after that, he left for a trip to England. When he returned home, he had with him 56 pieces of British ceramics. "When I came back from England with those pieces I put all my efforts into finding out about American works which comprise the major part of my collection," he said recently. Jean Sosin became a glass collector in the space of an afternoon by happening into a gallery showing contemporary glass. "That evening I told my husband I had seen something I could study and collect," she recalled.

A number of collectors have said that their life revolves around crafts. Their interests provide a circle of ties and relationships that cross state borders as they travel to meetings and important exhibitions. As Sue Knapp put it, "Collecting crafts is a wonderful way to meet people and have a good time."

Collectors of craft art display the same quality of enthusiasm that distinguished the great early accumulators of art. In a move that might be considered one of genius if it had been conscious, American society has democratized and modernized the collector's role, which was once restricted to individuals of great wealth. This democratization is one of the great strengths of craft art.

## NOTES

1. Herbert Read, "The Origins of Form in Art," essay reprinted in *The Man-Made Object*, ed. Gyorgy Kepes (New York, George Braziller, Inc., 1966) pp. 30-49.

2. For a brief, lucid discussion of the spuriousness of boundaries between craft and art, see Jonathan L. Fairbanks' essay in *Directions in Contemporary American Ceramics* (Boston: Museum of Fine Arts, 1984).

3. Edward Lucie-Smith, *The Story of Craft: The Craftsman's Role in Society* (Ithaca, N.Y.: Cornell University Press, 1981) p. 28.

4. Lisa Hammel, "The Expanding World of American Crafts," *New York Times*, June 28, 1984, p. C6.

5. *American Craft Magazine*, February-March, 1986, p. 70.

6. The article was written by Neal Benezra and appeared in Section Two on Sunday, October 19, 1986. The review of the exhibition by Grace Glueck was in the Home section on October 23, 1986.

7. Gyorgy Kepes, *Language of Vision* (Chicago: Paul Theobald, 1944) p. 188.

8. Lee Hall, "Can Craft Be Art?" *House & Garden*, January 1983, pp. 8 + .

9. *The Story of Craft*, p. 274.

10. Aline B. Saarinen, *The Proud Possessors* (New York: Random House, 1958).

11. Remarks made at a seminar in connection with the "Ornamentalism in Art" exhibition at the Hudson River Museum, Yonkers, N.Y., March 1983.

This piece by Mitch Ryerson shows a wry appreciation of American roots. *Highchair,* 1986. Curly maple, clothespins, washboard and soapbox labels, 43 inches tall. (Photo by Andrew Dean Powell.)

CHAPTER TWO
# THE ROOTS OF THE AMERICAN CRAFT TRADITION

All craft artists are deeply affected by the functional traditions of their media. Perhaps even more important, all Americans have been affected by the central place of the useful crafts in transforming—rather recently at that—a wilderness into a civilization.

Each school child learns in hundreds of anecdotes and stories that invention and artisanry are the basis for all that has been accomplished. Some examples that come readily to mind include the American rifles known as "widow makers"; the cotton gin, steamboat and Conestoga wagon; and Shaker gadgets and furniture. Long before the coming of the colonists, Native American hunting and gathering societies created pottery and baskets whose forms are acknowledged to have nourished today's craft movement.

The American predilection for the useful continued with the first Puritans, who came partly as a protest against privilege. These plain farmers and artisans eschewed high art, condemning it as full of popery. In building a country from an undeveloped land, they relied on the useful arts practically as well as philosophically. Regardless of religious persuasion, early colonists could all agree that "it is more noble to be employed in serving and supplying the necessities of others, than merely in pleasing the fancy of any."[1]

High art would come later and would be based on mastery of practical skills. In 1780, the future president John Adams wrote that "I must study politics and war that my sons may have liberty to study mathematics and philosophy, geography, natural history, naval architecture, navigation, commerce and agriculture in order to give their children a right to study painting, poetry, music, architecture, statuary, tapestry and porcelain."[2]

The idea that the past could be improved on, that the wrongs of European privilege could and should be righted here, was compelling to these early Americans. Some associated purely visual imagery with the pomp of the Church of England, against which they had rebelled. The sensuous shapes and colors of religious art diverted minds from the truth, and John Calvin himself warned against images as ends in themselves. Embellishment of useful objects harnessed art to use; crafts were worthier and more necessary.

An early North Carolina preacher described

This ceramic work by Mark Burns is funny on both a visual and conceptual level. *I Dreamed I Saw A Diamond In The Rough,* 1973, 11½ × 12½ × 15¼ inches. (Photo by Bernard Handzel, collection of Daniel Jacobs.)

some of his fellow colonists: "Men are of all trades and women the like within their spheres. Men are generally carpenters, joiners, wheelwrights, coopers, butchers, tanners, shoemakers, tallow-chandlers, watermen and whatnot; women, soapmakers, starch-makers, dyers, etc. He or she who cannot do all these things will have but a bad time of it."[3] From this versatility emerges a picture of a tinkerer who could make or fix almost anything. The model citizen was a small farmer or artisan who stood or fell on his own resources, who provided for his own needs. Independent, self-reliant, proud, manually accomplished, yet with an interest in learning and social improve-

ment: Similar words have been used to describe craftsmen in the latter half of the 20th century, who set out to find their own salvation in weaving, glass blowing, woodworking or pottery throwing.

Opportunities for economic and social improvement without reference to past origins created a sense of self-worth in Americans and a belief in the individual's ability to improve on the past. These enduring early values have given contemporary craftsmen the courage and necessary egotism to push off in new directions, sometimes against considerable negative opinion.

Whenever the pattern of existence has been

Though in the classical style, Michael Frimkess' ceramic vessel features figures clad in modern sports clothes and riding a bicycle. *Ecology Krater II,* 1976, 26 × 26 × 19½ inches. (Photo by Malcolm Varon, collection of Daniel Jacobs.)

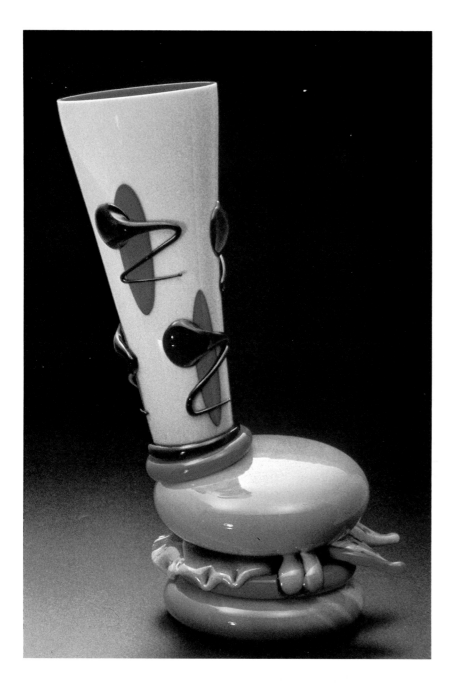

Robert Levin's glass sculpture pays homage to the all-American lunch. *Hamburger Cup #4,* 1986. Handblown glass, 12½ inches tall. (Photo by Dan Bailey.)

threatened, as in the Depression and again in the 1960s, early experiences and values have provided a model for change. Thus, in the 1930s, some socially minded individuals set up crafts cooperatives. Significantly, Aileen Webb, founder of the American Craft Council, first became interested in crafts when she organized workshops in the 1930s to help local residents in Putnam County, N.Y., where she had a summer home.[4] During the 1930s, the federal government also looked to the American craft tradition by establishing the Index of American Design (see p. 46) as part of the Federal Arts Project. Later, the nationwide questioning of purpose in the 1960s produced dropouts and rebels, some of whom turned to crafts to support themselves and to register a protest against contemporary society. A number of today's artists come from this tradition.

Humor has also been an important ingredient in the work of craftsmen. Some examples that come readily to mind include the ceramics of Robert Arneson, Clayton Bailey, David Gilhooly, Howard Kottler, Irvin Tepper and Mark Burns, the jewelry of Fred Woell and the glass of Dan Dailey.

Parallels have been drawn between the Funk movement in ceramics and Surrealism and Dadaism. But Funk, a form of Pop Art that debunked the establishment's most sacred myths, owes as much to an ingrained American love of earthy humor, puns and sarcasm. American fictional characters like Paul Bunyan, Tom Sawyer and that Connecticut Yankee, who visited King Arthur's Court and found it wanting, revealed a lack of respect for august personages and majority values. Some 20th-century American craft artists share the same attitudes. Michael Frimkess' "Ecology Krater II" on which contemporary figures are pictured each riding a bicycle, and Fred Woell's "Class of '85" pin are in the American tradition of humor.

The Bicentennial in 1976 led to a surge of interest in American craft traditions in virtually every corner of the country. Museums and historic buildings were opened, articles and books appeared on past craft traditions, enrollment in craft classes increased and the wide dissemination of information piqued the interest of some of today's craft artists and collectors.

But 1976 was not unique. Earlier celebrations also led to revivals of interest in craft traditions. The 1876 Centennial in Philadelphia, for example, included a reproduction of a simple log cabin filled with handmade objects. Twenty costumed "colonists" conducted visitors through the popular exhibit and explained the uses of the objects on display.[5] About the same time, the Philadelphia Museum of Art was organized to collect and exhibit examples of the technical and artistic achievements of American culture. Among its first acquisitions was a collection of contemporary and early American pottery.

Even though by the mid-19th century industrialism was firmly entrenched, there were always individuals who valued both the expression of craft and the values on which it was based. Eventually, as historian Oliver Larkin has noted, "When the democrats of the 1930s looked back to the Age of Jackson for their inspiration, not the least of their discoveries was the richness, variety and plastic worth of an everyday art which had been forgotten while more ambitious talents competed for patronage and fame."[6]

Folk craft was frequently rediscovered by a receptive public. At the Chicago World's Fair in 1933, for example, a group of weavers from Appalachia demonstrated their skill and sold their handwoven scarves and bedspreads. They

received a warm reception, recalled Lucy Morgan, founder of the Penland School in North Carolina and organizer of the trek from the mountains of North Carolina to the shores of Lake Michigan to publicize the newly established crafts school.[7]

The foregoing examples illustrate that the contemporary craft movement is not a postwar phenomenon as has often been claimed, based on the demands of World War II veterans for relevant cultural education. The ideas on which the craft revival are based are deeply woven into the

J. Fred Woell's funny and biting pin is an example of political and social humor. *Class of '85,* 1985. Silver with a handcut stone, 2½ inches tall.

The American love of the pun is evident in this piece by Joan Steiner. *Iron Hat, 1980.* Handstitched and constructed in satin and faile. (Courtesy Julie: Artisans' Gallery, New York.)

his fabrics and wallpaper) were quickly exported to the United States, where they profoundly influenced American cultural life. Beginning in the 1890s, there was a rapid proliferation of arts and crafts societies and other activities in the Northeast, Midwest and Far West, following the founding of the London Arts and Crafts Exhibition Society in 1888.[8]

In Boston, for example, the Society of Arts and Crafts was founded in June of 1897 and there was a notable revival of silversmithing. *Handicraft* magazine was published by the society beginning in May 1902. It disappeared in 1904 but was revived from 1910 to 1912. The Rhode Island School of Design was founded in 1877.

After the turn of the century, activities intensified in upstate New York. In Buffalo, Charles Rohlfs made furniture that was exhibited all over the world and Paul Wilhelm worked in copper, silver and enamel. In East Aurora, Elbert Hubbard established the Roycrofters craft workshops. In Syracuse, Adelaide Alsop Robineau set up a highly successful ceramic studio and published the magazine *Keramic Studio*; Gustav Stickley produced furniture and edited *Craftsman* magazine, which between 1901 and 1916 carried news across the country of the crafts revival.

In the Midwest, where Morris' fabrics, wallpapers and furniture were available at Marshall Field & Co., the activity appears almost feverish from today's perspective. The Chicago Arts and Crafts Society was founded in 1897. The William Morris Society was organized in 1903. Other groups included the Industrial Art League, founded in 1899, whose membership in 1902 totaled more than 400, and the Illinois Art League, whose Chicago chapter ran workshops in arts and crafts. The League also established industrial art libraries and museums in Illinois and

fabric of American experience.

While today's movement is unique in breadth of media and in the numbers of artists, collectors and galleries, early foundations set the stage for the present. The Arts and Crafts movement of the late 19th century anticipated many of today's attitudes and activities. William Morris led the movement, but Morris's ideas (as well as promoted arts and crafts through publications.

The Chicago Art Institute held annual decorative arts exhibitions between 1902 and 1921, and its first curator of arts and crafts was Bessie Bennett, a working craftsman. The Chicago Architectural Club also held exhibitions at the Art Institute between 1888 and 1928, frequently including decorative arts. The Society of Decorative Arts maintained a salesroom at the Institute, where members' work was sold.

In Chicago's Fine Arts Building were located the Kalo Shop, the Artists' Guild and the Wilro Shop. Elsewhere were the Craftery, the Krayle Shop, the Atlan Ceramic Club and the Swastica Shop. All sold handicrafts. Periodicals published in Chicago devoted to promulgating the values and objects of the Arts and Crafts movement included *House Beautiful, Common Clay, Ornamental Iron, The Fine Arts Journal, Forms and Fantasies, Builder and Woodworker* and *Ceramic Monthly.*

Although Chicago was the most important center for arts and crafts, Cincinnati, Cleveland, Dayton, Detroit, Minneapolis and St. Louis also had their crafts enthusiasts. The Minneapolis Chalk and Chisel Club (later the Minneapolis Arts and Crafts Society) was, for example, established in 1895. Most midwestern cities had art schools in which arts and crafts instruction was offered. These included the Cincinnati School of Art, Washington University Department of Art in St. Louis, the School of the Art Institute of Chicago, the Cleveland School of Art and the University of Kansas at Lawrence.

A tie between craft and architecture began in the Midwest with the Prairie school of architecture, whose most famous practitioner was Frank Lloyd Wright. Both movements shared ideology and stylistic beliefs, including an emphasis on the unity of exterior and interior, respect for natu-

Crackpot inventions are part of American humor. No home should be without Thomas Mann's cookie jar which lights up and dispenses cookies on demand through a voice-activated electronic circuit. *Oreo Cookie Jar Dispenser,* 1985. Acrylic on wood, 30 inches high. (Photo by Will Crocker.)

ral materials, a desire for simplicity, interest in Japanese art forms and a geometric and rectilinear style.

California experienced its own arts and crafts movement in the late 19th and early 20th centuries. At the World's Columbian Exposition in Chicago in 1893, California was represented in a large pavilion with details from its Franciscan

Charles Rohlfs' desk and swivel armchair were made circa 1900 in Buffalo, N.Y. (Photo courtesy Jordan-Volpe Gallery, New York.)

and early 20th centuries in the work of Ernest Coxhead and Bernard Maybeck. Maybeck built a number of shingled houses in the hills of Berkeley for professors on limited budgets. Furniture for some of the homes came from Lucia and Arthur F. Matthews' San Francisco studio. These painters designed furniture at a shop which they established after the 1906 earthquake and fire.

In Southern California the homes that Charles and Henry Greene built in Pasadena after 1893 made that city an architectural mecca before World War I. Around 1909, a group of architects and craftsmen known as the Arroyo Guild sought commissions for houses in which all elements, including furniture and landscaping, were integrated.

In the Pacific Northwest, similar attitudes and design ideas were put into practice. The Berry Shop in Seattle produced copperware. Architect Ellsworth Storey, a native of Chicago, came to Seattle in 1903 and designed fine wooden houses and furniture in the Arts and Crafts style. In 1906, the Oregon School of Arts and Crafts was founded in Portland.

The values of the Arts and Crafts movement began to fade from fashion after 1916. However, they did not cease to exist. Instead they remained in the culture awaiting the next major influence on today's craft movement—the ideas of the Bauhaus. Though it originated in Germany in 1919, the Bauhaus had far-reaching importance for much of the 20th century in America, especially after some of the leading Bauhaus thinkers settled here in the late 1930s and early 1940s.

The Bauhaus was both a creative center and an educational training ground for craftsmen and artists. Founder Walter Gropius aimed to break down the barriers between artists and technically

missions which were then being rediscovered. But there was also a booth in which craftsmen showed objects made by hand mostly of redwood. The following year, San Francisco's Golden Gate Park was the setting for the California Midwinter Exposition where crafts were exhibited. The forerunner of the San Francisco Art Institute was founded in 1874 and the California College of Arts and Crafts was initiated in 1907.

A distinctive Northern California style of domestic architecture emerged in the late 19th expert craftsmen by training students to be effective in both areas. In a statement of purpose in 1919, he wrote these prophetic, often quoted words:[9]

> *Architects, sculptors, painters we must all turn to the crafts! Art is not a profession. There is no essential difference between the artist and the craftsman. The artist is an exalted craftsman. In rare moments of inspiration, moments beyond the control of his will, the grace of heaven may cause his work to bloom into art. But proficiency in his craft is essential to every artist. Therein lies a source of creative imagination. Let us create a new guild of craftsmen, without the class distinctions which raise an arrogant barrier between craftsman and artist.*

Many of the most important Bauhaus thinkers came to the United States and taught in various universities, where they influenced countless students. Gropius himself taught at Harvard as did Marcel Breuer; Mies Van der Rohe joined the Armour Institute in Chicago (now Illinois Institute of Technology); Josef and Anni Albers came first to Black Mountain College in North Carolina and later to Yale University. After designing the buildings at Cranbrook Academy of Art, the Scandinavian architect, Eliel Saarinen became head of the art school in 1932. Saarinen and his patron, George Booth, conceived of the school in Bloomfield Hills, Mich., as an American Bauhaus.

Other Europeans who either were at the Bauhaus or who espoused the same values exerted an important influence on American craftsmen as role models and teachers. They included weaver Trude Guermonprez; Marguerite and Frans Wildenhain who established a pottery at

Gustav Stickley's Craftsman Workshops in Eastwood, N.Y., produced this china closet circa 1902. (Photo by Scott Hyde, courtesy Jordan-Volpe Gallery, New York.)

Tiburon, California; and the potters Otto and Gertrud Natzler, who also settled in California.

Even before the Bauhaus educators came to the United States, there were pockets of craft activity here. For example, there was still a public for ceramics. Between World War I and 1939, major colleges and the universities of Idaho, Montana, Oregon and Washington included ceramics in their curricula.[10] In 1932, the University of Southern California offered its first ceramics course, taught by Glen Lukens, and

Dirk Van Erp was active in San Francisco after the turn of the century. This table lamp, circa 1912-1920, is of beaten copper with a beaten copper shade. (Courtesy Jordan-Volpe Gallery, New York.)

of Modern Art in New York in the early 1930s.

Meanwhile, others began to concern themselves with the destitute inhabitants of rural backwaters. They attempted to aid this constituency while at the same time reclaiming indigenous traditional crafts. Three well-known activists are Lucy Morgan, Aileen Webb and Allen Eaton; but reason suggests there must have been others whose contributions will be revealed as scholarship grows. As a result of this outside help, in the southern Appalachians a number of settlement schools began to offer crafts instruction. In 1930 these groups provided the basis for the organization of the Southern Highland Handicrafts Guild. Participants included representatives of the Hindman and Pine Mountain Settlement Schools in Kentucky, Pi Beta Phi School in Gatlinburg, Tenn., John C. Campbell Folk School in Brasstown, N.C., and Penland.

The League of New Hampshire Craftsmen was organized in 1932 with the help of Eaton and the Russell Sage Foundation. Though the emphasis was on traditional crafts, a 1931 advance report recommended that "gradually the so-called fine arts be included in the general scope of this enterprise, for only as art expression becomes fine does it survive and merit support."[11] In 1934 the League held its first Craftsman's Fair at Crawford House in Crawford Notch. Prior to that time, local shops for the sale of crafts were established by the Guild, as were local guilds of weavers, potters and needleworkers.

The Index of American Design was initiated in 1935 as part of the Federal Arts Project.[12] It is a pictorial record of craft skills and objects mostly created by unsung craftsmen in all corners of the country. The Index was discontinued in 1939 before it was completed, as World War II approached. The completed plates were stored

the Ceramic National was established at what is today the Everson Museum in Syracuse, N.Y., in 1932. Regular exhibitions of ceramics from all over the country were a feature of this prestigious juried exhibition. (As noted earlier, the Ceramic National was reinstated in 1987 after being discontinued in 1970.) By the 1930s there was a full-scale revival of interest in traditional and functional crafts. Exhibitions of folk arts and crafts were held at a number of museums, including two organized by Holger Cahill at the Newark, (N.J.), Museum of Art and the Museum at the Smithsonian Institution. Despite its rather unceremonious ending, the Index played an important role in popularizing American craft skills and adding to the vocabulary of American artists, designers and collectors of the often untutored but beautiful forms of the past, especially since the objects illustrated in the Index were shown in slide lectures and exhibits across the country. Two books were published that include a number of the plates. Erwin O. Christensen's *The Index of American Design* has 400 and Clarence P. Hornung's *Treasury of American Design* has 900. After its conclusion, Holger Cahill, who was a backer of folk arts and the Index itself, said that its existence corrected a bias which had relegated the work of craftsmen to the back pages of our history.

While the Index was reclaiming the past in American crafts, others were working in the present in a variety of ways. During the 1930s, retail outlets for crafts existed in many localities. In New York, Aileen Webb established America House in 1940 as a retail shop for the work of craftsmen. Some craft guilds and rural schools offered objects for sale. In the west, American Indian outlets, such as Hubbell Trading Post, sold work to tourists. A national group organized by designer Russel Wright in 1940 and known as "The American Way of Education," featured the work of 65 craftsmen and small manufacturers. The objects were sold through department stores such as Macy's in New York.

In 1941, *Craft Horizons* magazine made its first appearance as a newsletter for America House. Within two years the American Craftsmen's Educational Council (now the American Craft Council) was established with backing from Aileen Webb. The goal was to foster communication among craftsmen all over the country and to promote the cause of crafts. The council turned *Craft Horizons* into its official publication in 1943. The magazine, now known as *American Craft,* and the council continue to reflect the development of craft. Both publication and organization, so long the only national voice of the craft movement, have been joined by many others.

In the late 1930s and early 1940s, émigré artists came to the United States as refugees, establishing themselves at colleges and in their own workshops in various parts of the country. These individuals would serve as teachers and role models for future American craftsmen, some of whom were soon fighting in Europe and the Pacific.

Despite the war, a number of exhibitions of crafts were held in the 1940s. In 1943, for example, a show of New England craft at the Worcester Art Museum provoked the director of the League of New Hampshire Craftsmen to write that "the show set a new height . . . . In effect, it raises contemporary crafts to the museum level. Instead of being artisans, we can now justly claim we are artists."[13]

The decade of the 1950s was a period of communication among craftsmen. One example gives the tenor of the times. In 1952, English potter Bernard Leach accompanied potter Shoji Hamada and Soetsu Yanagi, director of the Folk Museum in Tokyo, on a trip to the United States. Hamada, Yanagi and Leach, who is sometimes called the father of the studio pottery movement, traveled around the country proclaiming the values of the craft movement and acquainting craftsmen with the Japanese Zen Buddhist ceramics tradition. They spoke at the Archie Bray Foundation in Montana, where Rudy Autio and Peter Voulkos were making sculptural ceramics, and they also gave a memorable workshop at Black

*Black Plate,* a stoneware vessel by Peter Voulkos made in 1968, reveals the changes wrought by the process of breaking with and building on tradition that characterized the 1950s and 1960s. (Photo courtesy Garth Clark Gallery, Los Angeles/New York, collection of Aaron Milrad.)

Mountain College in North Carolina. This school had opened in 1933 as an experimental and utopian college dedicated to the arts. Besides Josef and Anni Albers, the faculty included Robert Turner (who set up its ceramics program) and Karen Karnes and David Weinrib, who were resident potters at the school. The summer program, co-chaired by Marguerite Wildenhain, attracted potters from all over the country.

Also in the 1950s, shops began to show handmade domestic pottery and imports. Keeg's in Seattle sponsored the first solo exhibition of Peter Voulkos' work.[14] At the same time, college art curricula began to expand to include ceramics and the art school population swelled with GI's as more students sought to work in craft media.

In 1956, the Museum of Contemporary Crafts was opened in New York by the American Craft Council and the following year at Asilomar, Calif., the first national craftsmen's conference was held under the same auspices.

Robert Ebendorf, now a professor at the State University of New York at New Paltz and a well-known jewelry maker, was a student at the University of Kansas in the early 1950s. He recalled that regional museums and university art departments sponsored annual exhibitions of new work on a fairly regular basis. A few early events were the Michigan Artist-Craftsmen annuals at the Detroit Institute of Arts; the Wichita (Kansas) National Decorative Arts Competition; the biennial Fiber-Clay-Metal competitions at the St. Paul (Minn.) Gallery and School of Art; and the Northwest Craftsmen's Exhibitions at the Henry Gallery of the University of Washington.

The 1960s continued the trend of heightened communications among craftsmen, and also introduced a new element—the widespread development of the crafts marketplace through craft fairs, shops and eventually galleries. Lee Nordness, who would organize in 1969 Objects USA, the most important exhibition of American crafts to date, was an art dealer in New York. As a specialist in contemporary American art, he traveled frequently to jury art shows. By the late 1950s he began to notice an occasional pot or a piece of jewelry done by one of the teachers or students. "I responded to this work immediately," he recalled recently, and presented some of it in 1963 at his Madison Avenue gallery. He called the exhibit "The Fine Art of Living," and invited 15 craftsmen to show their work. Although the show didn't sell well and he did not pursue the idea, Nordness continued to follow the careers of those in whom he had become interested. "As time went on, I saw they were being impeded in their development as artists because there were no galleries to show their work. They had to stay close to the popular taste in order to sell."[15]

Nordness, backed by the S. C. Johnson Co., which had already supported his influential traveling exhibition of American painting called Art USA, then organized Objects USA, which opened at the Smithsonian Institution with 308 objects in 1969. Nordness enlisted the help of Paul Smith, director of the Museum of Contemporary Crafts, to select work by ceramists, metalsmiths, glassmakers, woodworkers, weavers and enamelists across the country. The exhibition toured museums in the United States and abroad. The objects were purchased by the Johnson Co. and then donated to the various American museums hosting the show. The exhibition catalogue, Objects USA, included an essay by Nordness on the development of craft as art.

Nordness's thoughts were also contained in a short publicity piece for the exhibition. In it,

A portion of the Objects USA exhibition is shown. In the foreground is Richard Shaw's ceramic *Couch and Chair with Landscape and Cows* (1966-67). The vase directly behind the sofa is Robert Engle's *Harlow Pot* (1968). The feathery fiber work hanging at rear center is by Dominic DiMare. (Photo courtesy S. C. Johnson & Son, Inc.)

he amplified his views on the role craftsmen were playing in contemporary society: "Craft artists have humanized the object once more, given meaning and enduring values to the things we touch, use and live with in our intimate environments. In a world in which most objects are fabricated with a built-in obsolescence, are made to be thrown away, these artists have created objects which may one day tell a future century of the culture of our time."

He claimed that "placing paintings and sculpture into a convenient fine arts category and objects whether functional or non-functional into a crafts category no longer sustains any aesthetic validity. The presence of many an object made in clay or wrought in gold is as satisfying as a sculpture in bronze or a painting in oil."

The exhibition documented a bona fide new movement. It also contributed greatly to a new respect for craft. As a national show with excellent work from all over the country, Objects USA showed how widespread craft art had become and exposed to wide view objects that went beyond the old definition of craft.

It was not uppermost in anyone's mind to turn craft into art. Instead, the process of perfecting their craft placed some gifted practitioners on a pathway toward art. These individuals had turned around Walter Gropius' statement that "the artist is an exalted craftsman." The exalted craftsman had become an artist.

The legitimacy vouchsafed by the Objects USA exhibition led directly to the contemporary craft art movement in the 1970s, with its greatly increased number of exhibitions and artists, as well as collectors, publications and museum acquisitions. Eventually, a new synthesis, perhaps through another exhibition like Objects USA, will make the recent past intelligible. It then will become the next chapter of history.

---

## FOR FURTHER READING

Robert Bishop and Patricia Coblentz, *American Decorative Arts: 360 Years of Creative Design* (New York: Harry N. Abrams, 1982).

Eileen Boris, *Art and Labor: Ruskin, Morris and the Craftsman Ideal in America* (Philadelphia: Temple University Press, 1986).

Kenneth H. Cardwell, *Bernard Maybeck: Artisan, Architect, Artist* (Salt Lake City: Gibbs M. Smith, Inc., 1983).

Erwin O. Christensen, *The Index of American Design* (New York: Macmillan Co., 1950).

Robert Judson Clark, ed., *The Arts and Crafts Movement in America* (Princeton: Princeton University Press, 1972).

*The Craftsman in America* (Washington: National Geographic Society, 1975).

Sharon S. Darling, *Chicago Ceramics & Glass: An Illustrated History from 1871 to 1933* (Chicago: Chicago Historical Society, 1979).

*Design in America: The Cranbrook Vision 1925-1950* (New York: Harry N. Abrams, 1983).

Martin Duberman, *Black Mountain College: An Exploration in Community* (New York: E. P. Dutton, 1972).

Allen H. Eaton, *Handicrafts of the Southern Highlands* (New York: Dover Publications, Inc., 1983, reprint).

———. *Handicrafts of New England* (New York: Harper & Bros., 1949).

Lionel Lambourne, *Utopian Craftsmen: The Arts and Crafts Movement from the Cotswolds to Chicago* (New York: Van Nostrand Reinhold Co., 1980).

Oliver W. Larkin, *Art and Life in America* (New York: Holt Rinehart & Winston, 1960).

Edward Lucie-Smith, *The Story of Craft: The Craftsman's Role in Society* (Ithaca, N.Y.: Cornell University Press, 1981).

Coy L. Ludwig, *The Arts & Crafts Movement in New York State 1890s-1920s* (Hamilton, N.Y.: Gallery Association of New York State, 1983).

Randell L. Makinson, *Greene & Greene: Architecture as a Fine Art and Furniture and Related Designs* (Salt Lake City: Gibbs M. Smith, Inc., 1977, 1979).

Aline B. Saarinen, *The Proud Possessors* (New York: Random House, 1958).

Mary Ann Smith, *Gustav Stickley: The Craftsman* (Syracuse, N.Y.: Syracuse University Press, 1983).

Jeanne Madeline Weimann, *The Fair Women: The Story of the Woman's Building, World's Columbian Exposition, Chicago 1893* (Chicago: Academy, 1981).

Hans M. Wingler, *The Bauhaus: Weimar, Dessau, Berlin, Chicago* (Cambridge, Mass.: MIT Press, 1969).

## NOTES

1. Oliver W. Larkin, *Art & Life in America* (New York: Holt Rinehart & Winston, 1960) p. 10.

2. *America's Arts & Skills* (New York: Time-Life Books, 1968) p. 9.

3. Ibid., p. 15.

4. Lee Nordness, *Objects USA* (New York: Viking Press, 1970) p. 19.

5. *The Craftsman in America* (Washington: National Geographic Society, 1975) pp. 130-131.

6. *Art & Life in America*, p. 231.

7. Lucy Morgan & LaGette Blythe, *Gift from the Hills: Miss Lucy Morgan's Story of Her Unique Penland School* (Chapel Hill: University of North Carolina Press, 1958). The book was reprinted in 1971 but is currently out of print. Look for it in libraries.

8. Robert Judson Clark, ed., *The Arts and Crafts Movement in America, 1876-1916* (Princeton: Princeton University Press, 1972) This excellent exhibition catalogue contains a succinct history of the movement and I have relied on it in my account. See also Wendy Kaplan, *The Art That Is Life: The Arts & Crafts Movement in America, 1875-1920*, (Boston: Museum of Fine Arts, 1987).

9. Quoted in *American Decorative Arts: 360 Years of Creative Design* by Robert Bishop and Patricia Coblentz (New York: Harry H. Abrams, 1982) p. 359.

10. LaMar Harrington, *Ceramics of the Pacific Northwest: A History* (Seattle: University of Washington Press, 1979) p. 13.

11. Betty Steele, "The League of New Hampshire Craftsmen's First Fifty Years," (Concord, N.H.: LNHC, no date) unpaged pamphlet.

12. Milton Meltzer, *Violins & Shovels: The WPA Arts Projects* (New York: Delacorte Press, 1976). An account of the Index is given on pp. 80-84.

13. "The League of New Hampshire Craftsmen's First Fifty Years."

14. *Ceramics of the Pacific Northwest*, p. 27.

15. Interview with author.

To build connoisseurship, look critically at many examples of an artist's work. Wendell Castle, four console tables, 1978. Stained, dyed and painted wood. *Ready*, 40 × 40 × 17 inches. (Photo by Bruce Miller, courtesy Alexander F. Milliken, Inc., New York.)

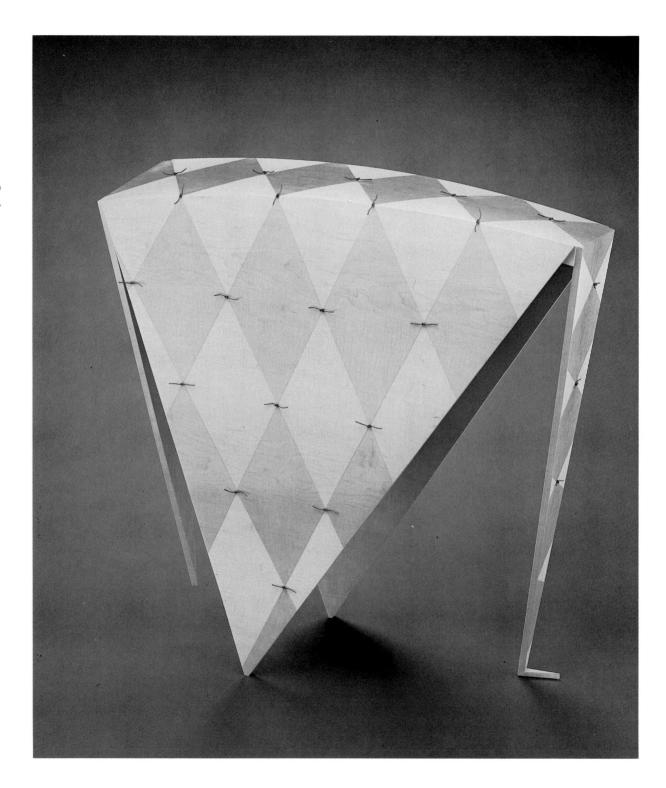

## CHAPTER THREE
# BUILDING A CRAFT ART COLLECTION

A person starts as a collector and becomes a connoisseur. The first stage is discovery, and indiscriminate accumulation; the last stage is selection, the tempering of initial enthusiasm with deeper knowledge. The movement between the stages can be deeply satisfying.

At first a collector may dwell uncomfortably in a place where "I don't know much about art, but I know what I like" happens to be true. Few are apt to verbalize a sentiment so likely to label one as an art Philistine. Yet this much maligned cliché has an element of truth. The latter part is true for everyone and the first may be, too, in the sense that art is mysterious and defies attempts to understand its essence. But it is actually the beginning of wisdom to admit the dreadful secret that you don't know much about craft art except that you like it and are willing to learn more.

William Warmus, formerly associate curator of 20th-century glass at the Corning Glass Museum in Corning, N.Y., says that the first naive phase is important for growth since it helps build knowledge at a time when enthusiasm and a desire to experiment are at their height. "The stage is often characterized by buying lots of items that are inexpensive. I think that's a positive attribute. It teaches a collector to take chances and helps him learn," he said. Eventually a collector may decide to part with some objects, as Jack Lenor Larsen, president of the American Craft Council and a fabric designer, has done. Or all may be retained. As collector Sue Knapp says, "We haven't sold anything. My view is that there are no mistakes in buying anything an artist has made. If something does not appeal after a while, we put it away and may take it out later." To Larsen, on the other hand, "objects are ephemeral. You live with them for a time and then you grow and go on to other things. Collecting is a series of expressions, each of which is important. Every step along the way has been valuable, although eventually I may no longer love the object as I mature."

The road to connoisseurship can seem perilous or, at best, poorly marked, but there are some things that facilitate intelligent choices. In this chapter we will first look at ways to become informed about craft art and how to develop a discerning eye and to hone a collection. Then we will consider the quality issue. A number of

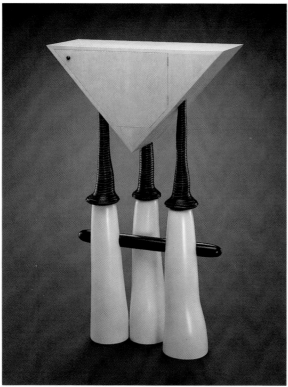

All tables on this page are by Wendell Castle. *Dr. Vermin's Attitude,* 57 × 34 × 15 inches. (Photos by Bruce Miller, courtesy Alexander F. Milliken, Inc., New York.)

*Little Incidents That Seemed Strange,* 57 × 48 × 18 inches.

*The Midnight Marriage,* 45½ × 58 × 21½ inches.

resources, such as books, periodicals, catalogues and organizations, are listed at the end of the chapter.

## BECOMING A COLLECTOR

Although the impulse to buy craft art often arrives before there is any knowledge of the field, it is rare for collectors of contemporary craft art to stay uninformed—many do a considerable amount of research in their quest for enlightenment about the objects they buy. Gallery owners and friendly shop proprietors are often a primary source of information. They may explain the work a budding collector admires; arrange for a meeting with the artist; issue invitations to openings to see more work and meet other collectors and new artists; provide reading lists and catalogues; lend magazine articles and books; even arrange introductions to galleries in other cities. Many collectors follow up on these preliminary gallery contacts with intensive reading and visits to other galleries, museums and artists' studios. They almost certainly begin subscribing to publications in the field. As they get to know more artists and aficionados, the web of relationships becomes ever more supportive.

To keep up to date, collectors of contemporary craft art rely heavily on exhibition catalogues, which offer the most authoritative information about current activities in the field. Since the essence of contemporary craft art is that it is happening now and the day after tomorrow—and few books can capture this immediacy—keeping files is usually essential. It would not be extraordinary for a collector to retain information on as many as 100 artists. Collector Daniel Jacobs, for example, follows about 200; Judith Schwartz, a collector and writer on ceramics, has a library of thousands of slides.

The more a collector studies and learns about ceramics traditions, the more there is to see in difficult work such as this sculpture by Viola Frey. *Untitled Junk Piece*, c. 1979. Ceramic, 24 inches. (Photo courtesy Garth Clark Gallery, Los Angeles/New York, collection of Garth Clark and Mark Del Vecchio.)

Robert Brady's figurative sculpture conveys an immediate sense of wonder and power. *Mum*, 1986. Stoneware, glaze and paint, 37 × 17½ × 15 inches. (Photo by Michele Maier, courtesy Braunstein/Quay Gallery, San Francisco.)

individuals interested in ceramics attend the annual meeting of the National Council on Education for the Ceramic Arts. Museums and galleries in the host city usually produce an extravagant series of special exhibitions and other events of interest to conferees. Schwartz noted that at one NCECA meeting recently she was able to see the work of as many as 60 important ceramists from all over the country in just a few days. "Otherwise you would have to travel for weeks to see so much work," she added. Furthermore, there was an opportunity to look at the output of new artists and to evaluate whether their work might become collectible. The conversations, parties and exchanges of information at such meetings are usually both enjoyable and useful.

A regular event for glass collectors is the annual meeting of the Glass Art Society. Artists, collectors and others mingle at a series of lectures, panel discussions, slide shows and impromptu meetings. A student show introduces new talent. Here again, galleries in the host city usually plan special exhibitions.

A similar outpouring of enthusiasm is present at annual meetings of the Society of North American Goldsmiths, and every three years, fiber artists meet at an event known as "Convergence." Woodworkers also hold meetings on a regular basis, although not on the scale of the other media. In addition, art centers, schools and museums host special events at which artists and collectors gather to discuss the state of the art. The best way to find out about important events is to subscribe to publications devoted to the media of interest.

As more collectors come on the scene, collectors' groups are springing up in various parts of the country. Some join groups devoted to

In addition, she subscribes to as many as nine specialized publications, including *American Craft, American Ceramics, Ceramics Monthly, Studio Potter, Art in America* and *Art News*, as well as several weekly art newspapers that report on gallery exhibitions nationwide.

Besides reading extensively and visiting museums and galleries, another way to quickly immerse oneself in a field is to attend meetings of organizations devoted to it. Large international gatherings of ceramists, glassmakers, jewelers and fiber artists occur on a regular basis around the country. Each year, for example, about 1,200

promoting artists they admire. (Gifts and pressure on curators for museum exhibitions can impact the development of interest in craft art in a particular locality.) Both the James Renwick Alliance and the American Craft Museum's Collectors Circle have national memberships. The Renwick group was founded in 1982 by a group of Washington-area collectors to support the Renwick Gallery, but it also supports other craft art activities. Benefits of membership include invitations to gallery openings and receptions for artists, monthly calendars of events and a quarterly newsletter. The group funds a variety of activities, arranges for artists to lecture at the gallery and has cosponsored symposia on crafts for collectors. It also purchases craft art for the Renwick. Recently, when the Smithsonian Institution considered eliminating the Renwick from its galaxy of museums in 1986, the collectors' group was instrumental in mobilizing public sentiment against the move.

The American Craft Council is the preeminent membership group for craft artists and enthusiasts. Its programs are extensive and membership includes free access to the American Craft Museum, as well as a subscription to the Council's magazine, *American Craft*, and access to the library, which has a good collection of catalogues and books on crafts. The museum associates program offers a chance to meet with others and to work for crafts appreciation.

Collector groups have also formed in a number of areas, such as Philadelphia, Detroit and Chicago. For example, the Contemporary Glass Group of Delaware Valley was founded in 1983 by glass artist Paul Stankard and the late Sy Kamens. Activities include arranging lectures by glassmakers, supporting glass education and providing a meeting place for area collectors.

The use of the sculptural form is a source of inspiration to many craft artists, such as Tony Hepburn. *Totemic Form I*, 1982. Ceramic, slate, brick and marble, 70 × 36 × 23 inches. (Photo by Vincent Lisanti, collection of Daniel Jacobs.)

Eleanor Moty's dramatic yet disciplined brooch is an example of one type of work that might be seen at a SNAG conference. *Faceted Brooch,* 1983. Silver and 14-karat gold, rutilated quartz and tourmaline crystal, 2 × 2 × 1 inch. (Photo by Jim Threadgill.)

## HONING A COLLECTION

As a collector travels from the first flush of enthusiasm to a more mature appreciation, refining what may be a jumble of objects into a collection becomes increasingly important. There are many ways to do this. One idea is to specialize in ceramics, glass or other media. Another is to select objects from a variety of media on some principle of organization or a belief in their overall excellence. A collector might indulge a particular interest by collecting figural objects in all media, work by women, Californians or midwesterners. Whatever the logic, collectors should be prepared for a time of confusion before judgment has matured and knowledge acquired on history, techniques and aesthetic issues.

Craft art objects are so appealing that it is tempting to buy pieces that reflect many different disciplines, styles and attitudes. Mixed collections can be exciting to assemble, but doing so successfully requires a great deal of time spent in learning to discriminate. Beginning in the 1960s, the collector Robert Pfannebecker has amassed more than 1,000 objects in all craft media. Pfannebecker has adopted a number of mentors from among craft artists, such as ceramists Wayne Higby and Richard DeVore and fiber artist Dominic DiMare, to help him expand his appreciation and discrimination. Higby wrote in a catalogue accompanying a museum exhibition of some of the Pfannebecker collection: "He is always in pursuit of good work and will track it down anywhere." Although Pfannebecker learns from mentors, his judgments are his own and by indulging them over the years he has collected many pivotal pieces. Pfannebecker said recently that it used to be easier to develop an eclectic collection. In his opinion, there are too many artists

Another important way to meet others and establish oneself as a collector is to take an active interest in one of the craft centers and schools around the country. Collectors are on the boards of institutions such as the Penland School of Crafts in Penland, N.C., the Pilchuck School in Stanwood, Wash., the Haystack Mountain School of Crafts in Deer Isle, Me., Anderson Ranch Arts Center in Aspen, Colo., and Arrowmont School of Arts and Crafts in Gatlinburg, Tenn. These and other schools occupy a special place in the American craft movement, having served as early promoters of the crafts.

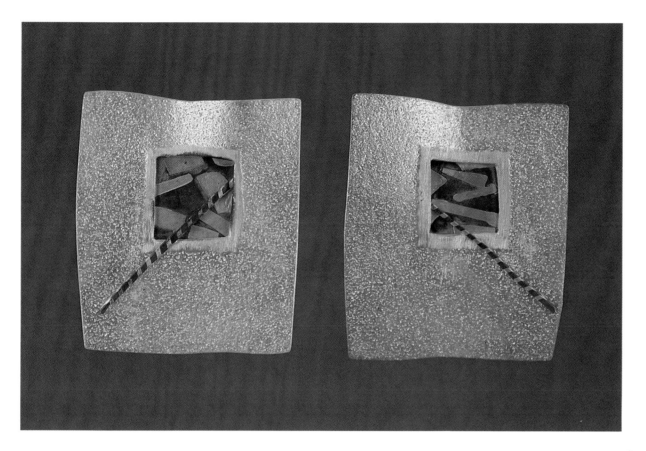

Micki Lippe's earrings present a similar sophisticated approach to art jewelry. *Through The Looking Glass,* 1986. Roll-printed sterling silver with brass, copper and gold centers. 1½ × 1¼ inches. (Photo by David Durham.)

working today for a single collector to keep up intelligently in all media.

Building a good collection takes a great deal of time. Daniel Jacobs, for example, devotes a part of almost every day to his ceramics collection. He may review slides sent by a gallery, work on his records, go to an exhibition or any combination of these. With role models such as Jacobs and Pfannebecker, the individual attempting to begin or increase a small collection may understandably feel overwhelmed. However, professional critics and curators note that it is possible to improve one's facility for making informed judgments.

William Warmus, for example, suggests doing exercises in looking. "Try to look at an object so freshly that it is as if you had never seen anything like it before. Examine your own reactions." He adds, however, that the development of connoisseurship is lacking today. Viewers are often so entranced by the beauty of the material and the virtuosity of the workmanship that they neglect to take a critical view. As an example, Warmus noted that "people are enthusiastic about Dale Chihuly's blown-glass baskets, but they don't tend to get eight of them in a row and consider which one they like best and why."

Making critical comparisons often requires developing one's visual memory. Ceramics collector Ruth Julian has a method of looking that helps fix objects in her memory. She concentrates on the object for about a minute, then turns away

Interest in the human figure crosses all media lines in craft art. The figure even inspires furniture makers, such as Alphonse Mattia. *Hors d'Oeuvre Server,* 1984. Ebonized walnut and dyed sycamore, 68 × 22 × 18 inches. (Photo by Andrew Dean Powell, collection of Dorothy and George Saxe.)

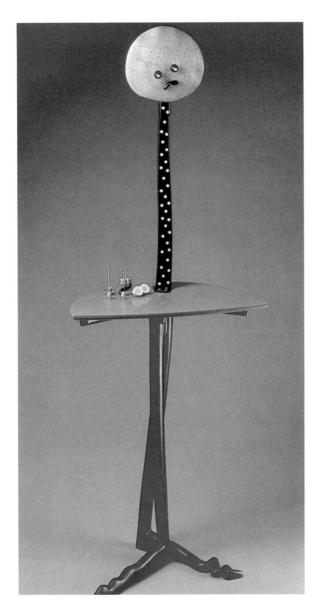

and tries to recall it. If she can't, she tries again.

After that first look, the next task is to consider the piece aesthetically. "Analyze issues such as shape, form, materials, workmanship, artistic ideas embodied in the piece, the posing of a problem and its solution," advises Warmus. Looking at art is a complex procedure that involves a first

response and numerous subsequent evaluations. The initial reaction is always intuitive. Then comes a more conscious evaluation, which includes looking at the form of the work, surface treatment, tactility (important in objects, though not in paintings), color relations, the ideas contained in the work and the feelings it engenders, and the skill of execution. A characteristic of good work, according to ceramist Robert Sedestrom, is that there is always something else to discover.

When the Armory exhibition mentioned in chapter 1 opened in 1913, reaction to some of the paintings was angry because the work challenged established ways of seeing. Viewers had no context for integrating the images they saw. But what had been strange and frightening also communicated new ideas that expanded the viewer's visual world. Craft art today is following the direction taken by painting at the beginning of the century, and craft artists are breaking away from traditional forms to indulge their own needs for expression. Craft art collectors are thus in the same position as earlier collectors of painting. Many report at first being drawn to the conventionally beautiful, easily understood forms, but deeper knowledge eventually leads them to appreciate more complex work. To the uneducated eye, this difficult or powerful work may often appear ugly, clumsy, inept or pedestrian.

When you see a tortured vase or teapot, it may be a bad piece, but when someone whose skills and knowledge are unquestioned makes a clumsy, lumpy object, the intellectually curious collector should be asking why. For example, since the ceramic telephone constructed by Robert Arneson in 1965 is plainly not beautiful in the traditional sense, a viewer might reasonably question why it has a place of honor in 20th-century ceramics. Is it a joke? Is it a wry admis-

This ceramic work by Robert Arneson, a quintessential example of Funk ceramics, is irreverently ugly on purpose. *Telephone,* 1965. (Photo courtesy of Allan Stone Galleries, Inc., New York.)

sion that making art is futile in a world where telephones are valued more highly than ceramic art? Is it a gesture of defiance by an individual who is perfectly capable of creating something that would conform to traditional ideas of beauty if he wanted to? The answer to all these questions is yes and other questions and answers may occur to viewers. The issues this piece brings up are complex, and its success lies in its power of communication.

Today, public tolerance for novelty of expression in art seems to be growing. This may be because viewers are visually well-educated through the daily barrage of images from advertising and television and are more open to receive provocative or even frightening communications. The darker pieces may eventually become the most prized as documents of contemporary experience.

Connoisseurship increases as a collector acquires knowledge of the historical development of a particular medium and of particular artists. Historic pieces, which will always grow in value because of their interest to scholars, are the early

The figure provides a format for an inexhaustible number of highly personal expressions, such as this leather mask by J. Pearson. *Bull Boy's Tattoo Pot Luck,* 1979. Tooled natural cowhide, 64 × 33 × 20 inches. (Photo courtesy of Julie: Artisans' Gallery, New York.)

Patti Warashina's fascinating early ceramic work is in Robert Pfannebecker's collection. *Metamorphosis of A Car Kiln,* c. 1971, 30 inches long.

examples of a new trend or school of thought. For example, a small and not particularly distinguished series of glass objects by Harvey Littleton is especially prized because the pieces were the first made of molten glass in a studio setting, and document the beginnings of the American studio glass movement. Wendell Castle's first *trompe l'oeil* piece, a chair dating from 1978, is another example of a historic work of craft art. But while owning a historic piece is the dream of a lifetime for some collectors, for others it might be of no interest. Since a collection is an extension of a collector's personality, that is perfectly all right. To gain an understanding of the principles guiding some collectors, go to exhibitions

of their collections and study the accompanying catalogues.

Deciding whether to acquire a work is easier if you approach the task in a questioning spirit rather than simply relying on your own impressions. For example, you might ask where other examples of the artist's work can be seen, about the other types of work the artist has done over his career, and whether others are working in the same general style. Additional concerns might include the way in which the artist is regarded by peers and critics, and whether museums have purchased or accepted the artist's work as gifts for their own collections. Collectors who can find answers to these questions are on their way to

Two similar works by Dale Chihuly offer the budding collector an opportunity to respond to similar but different forms. Both are from the *White Sea Form with Black Lip Wraps* series, 1986. Blown glass, top 12 × 16 × 12 inches, bottom 9 × 15 × 15 inches. (Photos by Dick Busher.)

connoisseurship and will reap the rich rewards of enhanced personal judgment. Keep in mind, however, that just because an artist is widely acclaimed does not mean that his or her work should be in everybody's collection. Buying the work of an unknown artist because it strikes a personal chord must surely be one of the greatest joys of collecting, especially when your judgment is eventually substantiated by history.

An effective method of increasing the ability to see critically is to look without any intention of purchasing, as curators and art historians do. "If you are a glass collector and find it absolutely impossible to go to an exhibition where glass is for sale and abstain from buying, then go to a museum where buying is impossible," suggests William Warmus. George Saxe, who describes himself as too impulsive in his buying habits, bought an instant camera several years ago and stated his intention to "take it to a gallery, snap a picture and then go away and study it to give us some distance and help us restrain our buying." At a 1987 exhibition of his glass collection at the American Craft Museum, Saxe said that the ploy has worked.

Curators and experienced collectors offer the following suggestions to beginning collectors.

**Always buy the best piece you can get.** This is not necessarily the piece on the cover of the catalogue (referred to as the "documented piece"), but generally there is agreement among those who have seen an exhibition as to which piece or pieces are best.

**Buy a piece you love and respond to emotionally.** "You always start with a gut feeling. Never forget that pit-of-the-stomach feeling. Look at that piece and ask: Does it move me?" says Penelope Hunter-Stiebel.

This plaque is as much about the pleasure of making art together as it is about figuration. Collaborative works are an important aspect of craft art. Four California ceramists made this portrait in clay: Arthur Gonzalez, Anthony Natsoulas, Lisa Reinertson and Jessica Berkner. *Four Davis Artists,* 1984. Ceramic and mixed media, 34½ × 48½ × 12¾. (Photo by Vincent Lisanti, collection of Daniel Jacobs.)

**Buy the piece that stretches you.** Buy the strongest piece you can possibly stand. The one that you like immediately may not have staying power, and you may soon tire of it.

These "rules" may suggest that collecting is just too much work, but those bitten by the collecting bug find the work a joy. The reward, which includes the possibility of shaping the future of an art form through one's choices, is a heady payoff for the extensive effort and expense. The public may identify museums as the great collectors, but museum curators know that the private collectors usually have the most wonderful collections. "Collectors can do things museum curators cannot do. They can take more risks, follow their intuition and take a chance on newer artists. If a curator wants to take a risk, he has to go through the purchasing committee—and 90 percent of the time they won't agree with him. A collector's risks may some day make a museum look great," said Warmus.

One measure of success is when a major museum calls and asks you to donate your collection or to loan pieces for exhibitions. Having taken a risk and acquired the early work of someone who eventually becomes well known

Wendell Castle's *trompe l'oeil* chair dates from 1978 and is a first example of his work in this genre, so it is a historic piece. (Photo by Steven Sloman, courtesy Alexander F. Milliken, Inc., private collection.)

and important, you may be approached to donate or sell the scarce and valuable early work.

To reach the highest standards of collecting skill, says Judith Schwartz, it is not enough to merely have examples of important artists' work. The most astute collectors have exemplary pieces, which are among the artist's finest work. No artist produces exemplary pieces every single time. When they do, they know it and so do collectors with sophisticated eyes. Schwartz notes: "I have an Arneson head but it isn't an exemplary piece. It is an example of his work. If I were putting together an exhibition, I would never include that head because it isn't the best. For me a successful collection is a collection of exemplary pieces. Of course, these will eventually be the more valuable ones so the collection's greater artistic worth will be reflected in monetary terms."

## PURSUING QUALITY

In conversations about why they collect craft art, collectors often express an appreciation of a work's quality. But what does the word *quality* mean?

On reflection it seems that there are at least three separate kinds of quality that might pertain when discussing objects. Technical quality relates to workmanship. Artistic quality concerns aesthetic issues and philosophical quality refers to the values that handicraft is supposed to impart to an entire culture within the ideals of the Arts and Crafts movement.

Technical quality can be described as honest workmanship in which appropriate materials have been handled correctly to produce an object that is a pleasure to use and look at because of the maker's skill and attention during production. Some examples include a teapot that pours but does not drip, whose handle stays cool to the touch even when filled with hot tea; a rocking chair that rocks well but doesn't risk catapulting the occupant backward; a rug that is soft underfoot and long-wearing. Some attributes of technical quality as it is judged in ceramic, fiber, glass, metal and wood objects are discussed in chapter 6.

The philosophical idea that craft excellence has a transformative power has figured prominently in the 20th century. In the 1950s and 1960s especially, craftsmen often were so committed to the ideal of quality that it extended beyond their work to encompass their way of life. Because a handcrafted object might enrich the life of the user almost as much as the maker, craftsmen

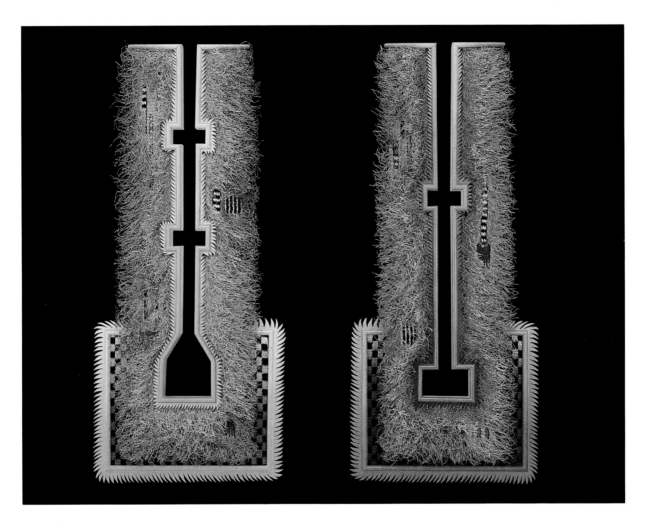

Collectors can choose audacious work such as Jane Lackey's bold twin fiber wall pieces. *Duo-Duo*, 1986-87. Rayon, wire and painted wood, each 55 × 24 × 3 inches. (Photo by E.G. Schempf, collection of B. Z. Wagman.)

could be exemplars and perhaps even help heal a troubled society.

Individuals who bought handmade objects in those days often did so out of a desire to surround themselves with things that could function symbolically as well as practically in the daily art of living. The very existence of crafts was a polemical statement against a culture felt to be inhumane and tawdry. Those who bought were not simply acquiring a wood salad bowl or a set of glasses, they were voting for a different way of life — participating even if vicariously in an attempt to remake society in a better way. To buy handmade objects was a small act of constructive rebellion.

This symbolism has largely disappeared today, though it remains a matter of historic interest. Few individuals are likely to relate the purchase of a wall hanging, a piece of art furniture or a ceramic vase to a political action. Furthermore, the marketplace has learned and profited from the exuberance, beauty and originality of craftsmen's wares, and manufactured products now display a sophistication and charm

Mayer Shacter's non-functional teapot is outside the current style in ceramics, but that needn't stop collectors, who have only themselves to please. *Big Grey Rock Walker,* 1986. Ceramic with lustre glazes, 10 × 12 × 4 inches.

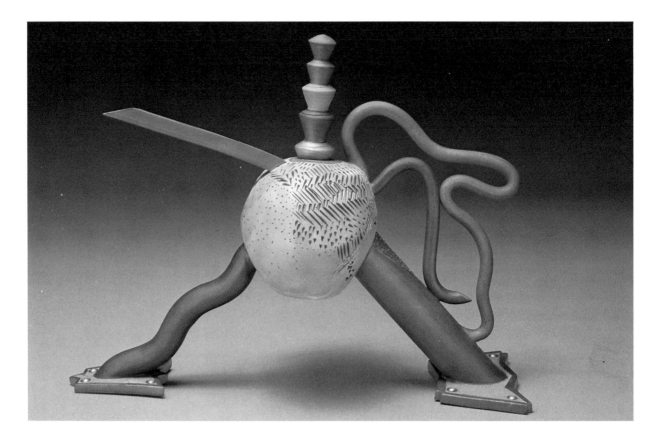

that were largely lacking in the 1950s and 1960s.

Nowadays the issues and language of art appear to be the focal points for many craft artists and collectors. But this can pose a problem for novices, since artistic quality is far more subjective than technical quality, which is likely to have quantifiable methodology to determine its presence or absence. Although there are aesthetic standards, it seems clear that pushed to its extreme, the idea of aesthetic quality is a matter of what the individual doing the evaluating likes and his or her verbal defense of the position. Still, there are some widely agreed-upon attributes, such as that good work keeps looking fresh, keeps saying something new, and that poorly executed, amateurish work requires at least an explanation

of intent. On the other hand, first reactions are not necessarily final. In the learning process, one's aesthetic senses change and develop. Artists often arrive ahead of their critics and collectors who may vigorously object to some new phase of work only to become convinced of its importance later on.

There is a continuum in collecting and more knowledge leads to greater discernment and appreciation of the more difficult pieces. Michael Monroe, curator-in-charge of the Renwick Gallery, equates quality with the cutting edge. "I look for a piece that challenges my visual awareness to a new level. My first reaction has to be almost unpleasant. It has to have a cutting edge. If a piece catches me off guard and lifts me to a new level,

then I want that piece. I try to project myself into the future to imagine if the work will still hold my interest in five years."

Like Monroe, Esther Saks, a Chicago area collector and gallery owner, is willing to endure discomfort in a search for works that will challenge her. She has discarded the old definite ideas she once had in favor of a broader standard. "Using clay in an iconoclastic way, stretching it, forcing it: These goals are valid, too," she says.

Attitudes such as these reveal a new willingness among collectors to be guided by the artists whose goals are to communicate rather than to entertain or soothe their patrons. A persistent

pattern in all contemporary art, this point of view was given expression in the 1950s in the ceramics of Peter Voulkos and his students at Otis Art Institute. These ceramists used clay as a means of communication, often of the ugly and the frightening, a departure that made a place for an idea of quality that ignored the role of tradition in the use of a material to control the aesthetic standards of the present.

There appears to be an increasing number of artists who are either not concerned about technical issues or philosophical quality, or who regard questions of intent and technique as a hostile challenge when asked by a collector. Yet there

Judy Moonelis' sculpture challenges accustomed ways of seeing. *Woman with Hand,* 1986. Ceramic, 56 × 40 × 26 inches. (Photos by Doug Long.)

Peter Voulkos' ceramic work reveals a new freedom in attitudes toward ceramic quality. *Wood-fired Bucket,* 1979. (Photo courtesy of Exhibit A Gallery, Chicago.)

The philosophical power of striving for excellence within a clearly defined tradition is conveyed by Alan Caiger-Smith, an English potter. He says that quality evolves at least partly from skill. "Shapes which are repeated begin to mature without undergoing any obvious changes . . . if you compare two pots made to the same measurement at an interval of about five years you find that the shape has become more agreeable simply by being often made . . . . The same with brush strokes . . . this is an important part of any work which involves repetition. It is a feature of the best peasant pottery. . . . There is a difference between inattentive repetition which leads eventually to something pretty vacant and facile, and repetition done with attention which is really a growing thing, giving rise to the process of maturing that you only see long afterwards . . . it is something that happens even with really skilled people."[3]

Michael Cardew, the English potter who was Bernard Leach's first pupil, explains why Shoji Hamada is his favorite potter: "Everything Hamada does is tremendously genuine. It looks like something made of clay and it looks 'kind,' Hamada's favorite word. Even photographs of his pots show a sort of warmth in the material . . . . The clay sits there and it glows. The treatment is right. No violence has been done . . . . Natural materials are used in a more or less natural or harmonious way and nothing artificial is imposed on them."[4]

On the other hand, nobody has proprietary rights to a material. Some people use it in what they consider a natural way. Some practice exquisite technique. Still others are interested in the expressions of the moment.

Conflicts between two philosophical opposites—an Apollonian sense of order and

is also discomfort with the idea of poor workmanship among both makers and appreciators of craft objects.

Glassmaker Harvey Littleton has noted that "it is up to each individual [artist] to decide whether a piece is or is not defective. Today, we have an increasing number of artists who are not concerned with how long a given form will last but with what impact it will have on people the first time they see it."[1] For himself, however, Littleton adds that "I could not sell a piece knowing it was bad to begin with—although I have seen a signed Tiffany piece with 'imperfect' in the signature. It was very checked but of such unusual color that evidently he could not bear to destroy it."[2]

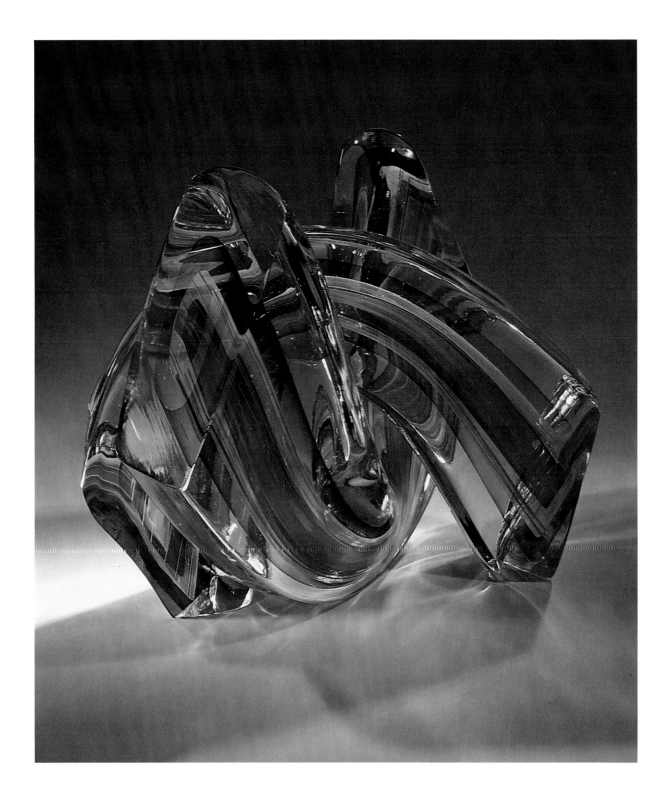

Harvey K. Littleton is the undisputed leader of the studio glass movement. *Blue/Green Crossed Form*, 1984. Glass sculpture, 13 × 13 × 13 inches. (Photo by Jon Littleton, courtesy Heller Gallery, New York.)

Alan Caiger-Smith's beautifully shaped bowl reveals the appeal of tradition. *Lustre Bowl*, 1982. Ceramic, 5 × 14⅜ inches in diameter. (Photo by Eric Shambroom, collection of Daniel Jacobs.)

structure and a Dionysian concept of creative freedom—have been occurring for centuries and are inevitable within art and life itself. Recognizing that art can come out of both impulses, collectors should be open to the fact that there are different ways of looking at material. This is part of the dynamic of art. While those who care about tradition and technique are building an academy, those who don't are busy breaking out of it.

One might speculate that one reason for what some see as a battle between contemporary craft and contemporary art is that the latter is presently progressing on a Dionysian course while craft has heretofore traveled on the Apollonian path. Investigating the implications of these contrasts in detail might lead to a new understanding and ability to communicate about differences in approach within the arts and would certainly be a fascinating voyage of discovery.

The traditional view of craft art as a personal exploration of form within a framework of tradition raises an answering chord in many appreciators of craft art. Yet, such a point of view differs markedly from contemporary art attitudes endorsed by those restless personalities who seek

David Shaner's quiet and controlled covered vessel represents the Apollonian way at its best. (Photo by Marshall Noice.)

to use craft media as a means of investigating a more violent confrontation between self and society, passion and intellect.

The heat still generated by the issue of the primacy of tradition and technique versus fearless experimentation makes it clear that the role of quality in craft and craft art is far from resolved. Perhaps it is unresolvable. Are consummate skill, honesty of workmanship and durability central or is freedom to experiment, to bend a material to the artist's will, to disregard tradition if need be, paramount?

Those collectors who believe that artists must

be accorded total freedom will have no trouble adopting the latter point of view. Those who see in handicraft a disciplined way of life that has lessons for contemporary society may be more attracted to the first idea. Less ideologically committed collectors may change their minds from time to time or straddle the line.

The conflict is particularly intense for those who have participated in the growth of craft art since the 1950s. These individuals are more likely to have believed once or even now that the craftsman's way of life has curative powers. It seems as if the heated discussions on quality mean that

Ginny Ruffner's glass sculpture is vivid with color, life and excitement. *Ghost Turnips in the Sky*, 1986. Lampworked glass, pastels and pencil, 25 × 19 × 12 inches. (Photo by Michael Siedl.)

some of us hope that our craftsmen can somehow save the world.

Jack Lenor Larsen said in a speech before several crafts groups in 1984, entitled "American Craft, 2000 A.D.," that it is craftsmen who have "dispelled the invasive mediocrity of mass culture" by melding materials, process and form into worthy objects. To paraphrase his remarks, once we recognize excellence in one area, we can seek it, appreciate it, follow and nurture it in all areas. Craftsmen, in this view, offer solutions to life itself by being "in touch, center-grounded and alive." They can lead the rest of us to utopia by proving at least by example that an integrated life is possible.

Karen Johnson Boyd is a collector, gallery owner and member of the Johnson family, whose pioneering support of crafts included sponsorship of the Objects USA exhibition. "To me, quality occurs when the artist remains true to himself and his own creativity and does not pander to the demands of the collecting public," she said. "It is an important part of the battle to keep the quality of our life up by teaching people that there are high standards and what those standards are. Craftsmen and collectors jointly are very concerned with quality. One reason for jurying exhibitions is to constantly keep the quality issue before the public and to keep the quality up."[5]

## NOTES

1. Harvey K. Littleton, *Glassblowing: A Search for Form* (New York: Van Nostrand Reinhold, 1971) chapter 4.

2. Ibid.

3. Elizabeth Cameron and Philippa Lewis, *Potters on Pottery* (New York: St. Martin's Press, 1976) p.44.

4. Ibid. pp. 52-53.

5. Interview with author.

## RESOURCES FOR COLLECTORS

Books, periodicals and organizations within a specific craft medium are listed at the end of each section in chapter 6, but for an overview of the entire field, the following resources are useful.

Those who live near an art school or university with a large craft art department may find it helpful to visit the library, since school libraries buy reading material that supports the activities of the school. Often individuals with a serious purpose will be admitted to a school library on request.

Information on the location and programs of 2,500 art schools is found in the *American Art Directory*, published every two years by R. R. Bowker, New York. This reference book also describes the activities of approximately 3,200 American and Canadian museums and art organizations and lists corporations with art holdings on public view, art publications, state and regional arts councils and even the names of newspaper art critics. The *Official Museum Directory*, published by the American Association of Museums, has information about museums not listed in the *American Art Directory*. An interesting organization to know

of is the Art Libraries Society of North America (ARLIS/NA), which was established in 1972 to promote the profession of art librarianship. The group publishes a quarterly, *Art Documentation*, which sometimes includes annotated bibliographies on subjects of interest, such as textiles. (See "Organizations" p.77.) All of these reference guides can be found in the reference department of many public libraries.

## BOOKS

Thomas Albright, *Art in the San Francisco Bay Area, 1945-1980: An Illustrated History* (Berkeley: University of California Press, 1985).

Joseph Alsop, *The Rare Art Traditions: A History of Art Collecting & Its Linked Phenomena* (New York: Harper & Row, 1982).

*Craft Today: Poetry of the Physical* (New York: American Craft Museum, 1986). This is a catalogue but has a substantial essay on the development of craft art.

Barbaralee Diamonstein, *Handmade in America, Conversations with Fourteen Craftsmen* (New York: Harry N. Abrams, 1983).

Julie Hall, *Tradition and Change: The Craftsmen's Role in Society* (New York: E. P. Dutton, 1977).

*High Styles: Twentieth-Century American Design* (New York: Summit Books & Whitney Museum of Art, 1985).

Robert Jensen and Patricia Conway, *Ornamentalism: The New Decorativeness in Architecture & Design* (New York: Clarkson & Potter, Inc., 1982).

*Living Treasures of California: California Crafts XIV* (Sacramento, Calif.: Creative Arts League of Sacramento and Crocker Art Museum, 1985). This 86-page catalogue of the work of craftsmen designated "living treasures of California" has an essay on the past 35 years of craft activity by Eudorah Moore.

Lee Nordness, *Objects USA* (New York: Viking Press, 1970). Though out of print, this historically important catalogue is well worth searching out.

David Pye, *Nature & Aesthetics of Design* (New York: Van Nostrand Reinhold, 1982).

————. *Nature & Art of Workmanship* (Cambridge: Cambridge University Press, 1968).

Soetsu Yanagi, *The Unknown Craftsman: A Japanese Insight Into Beauty* (New York: Kodansha International, 1972).

## PERIODICALS

Besides the national periodicals such as *American Craft*, regional publications are also useful for keeping abreast of local exhibitions and new artists. In addition to the list of periodicals found in the *American Art Directory*, the well annotated *Magazines for Libraries*, published by R. R. Bowker, and the exhaustive *Ullrich's International Periodicals Directory* list craft art magazines. All these directories are found in many public libraries. If available, *Magazines for Libraries* is best when making subscription decisions, since each publication listed is described in some detail.

The *Art Index*, which has been published since 1932 by H. H. Wilson, New York, is a good research resource since it indexes the articles in each of the 231 periodicals it covers. Though accurate at publication, the listings here should be confirmed in a current directory.

## NATIONAL PERIODICALS

**American Craft** (bimonthly)
45 West 45th St.
New York, NY 10036

**Archives of American Art Journal** (quarterly)
Smithsonian Institution
Washington, DC 20560

**Art in America** (monthly)
150 East 58th St.
New York, NY 10022

**ArtNews** (monthly)
5 West 37th St.
New York, NY 10018

**Craft International** (quarterly)
247 Centre St.
New York, NY 10013-3216

**Crafts** (bimonthly)
British Crafts Council
12 Waterloo Place
London, SW1Y 4AU
England

**New Art Examiner** (monthly except August)
1116 F St. NW
Washington, DC 20004

## REGIONAL PUBLICATIONS

**Art New England** (quarterly)
353 Washington St.
Brighton, MA 02125

**Artspace**
Box 4547
Albuquerque, NM 87196

**Artweek** (weekly, biweekly June-August)
1628 Telegraph Ave.
Oakland, CA 94612

**Dialogue: An Art Journal** (bimonthly)
Box 2572
Columbus, OH 43276-2572

**Metropolis** (10 issues a year)
The Architecture & Design Magazine of New York
177 East 87th St.
New York, NY 10128

**Northwest Arts** (biweekly)
588 NE 98th St.
Seattle, WA 98115

**Texas Arts Journal** (quarterly)
Box 7458
Dallas, TX 75209

## COLLECTOR CATALOGUES

Each of the catalogues listed here has been selected because it provides an interesting example of the way in which an individual has shaped a collection. These few are only a tiny sample of the many catalogues that have been published.

*The Fine Art of Private Commissions* (Washington, D.C.: The George Washington University Dimock Gallery, 1983). Ronald D. Abramson Collection.

*A Passionate Vision Contemporary Ceramics from the Daniel Jacobs Collection* (Lincoln, Mass.: DeCordova Museum, 1984).

Edward Jacobsen, *The Art of Turned Wood Bowls, A Gallery of Contemporary Masters And More* (New York: E. P. Dutton, 1985).

*The Jewellery Project, New Departures in British and European Work 1980-83* (London: Crafts Council Gallery, 1983). A collection made on behalf of Malcolm, Sue and Abigale Knapp by Susanna Heron and David Ward.

*The Fred and Mary Marer Collection* (Claremont, Calif.: Lang Art Gallery, Scripps College, 1974).

*Surface Function Shape — Selections from the Earl Millard Collection* (Edwardsville, Ill.: Southern Illinois University, 1985).

*A Decade of Ceramic Art 1962-1972 From the Collection of Prof. and Mrs. R. Joseph Monsen* (San Francisco: San Francisco Museum of Art, 1972).

*Robert L. Pfannebecker Collection* (Philadelphia: Moore College of Art, 1980).

*Contemporary American and European Glass From The Saxe Collection* (Oakland, Calif.: The Oakland Museum, 1986).

## MAIL-ORDER BOOKS AND CATALOGUES

Besides documenting the work of individual artists, exhibition catalogues assay the state of the art and contain the scholarship needed by collectors to accurately assess their field. Few early craft catalogues are still available, but a collector can look at some of them at the library of the American Craft Council in New York. In addition, some of the American Craft Council's catalogues can still be purchased and a few other institutions have kept some catalogues in print or have reprinted them.

Search for out-of-print catalogues and books on craft art through mail-order book dealers and secondhand bookstores. One catalogue specialist is Worldwide Books, a division of Kraus-Thomson Ltd. However, although their *Worldwide Art Catalogue Bulletin* has a stock of 11,000 catalogues, few are on craft art. Worldwide Books publishes quarterly bulletins and a cumulative annual index of the catalogues and books it sells. Special indexes cover specific subjects such as ceramics, glass, metalworking, textile and fiber arts and decorative arts.

**Worldwide Books**
The Worldwide Art Catalogue Bulletin
37-39 Antwerp St.
Boston, MA 02135
617-787-9100

**Museum Books, Inc.**
6 W. 37th St.
New York, NY 100018
212-563-2770

**Jaap Rietman, Inc.,**
134 Spring St.
New York, NY 10012
212-966-7044

**George Wittenborn Books**
1018 Madison Ave.
New York, NY 10021
212-288-1558

**Irving Zucker Art Books**
256 Fifth Ave.
New York, NY 10003
212-679-6332

**The Book Exchange**
90 W. Market St.
Corning, NY 14831
607-936-8535

## ORGANIZATIONS

**American Craft Council**
40 W. 53rd St.
New York, NY 10019

**American Association for State and Local History**
172 2nd Ave. N.
Nashville, TN 37201

Publications on conservation and care of art objects; send for catalogue

**Art Libraries Society of North America (ARLIS/NA)**
3775 Bear Creek Circle
Tucson, AZ 85749

**James Renwick Alliance**
5240 Nebraska Avenue, NW
Washington, DC 20015

**Renwick Gallery of the National Museum of American Art**
Pennsylvania Avenue at 17th St. NW
Washington, DC 20560

Cynthia Schira's work is sold primarily through galleries. *The Kingdom of Wu,* 1985. Woven cotton, rayon and mixed fibers, 43½ × 55 inches. (Photo by E. G. Schempf, courtesy Miller/Brown Gallery, San Francisco.)

# CHAPTER FOUR
# WHERE TO FIND CRAFT ART

Galleries, craft shops, street fairs, art expos, artists' studios and wholesale decorating showrooms all serve as outlets for craft art. Once it was possible to find a remarkable piece at a street fair or gift shop. But nowadays, the expansion of opportunities to sell their work has given craft artists more of a choice about where to place it. Seeing a selection of good work, therefore, presupposes looking for it in art and craft galleries and shops and at juried exhibitions and fairs.

## GALLERIES

Henry Kahnweiler, the dealer who was representing Picasso, Braque, Derain and Vlaminck by the time he was 25, set the pace when it comes to modern art dealers. Not only did he represent these artists exclusively, but "he lived with them on a day-to-day basis . . . . He knew exactly what they wanted, and how to get it for them. Picasso, for instance, was in very poor financial shape when Kahnweiler first met him. Sensing that Picasso wanted to live, 'like a poor man with plenty of money,' Kahnweiler fixed it."[1] This dealer's ability to be with artists in the right way enhanced his usefulness to collectors since, until

the dealer's death, his gallery in Paris was the best place to see Picasso's work.

Without dealers, artists and collectors might never connect and the world's store of art would be far poorer, since when collectors make their wills museums are often the beneficiaries. But dealers make their living from selling art; when their artists prosper, so do they. Their ambiguous role makes them power brokers between artists and their public. Collectors tend to put themselves in the hands of dealers and then, as if in resentment for a usurpation of authority, to denigrate them.

Whatever else they may do, however, successful dealers are hard workers who over the years have developed a wide knowledge of their field. They know many artists, other collectors, museum curators and art consultants, are aware of important upcoming exhibitions and in general can be of great help in guiding collectors to the excellent work they seek.

This is their stock in trade as much as the works they may exhibit. "My responsibility is to provide the sum total of my experience. This may mean telling a collector not to buy work, or advising my client to buy work from another gallery

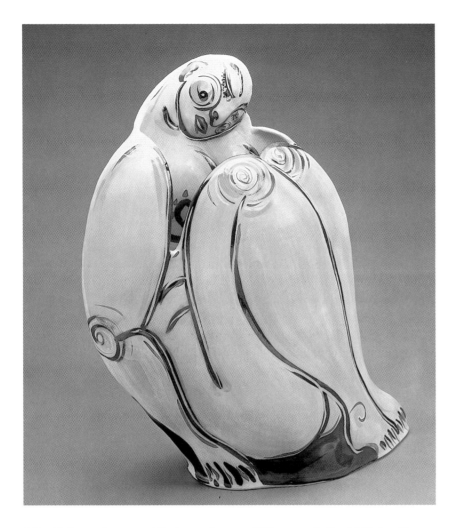

Akio Takamori,
*Woman in
Meditation,*
1986. Porcelain,
23 inches tall.
(Photo courtesy
Garth Clark Gal-
lery, Los
Angeles/New
York.)

gallery earns a commission from the artist, usually ranging from 40 to 50 percent. Commissions are increasing due to higher costs of doing business.

Gallery services valued by collectors include personal contact with a gallery principal, willingness to provide slides and information about gallery artists and to arrange personal introductions, if appropriate, and appraisals in their fields of expertise. (A bill of sale can be used as an appraisal at the time of purchase but appraisals should be updated over the years as the value of the work changes.)

Following the Kahnweiler model, a gallery that serves its artists well can be useful to collectors. Some policies that artists seek in a gallery are fair methods of payment, insurance against theft and damage to work, good record keeping, a well-maintained space and written contracts, good contacts in the museum and collector worlds and an active program of publicity. But, illuminating the personal qualities that govern art-world relationships, many artists will waive all these requirements in return for an association with a dealer who is enthusiastic about their work and can communicate that enthusiasm.

Unlike painters, craft artists tend to be represented by more than one gallery so that their work is shown all over the country. Collectors who want to see a particular craft artist's complete output should ask which galleries regularly represent that artist. The effect of multiple galleries is to make a relationship between artist and avid collector closer, since dealing directly with the artist is the only way to really know the true situation in terms of output and its location. For many collectors, this is one of the attractions of collecting craft art.

One way that some artists deal with what can become inordinate demands on their time is by

if it is good, even if I lose a sale," said Helen Drutt, owner of the Helen Drutt Gallery in Philadelphia.

A dealer can help his or her client arrive before others. "I may tell a collector to buy work which is new and difficult. My job is to spot the comers and get work for my collectors before it becomes too expensive," said Ruth Snyderman, of the Snyderman Gallery, also in Philadelphia.

Galleries do not own the work they show. They accept it on consignment from artists whose representatives they therefore become. In return for showing, selling and promoting the work, the

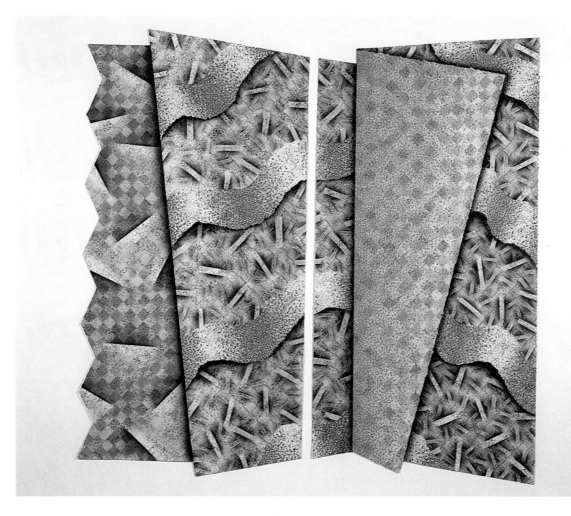

Glenn Brill, *Many Roads,* 1985. Mixed media on woven paper, 58 inches square. (Photo courtesy The Allrich Gallery, San Francisco.)

maintaining a special relationship with a particular gallery, which is sometimes referred to as the mother, or parent, gallery. "A collector should be able to go to a mother gallery to find the best examples of currently available works and complete information on the artist," said Barbara Fendrick, the Washington, D.C., dealer who represents metal artist Albert Paley in this way.

Issues centering on gallery representation and policies are among the most volatile in the rapidly changing craft art world. As a result, it is impossible to make definitive statements on gallery-artist relations and, when in doubt, each collector should feel comfortable about asking what an artist's relationship is with a specific gallery.

When buying through galleries, it can be useful to be a known collector, since many individuals typically vie for the best pieces. Collectors are sometimes given an opportunity to buy ahead of the opening, thus getting a head start. (Gallery courtesy is often extended to a collector following a particular artist, who is not a gallery regular but who asks to come early.

Gammy Miller, *Scroll Basket,* 1985. Waxed linen, paper, ash and stone, 3½ inches. (Photo by David Arky, courtesy Elaine Potter Gallery, San Francisco.)

Some galleries will not go this far but will accept work for resale on consignment. The consignor should expect to pay a commission for this service (see p. 114). The ethics of the marketplace dictate that collectors and artists deal fairly with a gallery by not negotiating separate agreements and withholding the gallery's commission.

Galleries representing painters and sculptors have not been receptive to representing artists working in craft media, particularly in New York. On the West Coast, a mix of media is more likely to be found in art galleries.

Despite acts of generosity and concern for collectors, dealers often find themselves on the defensive. According to Michael Heller, co-owner of the Heller Gallery in New York specializing in work by glass artists, some collectors have erroneous ideas about galleries.

> *Misconception number one is that we are making a lot of money. Actually, the commission often hardly covers the cost of doing business, including shipping and selling. Many collectors demand discounts. Museums and sales agents get discounts as a matter of course. The opportunity for enormous profits is not great; there are very few pieces that command as much as $25,000.*

> *Misconception number two is that the best work is in the artist's studio and a variant is that the best work is hidden in the back of the gallery or down in the cellar. We take clients on a tour to dispel that myth.*

> *There are collectors who view their collection as they do their car. They want to trade part of it in next year. If someone buys a piece, feels it was a mistake and tells us immediately we would probably go along, especially if the collector exchanged it for another work by the same*

Collectors interested in acquiring a piece by an artist whose work is in demand usually put their name on a list which the artist's dealer keeps. When the collector's turn comes, he or she is given the opportunity to buy the available piece. If the piece is not bought, the collector's name goes back to the bottom of the list.

Services offered by some, but not all, galleries include return of work purchased there in trade, usually for another piece by the same artist.

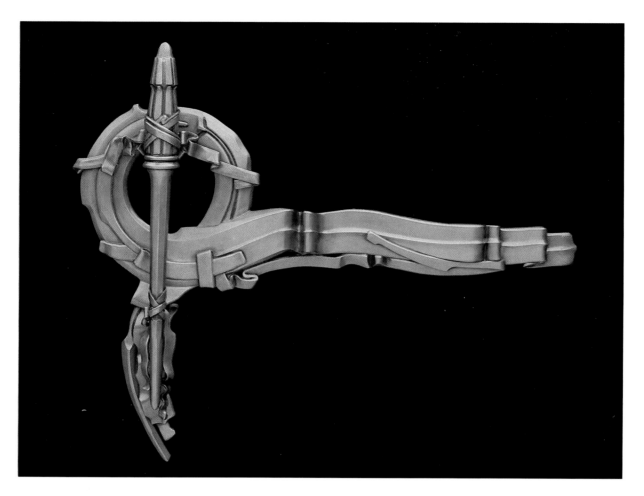

Albert Paley, cast bronze door handle, 1987. Wortham Theater Center commission, Houston. (Photo by Bruce Miller, courtesy Fendrick Gallery, Washington, D.C.)

*artist. However, we are the artist's representative. We don't own the work, so once we tell the artist it is sold, it is difficult to take it back.*

*For most collectors we recommend two-thirds of their budget each year be spent on well-established artists, leaving one-third for exciting impulse buys. 'Buy less but buy better' is a good idea especially if you have a small budget.*

## CRAFT SHOPS

Craft shops are usually delightful places where a rich profusion of functional and decorative crafts are sold. Although shops sell objects, not artists, in many instances the staff's enthusiasm for the work causes them to function as quasi-galleries. Sales personnel (who are often the owners) are typically knowledgeable about crafts and about the makers whose work they show. There is little or no pressure to buy and a low-key, informal atmosphere is the rule. Often shops arrange for commissions and special orders, provide information on craft media and artists and even offer a reading list for beginning collectors. Exhibitions may be arranged and a library of slides of work not on display may be available to view.

Shop policies on returns are those typical of

Jonathan Bonner's *Gator Candlesticks* (1986, copper, patina, 14 inches) are sold in craft shops. (Photo by Andrew Dean Powell.)

retail stores. It would be out of place to offer less than the price marked on the object, while polite bargaining is not atypical with galleries. A customer should expect to pay for a piece in entirety before taking it home, although payments over time may be possible. As a rule, shops will not finance a purchase, except through a credit card or store charge card. Returns of merchandise are likely to be allowed within certain time limits. Some craft shops have also adopted other standard store practices, such as bridal registries and sales.

Craft shops provide a place for young artists to sell their work and for beginning collectors to buy. Since prices tend to be lower than at galleries, many collectors begin their career with purchases through craft shops and a number of galleries started out as craft shops.

## CRAFT FAIRS

In the 1960s, the craft movement burst forth so rapidly that there were no marketing structures available to support the talented individuals who were creating such wonderful objects. Fairs, which are a direct method of putting buyer and seller together without the intercession of middlemen, made these transactions possible. As a result, fairs have nostalgic associations for many collectors and artists who first discovered one another in this way.

After a period during which they were denigrated as demeaning to artists and a waste of time for collectors seeking high-quality objects, the lustre of fairs as an appropriate meeting place for artist and collector has returned. New fairs are springing up, including giant art expositions at which major international galleries exhibit the work of their most illustrious artists. In 1985, for example, the Chicago International Art Exposition at Navy Pier drew over 40,000 visitors to see more than 10,000 works from 100 of the nation's top galleries and 50 foreign galleries. The event was established in 1980 and shows every sign of continuing to grow, in a sense bringing us full circle from the fair as a means of showing work galleries refused to show, to the fair as a marketplace for the work of established artists. Fairs such as the Chicago Art Expo offer collectors an excellent opportunity to sample the offerings of galleries that would otherwise require considerable time and expense to visit.

Specifically for craft art, the juried fairs run by American Craft Enterprises are among the best. This marketing organization was set up by the American Craft Council to provide opportunities for craftsmen to sell their work. In 1987, the group's roster of fairs included events in Baltimore in February, Minneapolis in April, West Springfield, Mass., in June and San Francisco in August. (The Springfield Fair was moved from Rhinebeck, N.Y., in 1984.)

Craftsmen from all over the country may apply to be in one or more of the fairs. Each year a new jury of peers is elected by the preceding year's exhibitors, crafts retailers and other authorities. The jury reviews the thousands of

Silas Kopf shows his work at craft fairs. *Telephone Cabinet*, 1987. Marquetry using various woods, 73 inches tall. (Photo by David Ryan.)

applications submitted for each fair. Collectors may choose to attend the opening benefit preview, if scheduled, or on the weekend. The first two or three days are limited to wholesale buyers.

Carol Sedestrom, president of American Craft Enterprises, said in 1987 that approximately 6,000 applications were received for that year's fairs, more submissions than in any previous year. The group added the Minneapolis fair in 1987, in cooperation with the Minnesota State Arts Board and the Minnesota Crafts Council. May 1987 marked the first appearance of a fair specifically geared to collectors, sponsored by the American Craft Council, at which one-of-a-kind pieces by 100 nationally-known craft artists were for sale at the Seventh Regiment Armory in New York.

Other fairs having venerable histories and excellent reputations are held in various parts of the country. A few of these are the fairs in Morristown, N.J., Winter Park, Fla., Guilford, Conn., the Smithsonian Institution's craft fair in Washington, D.C., and the fair run by the Women's Committee of the Philadelphia Museum of Art. The Philadelphia group has used some of the funds raised to purchase craft art for the museum's permanent collection.

Each fair has its own traditions and ambience. Some tend to emphasize high-quality original work while others provide opportunities for a pleasant outing. In general, indoor fairs are more likely to emphasize quality. For one thing, some objects, such as fiber art, are too fragile to subject to the chance of bad weather. Some well-known fairs, such as the WBAI Crafts Fair held at Columbia University in New York just before Christmas, are primarily intended for gift-buying. Others, such as the fair sponsored by the Ann Arbor Art Association, celebrate the spirit of the place in which they are held. A number of fairs stress traditional crafts.

## DEGREE SHOWS

A good way of keeping up with new talent is to attend the graduate or degree shows virtually all degree-granting art schools have, generally in the spring just before school ends. As a rule, all those being awarded master of fine arts degrees (sometimes those receiving bachelor's degrees as well) exhibit work they have completed in the preceding year or so. The work is for sale, often at low prices. A number of schools also have a faculty show at which work is for sale.

There is a difference of opinion about the value of attending and buying from student exhibitions. Some collectors prefer to wait until an artist has been out in the world for a while and producing and selling regularly through fairs, shops or gallery exhibitions. The risk obviously is that the student will abandon art for another field, leaving a collector with a single example of work when there is to be no more. On the other hand, more than one collector has noted that early work often has a special vigor.

Some of the more interesting graduate shows are in schools where a powerful artist is teaching. Recognizing that each person's list is likely to be different, here are a few schools whose graduate shows have interested collectors: Cranbrook Academy; the University of Washington at Seattle; Southern Illinois University at Carbondale; the University of Wisconsin at Madison; the University of Michigan at Ann Arbor; State University of New York at New Paltz; Philadelphia College of Art; University of Delaware; Rhode Island School of Design; The School for American Craftsmen at Rochester (N.Y.) Institute of Technology; Alfred Univer-

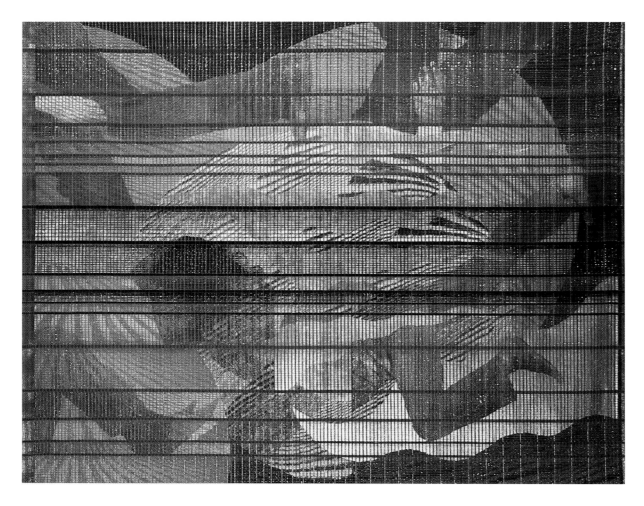

Gerhard Knodel teaches at Cranbrook Academy, whose degree shows regularly attract collectors. *Guardian of the Second Corner*, 1987. Woven cotton, linen, Mylar, metallic gimp, 70 × 54½ inches. (Photo by artist.)

sity; University of California at Davis; San Francisco Art Institute; and California College of Arts and Crafts in Oakland.

To learn about graduate shows, contact the school's art gallery or art department and ask to be notified, suggests Robert Ebendorf, jewelry professor at SUNY New Paltz. He said that collectors and young artists both benefit when a collector attends a degree show. "Students, especially those making esoteric pieces, really need to learn how to talk to collectors and museum people, because this will be the only market for their work," he said.

## BUYING DIRECTLY FROM THE ARTIST

Some artists prefer to sell their work themselves instead of through galleries. They may maintain a salesroom attached to their workshop, which is open by appointment or during regular hours, open their studio to the public a few times a year or on weekends, or simply be willing to see a collector by appointment.

Craft cooperatives sometimes schedule special events for the public. For example, the Bay Area Studio Art Glass group (BASAG) has been holding open houses to show the work of its 22

Toshiko Takaezu handles her own work. *Closed Form Ceramic,* 1979, 8 inches tall. (Photo by Bernard Handzel, collection of Daniel Jacobs.)

members since 1979. (Write Julia Peterson Maslach, 44 Industrial Way, Greenbrae, Calif. 94904). Group members also sell through galleries throughout the country and prices are the same as at the galleries, but the opportunity to see a great deal of work and meet and talk to the artists is a draw for collectors.

Craftsmen sometimes band together for publicity. The Asparagus Valley Potters Guild around Springfield, Mass., published a pamphlet in 1984 listing 21 potters with addresses, phone numbers and brief descriptions of their work. Craftsmen working in and around Penland, N.C., have published a map listing open studios.

In urban centers such as Chicago, Washington, D.C., Baltimore and New York, some artists have established cooperative galleries and some buildings contain a number of studios along with exhibition space. One such cooperative—Lill Street Studios in Chicago—is a non-profit group that provides working space for ceramists and maintains a professionally run gallery. Its regular exhibitions are listed in Chicago arts publications. The Pindar Gallery in New York, the Northwest Gallery of Fine Woodworking in Seattle and the Torpedo Factory in Alexandria, Va., are several others at this writing. Further information may be obtained by contacting the Association of Artist-Run Galleries at 164 Mercer Street, New York, N.Y. 10012 (212-226-3107). Many of the groups are ephemeral and finding out about them is serendipitous. Check for information at craft fairs and craft shops in an area. Good sources for information about crafts-producing areas are the arts councils found in every state. A list of arts councils is printed in the *American Art Directory.* Although prices may be lower at cooperative galleries and artist's studios since there are fewer marketing layers, the greater advantage is an opportunity to see a larger quantity of work and to interact with the artists.

## PRIVATE DEALERS AND CONSULTANTS

Private dealers and consultants are usually individuals with an excellent background in the craft world. They may have operated a gallery in the past. Their contacts with dealers, artists and collectors as well as with museum curators and others in the field make it possible for them to take on special assignments. These may include advising beginning collectors, helping corporations to put together a collection of craft art, and acting as go-between in commissions, especially for interior designers and architects who may be seeking a special work for a public or commercial installation. The art market has included such consultants for many years, but recently individuals who are knowledgeable about craft media have also been finding clients for their services.

In some instances, dealers who once had galleries continue to guide and advise long-standing clients, perhaps ferreting out the best examples of an artist's work, turning up new artists and procuring their work before it becomes prohibitively expensive. Such long-time dealers may also maintain relationships with one or a few artists whom they formerly represented and may continue to act as agents for these artists. Collectors may therefore find it best to seek out such dealers for particular artists' work.

The names of consultants and private dealers are not generally listed in any directory but a collector who attends exhibitions, reads catalogues and current publications will eventually come across them, or conversely, dealers and consultants may find collectors as they become known.

Consultants charge for their services on a per diem or per project basis or they may earn a commission on work that is sold. If you hire a consultant on a fee basis and a purchase is involved, you may reap the benefit of saving money on the purchase since the consultant may not take the commission. Agreement on payment for time and services should naturally occur before beginning to work with a consultant.

## OTHER MARKETING METHODS

Some craftsmen, especially producers of multiples, are seeking markets with retailers such as furniture and department stores and gift shops. They make it easier for these retailers to buy their work by taking space at trade shows and permanent showrooms, such as the National Crafts Showroom in New York, representing about 200 craftsmen, and the American Crafts Showroom, which is open during the twice-yearly national wholesale furniture market in High Point, N.C.

These efforts mean that crafts are more visible than they used to be and easier to find in traditional kinds of stores. Some craftsmen are represented in showrooms used by interior designers and architects.

## COMMISSIONING CRAFT ART

There are important differences between an order for custom work and a request for something beautiful from a particular artist. Both are valid examples of the virtues of commissions, but the collector should be clear about which he or she is seeking. Some artists will be perfectly happy to make a set of pillows for your pink couch. Others won't. The way to find out is to ask.

Some examples of typical commissions for custom work include: furniture; ornamental iron such as fireplace grates, steps or railings; ornamental glass panels, windows or partitions; large-scale fiber pieces; clothing for a special occasion; jewelry; a set of goblets, a dinner service and flatware.

On the other hand, you may admire an individual's work and want an example created specifically for you. Ronald D. Abramson, an attorney in Washington, D.C., and his wife,

Kathie Stackpole
Bunnell, stained
glass room
divider, 1982.
Commissioned
for John Denver
residence, Aspen,
Colo. (Photo by
Peter Stackpole.)

Anne, have commissioned many pieces, including an addition to their home to house some of their extensive glass collection. In 1983, an exhibition of 24 works made for the Abramsons was held at the Dimock Gallery at The George Washington University in Washington, D.C. In the catalogue, Abramson wrote that he did not usually attempt to influence the outcome of a commission. He simply presented a problem and asked an artist to solve it. The parameters are thus often very loose. The price and a general idea of what is to be made are specified. When it will be ready, how it will be used and precisely what it will look like are all open, he says.

"The letters back and forth are free and flowing. They are the ultimate artist's statement," in contrast to the formal statements by artists often found in catalogues. "These letters are very much from the heart. I touched and was touched by the energy which exists between the artists and their art."

One of the most ambitious commissions for art work in recent years resulted in an exhibition of jewelry of nonprecious materials. Malcom and Sue Knapp, New York collectors whose multifaceted collection includes ceramics, fiber art, wood and jewelry, were enthusiastic about the work of some Dutch and English jewelers, which they saw in the home of London jeweler Susanna Heron and photographer David Ward. So they commissioned the two London artists to make a collection of interesting new work, imposing a purchase limit of about $20,000. The Knapps had in mind exhibiting the work in the United States because they wanted American artists and the public to be able to see it.

"This was new ground for us. Instead of commissioning an object, we were commissioning an idea," said Malcolm Knapp. The jewelry was shown at the British Crafts Council Gallery in London in 1983. Although it was not publicly exhibited in this country, a catalogue was published which, according to Knapp, became a source of inspiration to jewelers here and in other countries.

Many artists enjoy working by commission. Some, such as the metalist Albert Paley, work primarily in this way. Collectors can commission a work through an intermediary such as a gallery or consultant, or directly from the artist. Dealers and consultants can help narrow the search for an artist, since they know the work of many artists. They can find a number of candidates and, without embarrassment to a collector, procure slides of the artists' work and help evaluate the candidates. They can also draw up a suitable contract.

Sometimes, the professional acts as the contracting party with a collector and handles all details including delivery, installation and repairs, if needed. However, a more satisfying experience may result when client and artist work together directly.

Ed Carpenter, a Portland, Oregon-based artist working with flat glass, has completed more than 40 commissions. He said his best experiences have been with clients who were deeply involved with all aspects of the project. He advises full disclosure to the artist selected for the commission.

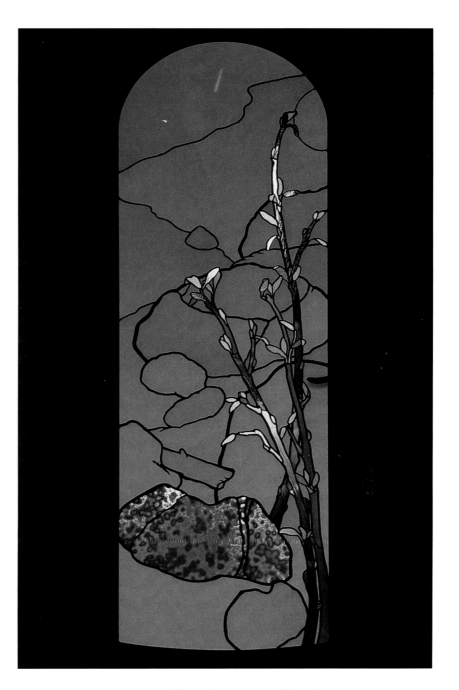

Kathie Stackpole Bunnell, *Willow Door,* 1982, John Denver residence. (Photo by Peter Stackpole.)

Even if a third party, such as an architect or consultant, is involved, the client should talk to the artist, leveling about budget, time considerations and goals.

You can find artists by consulting slide registries, such as the one maintained by the American Craft Council with the names of 2,000 artists. Published lists are another aid, such as "The Guild: A Sourcebook of American Craft Artists," issued annually by Kraus-Sikes, Inc., 150 W. 25th St., New York, N.Y. (212-242-3730). The directory lists individuals who will undertake lighting, furniture, tapestries, rugs, tiles and architectural metal, among other specialties, and shows examples of their work.

Finding an artist at a fair can be a good method because there is an opportunity to talk about what you want directly with the individual maker and to see his or her work. Craft guilds found in many states maintain slide libraries of members' work and information about commissions, approximate delivery time needed and a rough price range. Craft schools and craft departments of universities may also help.

A written contract can help keep a commission from going awry by spelling out the rights and obligations of each party. The Art Law Committee of the Association of the Bar of the City of New York has drafted a sample commission contract. Though it is for public art commissions, the areas covered, which include quality and defects, fidelity of the work to the original proposal, copyright and artist's rights, are of concern in private commissions, too. Copies are available for $5 from the American Council on the Arts, 570 Seventh Ave., New York, N.Y. 10018. Several books that cover legal issues also have sample contracts, and discuss a variety of legal questions in art collecting as well. See, for example, Tad Crawford's *Legal Guide for Visual Artists* (New York: Madison Square Press, 1987), when commissioning an object. (See also p. 97).

At this writing, a series of meetings on legal issues in commissioning, including contracts, conservation and copyright, is being conducted by the National Endowment for the Arts' Visual Arts Program office. A manual on these subjects will be published eventually by the Arts Extension Service of the University of Massachusetts, Amherst.

## PAYING FOR CRAFT ART

Most of the 308 examples of craft art assembled by Lee Nordness and Paul Smith for the Objects USA exhibition cost less than $500, according to Nordness.

"We paid $250 for one of Ken Price's cups and thought it was outrageous," he recalled recently. Today the cups sell for $10,000 each, he said. Several works by Robert Arneson, including an "Alice House," sold for $500 or less. Today a piece in the "Alice House" series might sell for $20,000, Nordness estimated. A ceramic vessel by Beatrice Wood, today $4,000 and up, according to her dealer, Garth Clark, was $500.

On the whole, added Nordness, currently a private dealer, functional work has gone up in price less than sculptural work, but prices have substantially increased for high-quality crafts of all types.

Others tell a similar story. "When I began ten years ago, a top price for glass was $150 to $200," recalled Douglas Heller, co-owner of the Heller Gallery. Today, it is not unusual for works by major craft artists to command four and sometimes five figures. Prices for the work of superstars such as Harvey Littleton and Wendell Castle are in this range. Castle's major pieces can go up

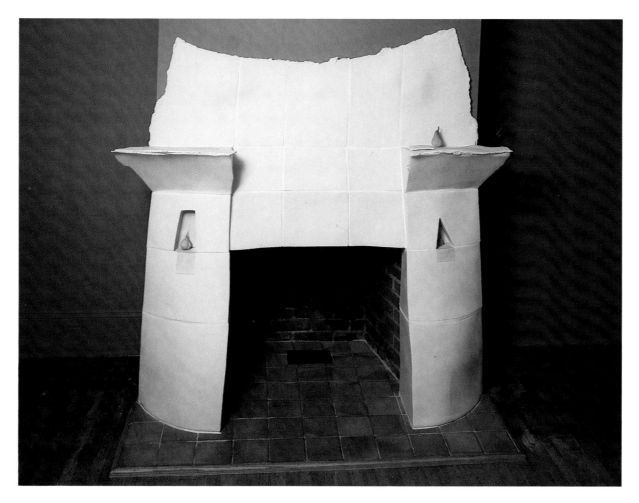

Paula Winokur, *Fireplace Site IV*, 1985. Porcelain, slab construction. Private residence commission. (Photo by Will Brown, courtesy Helen Drutt Gallery, Philadelphia.)

to six figures, says Alexander Milliken, who shows his work at the Milliken Gallery in New York. Peter Voulkos commands prices of from $5,000 to $50,000 for his work, according to Alice Westphal of Exhibit A Gallery in Chicago.

Since craft art collecting is not merely a rich person's game, enthusiasts have had to become creative about paying for the work they admire. Methods of doing so include paying over time (possible when buying both through galleries and directly from the artist), bartering (possible when buying directly from the artist) and borrowing money for purchases.

Some galleries accept payment over time, usually on a monthly basis. Often, these payments do not include additional interest, so the gallery in effect finances the purchase. Galleries often give a discount of approximately 10 percent to bona fide collectors who pay for work immediately. Each gallery may have its own test of "collector," but in general the term applies to an individual who has already acquired a number of works from this or other galleries, regularly attends exhibitions, holds membership in special-interest societies or displays knowledge of the field.

Jim Wallace, *Lowenberg Gates,* 1984. Forged steel and bronze, 7 feet high. (Photo courtesy National Ornamental Metal Museum, Memphis, Tenn.)

Decisions about advancing credit are based partially on other issues, such as how good a customer the collector is, his or her financial worthiness and even on feelings of friendship. As art lovers themselves, gallery people try to make it easier for someone who they sense loves certain work to buy it.

Artists, too, are often willing to accept monthly payments, especially from collectors whose apparent financial resources do not make it possible to pay for a work all at once. As a rule, expect the title to remain with the gallery or artist until the work is paid for. The issue of where the work resides before it is paid for is open to discussion.

A way of acquiring a piece that one cannot afford at the moment is to buy it as it is about to go on tour. Although the piece may be broken in transit, if it isn't, the collector ends up with a documented piece which has been on national exhibition and has enough time (often a year or two may elapse) to save up the money.

Some individuals who are seeking large sums of money for further purchases may be able to borrow the money using the art as security, according to Gideon Strauss, principal of Rosenthal Art Equities, Inc., in New York. The company makes such loans, usually for amounts of $50,000 or more, on a nationwide basis. An advantage to borrowing from a firm such as Rosenthal is that a collector is able to obtain funds quickly to purchase an object which would otherwise go to someone else. Some clients have a line of credit so that they can be certain of obtaining cash if they need it to make an art purchase.

Strauss, who says he is a collector himself of handmade paper art objects, said the firm lends money only on art that "has made its way into the auction catalogues of Sotheby's, Christie's or other prominent auction houses." This policy at present effectively eliminates much craft art because auction markets have not yet been well developed.

Although past banking practice has not supported lending money to buy art using the art as collateral, there have been some changes in recent years. At Chase Manhattan Bank in New York, for example, banking policy now permits such loans to high net-worth clients. The amount available depends not on the value of the art but on the value of the assets of the individual who wants to borrow the money. As a rule, interest rates are pegged to the prime rate, running about two percent above it. However, rates and amount available are open to negotiation. Most banks in the United States are actively seeking to increase their market share among wealthy clients. Consequently, many have set up private banking departments geared to serve the needs of this type of client. Those interested in obtaining a bank loan to buy art should broach the subject with their banker.

Bartering is another way to acquire artwork. Artists who collect frequently trade their own work for someone else's. Collectors can't trade art objects but they can trade services or merchandise to which they have access. Among objects and services artists have bartered for are: legal, financial, medical and dentistry services, catering, carpentry, consumer goods, labor in the studio and artist's supplies. As one collector who barters explained, there is always a polite way of asking if an artist would consider bartering.

Collectors should realize, however, that bartering does have tax implications. According to the Internal Revenue Service, goods received have a monetary value and must be treated as income by the artists who receive them. The individual who renders a service and receives a pot or a fiber artwork or a glass sculptural form in return for that service should report as income the monetary value placed on the object.

If an artist and a dentist barter, they are both expected to treat the goods or services they receive as income. However, each can deduct the cost of materials and labor elsewhere, so in many instances the barter arrangement will have no tax consequences. If a collector receives an artwork from an artist in exchange for a service that is not in his or her regular line of business, there are no tax consequences, according to the IRS.

The actual purchase price of an artwork is not the only expense a collector incurs in pursuit of art objects. The cost of catalogues, travel to exhibitions, phone calls, hotels, insurance, conservation and storage can add up to a substantial figure. However, since collecting art (even if some pieces are later sold out of the collection) is considered a hobby by the Internal Revenue Service, none of these expenses may be deducted from income taxes.

An individual who purchases crafts as decorative and art objects for a place of business can purchase them through the business, deducting the cost of insurance and conservation as a legitimate expense. However, the IRS stresses that these objects must remain at the business and not be taken home and mingled with a personal collection.

An art dealer may deduct from income any expenses incurred in pursuit of stock for his business. Those extremely active collectors who may also be in a related business, such as interior design, retailing or architecture, might find it worthwhile to investigate the legal requirements, costs and advantages of establishing such a busi-

The power of
Robert Arneson's
later work has
created demand
for the earlier
pieces as well.
*Huddle,* 1973.
Terra cotta,
17 inches high.
(Photo courtesy
Alan Frumkin
Gallery, New
York.)

ness by speaking with a knowledgeable tax attorney or accountant. (To set up a business, it isn't necessary to consult an attorney, but there have to be all the earmarks of a business in terms of buying and selling, business cards and so forth.)

Many collectors are tantalized by the fact that foundations may deduct expenses connected with collecting art. However, Norman Donoghue, a Philadelphia attorney with a special interest in art and a board member of the Wharton Esherick Foundation, explained that rules governing art foundations are restrictive and explicit. Setting up a foundation is a costly process and those interested in considering this should obtain appropriate legal advice before proceeding.

Anyone can seek recognition and tax-exempt status from the Internal Revenue Service by establishing a foundation. If tax-exempt status is granted, then contributions must be used in furtherance of the tax-exempt purpose. If, for example, the stated purpose is to establish a study collection of contemporary studio glass open to qualified students, then deductible foundation expenses would have to be in support of this goal.

Collectors eventually may need advice from an accountant or tax attorney when it comes to disposing of their collection or some part of it, either through bequest or as a charitable contribution. It's wise to find a qualified attorney along the way so that questions regarding financial and legal issues can be settled as they come up. Finding individuals qualified to advise about art collecting can take more digging than would simply finding a competent lawyer. Some possible techniques: Look for an attorney who is active at a local museum or on an arts group's board of directors. Ask gallery owners and museums for the names of attorneys who represent them. Call the local Bar Association for a referral; in a number of localities, volunteer groups of lawyers for the arts provide free or low-cost legal service to artists. Though these groups don't generally make referrals, they might be willing to say how to begin a search for a lawyer with expertise in art matters.

The Practicing Law Institute in New York holds seminars every two years on the subject of representing collectors. Speakers include attorneys and other experts who present information of interest to collectors concerned with legal and financial aspects of collecting. These seminars are open to collectors. Information on the seminars and on how to obtain the Casebooks, which include the papers presented by all the speakers, is available from Practicing Law Institute, 810 Seventh Ave., New York, N.Y. 10018.

## GUIDELINES ON COMMISSION CONTRACTS

Comprehensive contracts for the creation of crafted objects should include consideration of the following points.

### Phase One

Agreement for preparation of design specifications should include:

Design Fee

Form artist's presentation will take (drawings, models, maquettes, or detailed rendering)

Number of designs to be submitted

Date of completion for design proposal

Terms to terminate project at design phase

Ownership of submitted designs

### Phase Two

Commission for actual construction of object should consider:

Nature of piece(s) to be built in terms of dimensions, materials and design

Price and payment schedule

Production schedule

Insurance of work in progress

Copyrights

Inspection of work in progress

Grounds for termination of agreement

Delivery and installation

Ownership and transfer of title

Warranty

Artist's rights

---

## NOTES

1. John Russell, "A Book That Shows Art Dealers To Be Human, Too," *New York Times*, August 12, 1904, p. II-27.

## SLIDE REGISTRIES

The following list is far from exhaustive. These and other registries can be used to locate an artist for a commission or to update addresses and keep track of changes in working style of artists in a collection. Where available, telephone numbers are listed.

**American Craft Council Library**
Room 201
45 West 45th Street
New York, NY 10036
212-069-9422

**Art Information Center**
280 Broadway, Suite 412
New York, NY 10007
212-988-7700

**Arts, Inc.**
Box 32382
Washington, DC 10007

**Boston Visual Artists Union**
3 Centre Plaza
Boston, MA 02108
617-227-3076

**Center for the Visual Arts**
1615 Broadway
Oakland, CA 94612

**Illinois Arts Council**
111 N. Wabash Ave.
Chicago, IL 60602
312-793-3520

**National Slide Registry of American Artists & Craftsmen**
806 15th St., NW, Suite 426
Washington, DC 20002

**United States Fine Arts Registry, Inc.**
Dept. 986R
309 Santa Monica Blvd.
Santa Monica, CA 90401

This art quilt by Terrie Mangat will be as colorful 100 years from now if it is protected from fading. *Ladies Exercise,* 1982, 87 × 62 inches.

## CHAPTER FIVE
# ONCE YOU GET IT HOME

Acquiring an art object is merely the first step in a chain of stewardship that will eventually require the collector to consider insurance, documentation, effective and safe display and conservation, as well as the eventual transfer or disposal of a collection. This chapter covers these subjects.

### INSURANCE

Most individual homeowners have insurance policies which cover unlisted personal effects. Because of the theft limitations of $500 to $1,000 on items such as jewelry and silver, these homeowner policies are inadequate as a safeguard for even the smallest collection.

It is possible to purchase a homeowner policy on a replacement-cost basis, which includes the cost of replacing a collection. But better coverage is available for less in a fine arts policy, which can be written as a personal articles floater to the homeowner policy you already have or as an entirely separate policy. There are no benefits for a collector in selecting one course over the other. In each case, new items may be added to the policy as they are acquired. Fine arts policies can

be tailored to suit a particular collector's needs. This is especially true when you have selected an insurance agent who is knowledgeable about various options and underwriters.

A desirable feature of any fine arts policy is automatic coverage for newly acquired items. There is usually a 30-day grace period. During this time, you are expected to notify the insurance company of your acquisition, to supply a bill of sale as a current appraisal and to pay for coverage from the date of acquisition, not the date of notification.

Losses of any type are covered in a fine arts policy, unless specifically excluded. Typical exclusions include wear and tear, gradual deterioration, damage from moths or vermin, damage that occurs while an object is being restored or repaired and breakage. You can usually remove the breakage exclusion by paying a higher premium.

As a condition of obtaining a fine arts policy, you will be asked to supply an up-to-date appraisal or current bill of sale for each item to be insured. You may also be asked to supply details about your home and its construction, your neighborhood and any steps you have taken to minimize

Complex works with many small parts, such as this piece (both pages) by Mario Rivoli, are better displayed in a protected setting. *Winged Faun,* 1985. Assemblage with found objects. (Photos by Bob Hansson, courtesy Julie: Artisans' Gallery, New York.)

loss from theft or fire, such as installing a burglar alarm or smoke detectors.

The insurance company may send an inspector to check your home and to make suggestions about safety and security. For example, Chubb Insurance Co., an underwriter specializing in personal property insurance, sends an inspector out when the value of the home or its contents is $300,000 or more. The inspector's job is not only to safeguard the company, but also to help the insured minimize loss risk.

Fine arts insurance rates are determined by overall loss statistics in your locality, as well as by state regulation and the effects of competition. At this writing, fine arts insurance rates are low in comparison to the cost of insuring other types of personal property, such as jewelry and furs. Rates range from a low of about 15 cents to a high of about 50 cents for each $100 of value. Those who live in or near large cities pay more than those who live in rural or remote areas of the country. One underwriter estimated that insuring art objects in parts of Texas, for example, could cost 35 cents per $100, while insuring jewelry in the same locales would be $1.90. So it would cost only about $350 a year to insure a $100,000 fine arts collection, while the same amount of jewelry would cost $1,900 a year in insurance premiums.

There are two types of fine arts insurance policies available to most collectors. Most commonly, a list of every item to be insured is prepared and a value is assigned to each item. This figure (determined by appraisal) is what you and the company agree will be what you recover in case of a loss.

You can also buy fine arts blanket coverage, which does not necessarily have an agreed-upon value for each item. Instead, you estimate the total worth of the collection and buy insurance for the total. Of course, an itemized list is required to estimate the worth of a collection and the cost of replacement. But you do not need to obtain an expert appraisal for every item. If you suffer a loss, the insurance company will ask you to determine the value of the item. Usually you will be asked for verification of your estimate in the form of a statement from a dealer or perhaps from the artist who made it.

An important advantage of blanket coverage is that you can be reimbursed on current market value rather than on an appraised value determined perhaps several years prior to the loss. Blanket coverage is also useful if you have a large collection of currently unappraised items and would find it costly and time-consuming to obtain qualified appraisals for individual items. If you trade often, so that the individual items change but the total value does not vary much, this type of coverage is appropriate.

While the cost of both forms of fine arts insurance is approximately the same, beginning collectors often feel most comfortable with a specific appraisal value attached to each item. As one acquires experience and builds a larger collection, the blanket coverage method gains appeal. In both instances, collectors should keep track of changes in value due to appreciation. Most authorities recommend reappraisal at least every three years.

As a collection becomes more valuable, additional options become available. Insurers offer those whose collections are worth $1,000,000 and more an opportunity to insure in the way that museums do, that is, to buy coverage for an amount less than the value of the total collection. For example, an individual with a collection worth $2,000,000 might decide to buy

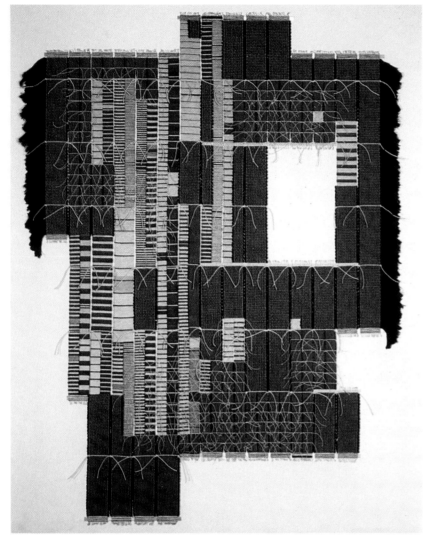

Textiles can usually withstand the rigors of a traveling exhibition. Blair Tate, *Resource,* 1987. Woven linen and cotton, 98 × 75 inches. (Photo by Jeffrey Schiff.)

Museum-type policies are most likely to be available through a specialist in fine arts insurance. These firms often deal with clients from many parts of the country. Some specialists are listed at the end of this chapter. Knowledgeable agents can also be located through referrals from galleries and museums.

Some collectors elect to forego insurance, putting the money they might spend on premiums into a home security system or saving it as a form of self-insurance. Since insurance dollars can't replace unique objects, this attitude is certainly understandable if an individual is comfortable with it. A tax loss can be taken if an art object is damaged or stolen. Those planning on using such a write-off as a means of self-insurance should be aware that the Internal Revenue Service allows a deduction of only the original cost or the value of the object at the time of loss—whichever is lower. Furthermore, if you should have an insured loss, the IRS expects you to replace the loss with objects of like kind and quality. Otherwise you will be asked to pay capital gains taxes on the insurance windfall.

## SAFETY PRECAUTIONS
### In Transit:
- Be careful all property is properly packed and unpacked.
- If hand-carrying, have at least one other person accompany you. If you travel by bus, train or plane, the artwork should be held at the seat, not in the baggage section or in an overhead luggage section. Never leave the work unattended.
- If you are carrying the object in a vehicle, make sure it is not left unattended.
- If you hire a transporter, opt for a fine arts mover, who will adhere to professional stan-

$1 million's worth of insurance, considering that only half of the collection could be destroyed in any single catastrophe. A loss of up to $1 million would be totally covered, no matter which items were destroyed or stolen, yet the premium savings would be substantial. Another way of saving on premiums is accepting a high deductible (perhaps $1,000 or more).

dards including carrying insurance and transporting the work in a locked, alarmed van.

**At Home:**

- Securely lock the residence at night and when leaving the premises. Turn on the alarm system before going to bed or out.
- Keep the phone number of the local police handy and call if any suspicious activity is observed on or near the premises.
- Do not invite strangers into your residence.
- Small portable works of art should be displayed well away from doorways and other exits.
- Require and check references of those you hire.
- If you intend to be away for an extended period of time, give the residence an occupied appearance. Continue mail and newspaper deliveries, but have someone pick them up. Have neighbors use your trash cans. Leave a car in the driveway. Place timers on lights so they come on and go off at the usual hours.
- Let the police know you plan to be away.

**Courtesy Huntington T. Block Insurance, reprinted with permission.**

## LOANING YOUR COLLECTION

Collectors have to weigh the advantage of loaning their objects, which may increase their value, against the risk of damage, destruction or loss. Fragile glass, ceramics and fiber works do get broken in transit more often than a novice might imagine, so before agreeing to make a loan, a collector should make sure that skilled and experienced art movers have been engaged, that care will be taken in crating, transport and unpacking and that the borrowing institution has adequate security, fire protection, climate control and safe lighting. Some institutions furnish facility reports explaining these issues. They will

The best time to collect documentation information is when a work is acquired. Dan Dailey, *Gliders in City Air—Bird Vase Series,* 1982. Blown glass vessel, 11 inches tall. (Photo by Susi Cushner.)

Narcissus Quagliata, *Portrait of Andrew Lewis,* 1983. Stained glass, 59 × 65½ inches. (Photo by Bill Kane.)

also make changes in standard loan agreements to meet a lender's demands.

A collector may, for example, wish to be able to withdraw a work before an exhibition has concluded or before it travels to another institution. Or he or she may specify as a condition of the loan that a photo of the object be included in the catalogue. Some collectors lend only to an exhibition which will be accompanied by a catalogue. Under some circumstances, a collector may elect to renege or withdraw work from an exhibition if the display or other conditions do not meet expectations.

The borrowing institution generally assumes

all costs of moving, packing and shipping an artwork and pays for the insurance. As a rule, however, the lender is expected to supervise the packing and may make recommendations about packing and shipping.[1] On rare occasions, a museum may send a courier to personally pick up an artwork, but this is to be expected only for the most fragile and valuable objects.

The lender will be asked to sign a loan agreement and to indicate the value of the object for insurance purposes. "That figure becomes sacrosanct and is the amount you will recover in case of a loss, so make sure it is accurate," notes Huntington Block, a broker specializing in fine arts insurance.

## DOCUMENTING THE COLLECTION

Keeping records may seem pointless or an affectation to a collector having only few art objects. But good records assume greater importance as a collection grows. For some, keeping and perusing these records, which are a kind of personal history, become highly enjoyable aspects of collecting. It's easiest to obtain the pertinent information at the time of purchase, so those just starting out are wise to set up a system for recording and filing the appropriate information early in their collecting careers.

Records serve a variety of purposes. Invoices and descriptive information are necessary to insure the work. As a collection increases, accurate records may be the only way to tell if something is missing and, in the case of theft, may make it easier to trace the object. If questions of valuation ever arise, records will make it easier to respond; if future restoration is required, a record of materials and methods of construction may prove helpful. Keeping good records will also help

scholars trace the development of the field.

At a minimum, you need to write down the name of the artist, date and place of purchase and price paid. A description of the object such as title, if any, measurements, materials and a brief summary of construction methods is useful. A photo (the instant variety or a slide), is often made and facts such as the piece's exhibition history may be included.

Ideally, the owner of any contemporary artwork should be able to trace it back through previous owners to the artist who made it, as museums attempt to do for contemporary works in their possession. Typical facts recorded by museums besides those just enumerated include history of ownership, method of acquisition, places exhibited or published and pertinent historical facts. Photos of the work are taken and data on insurance valuation is included, as are biographical information on the artist and a listing of the copyright holder. (To reproduce a work, its owner must obtain permission from the copyright holder, if any.)

Museums generally assign each item in their collection an accession number before going on to document it in the manner just described.[2] One numbering system includes information on year of acquisition, order received within that year and number of the item within the acquisition. A three-part number separated by decimal points is allocated. Thus, an accession number of 79.01.04 would be deciphered as the first accession in 1979 of a group of at least four items of which this is the fourth item.

To keep items from getting lost, each object in a museum collection is indelibly marked with its correct accession number. On firm surfaces, artists' oil paints are often employed. On textiles and baskets, the registration number may be

Metal objects have been called the conservator's dream because they withstand the elements beautifully. L. Brent Kington, *Weathervane,* 1987. Forged bronze, 52 × 26 inches.

placed on a cloth laundry-marking tag and then gently sewn to the object. Collectors who plan on a large number of acquisitions might consider emulating museums in numbering. The accession system is easily mastered and ensures objects will not become misidentified over the years.

Besides keeping a record of items (on computer, index cards or in a logbook), many museums and quite a few collectors also maintain folders in which documents such as correspondence, bills of sale, exhibition announcements and articles about works they own are saved. These may be filed by artist in acid-free paper file folders, envelopes or boxes and kept in standard file cabinets, or they may be kept in scrapbook form.

Regardless of whether a computer, index card system or logbook is selected for record keeping, a printed form consisting of a series of headings or captions with space for entering the appropriate information is best. The use of a form prevents unintentional omissions of information and

ensures that the data will appear in the same relative position on each entry.

Collectors do not have to know how to program in order to store records on a computer if they purchase a data management or file program, which can then be adapted for any type of collection. An important advantage to computerizing records is the ability to generate a variety of lists and breakdowns, according to collector Andrew Lewis, who transferred his records from paper to computer. Lewis, who used a standard filing program and an Apple II computer, also found it much easier to keep track of insurance records on the computer.

Lewis stressed that it is best to use pencil and paper to develop a form and work with it until it is satisfactory before computerizing the information. The form he created includes data such as the artist's name, item and number, medium, title, size and dimensions, location, cost, where purchased, address of outlet, amount insured for, check number or charge and comments. The information is stored both on disks and printouts. At least one list is on file outside his home along with photos of the objects in the collection.

Some collectors find art index cards developed primarily for galleries to be helpful in keeping records. One excellent card (shown at right) has a pocket for a slide. The 5 × 8 card, which has a section on the back for notes and references, was created by William Soghor, an art appraiser and photographer. Soghor also publishes the same card blank. Either version is useful for private collectors, too.

Collectors who have already acquired a number of objects, but have few or no records, can begin keeping records with their next acquisition. Then they can slowly update the earlier records as well as possible. Collectors may also rectify the

| | ARTIST | | NO. | PRICE |
|---|---|---|---|---|
| | TITLE | | DATE | SOURCE |
| | MEDIA | SIZE | | |
| | DESCRIPTION | | | COSTS |
| | | | | |
| | PHOTOGRAPHS | | | |

| | DATE OUT | DATE IN | ORIGIN OR DESTINATION | PURPOSE | |
|---|---|---|---|---|---|
| LOCATION | | | | | |
| | | | | | |
| | | | | | |
| | | | | | DISPOSITION |
| | | | | | |
| | | | | | |
| | | | | | |
| | | | | | |

Sample copies of the Soghor ArtIndexcard are available free. Request the Gallery-Collector or blank card from William Soghor Co., Box 6366, Yorkville Station, New York, NY 10128. Specify intended use by collector. Copyright 1977 William Soghor. Reprinted with permission.

situation by employing an individual to catalogue their collection or to make a written inventory.

Appraisers are sometimes employed in this manner, though as a rule the appraiser's primary role is to evaluate a collection being sold or donated to a charitable institution.

Art consultants also do inventories. Soghor, for example, has been employed to identify, measure and photograph objects as well as to provide a written description of them. Graduate art history and museology students represent another source of help in creating an inventory. Collectors who are interested should write or call a nearby graduate art department for information about qualified students who might undertake such work.

## DISPLAY AND CONSERVATION

A primary motivation for collecting art is to be able to experience the joy of living with it in daily life. Consequently, a method of display that permits both access and safety is best.

Some media are more impervious to the elements than others. Metal has been called a conservator's delight because of its durability and minimal deterioration. Ceramics have lasted thousands of years. Glass, so long as it is not

Although painted feathers look intensely fragile, the ones in this wonderful necklace by K. Lee Manuel have a natural ability to repel water and the artist has employed waterproof paint. *Rope Trick in the Bamboo Grove,* 1987. Painted feathers glued on leather. (Photo by David Reese, courtesy Elaine Potter Gallery, San Francisco.)

dropped, is quite durable. Wood, however, can be destroyed by water or by wide swings in temperature and humidity. Textiles and paper are perhaps the most fragile, since they are sensitive to heat, water, light, dirt, insects, mold and careless handling. Most objects can be slowly destroyed by rough handling.

Since most crafts are made of organic materials, an ideal environment is one in which temperature and humidity remain rather constant. A temperature between 60 and 75 degrees Fahrenheit and humidity between 40 and 65 percent are considered acceptable. If your environment deviates widely from these norms or registers extreme variations, it can be brought up to par through installation of devices such as air conditioners, heaters, humidifiers or dehumidifiers.

Other hazards to beware include excess heat, sunlight or artificial light that is too bright, and airborne dirt and dust. Placing objects so they are protected from these destroyers can minimize problems.

Placing a delicate object on a pedestal—perhaps even enclosing it in a plexiglass case—can be a good safeguard. Standing a large, sturdy piece on the floor and directing a light onto it is another way of displaying an object and (if it is not top-heavy) keeping it fairly safe.

Grouping pieces on shelves along a wall according to some unifying principle such as color, material, subject matter, shape, texture or contrast is also effective. In homes, too many pedestals may be unappealing and a method combining traditional techniques seems to work best.[3]

Furniture and accessories to display objects can be found in furniture departments, where pedestals in varying sizes and materials (wood and plexiglass are most common) as well as glass tables and shelves, wall systems and etageres are widely available. Specialized accessories for display include revolving turntables (either manual or electric) and armatures that can be constructed to dramatically display wall hangings, quilts and other collectibles. Quilt collectors often display quilts on the wall, using wooden dowels as mounts.

Often artists are the best source of good ideas on displaying their work. Glass artist Sydney Cash has included a pedestal display unit with some of the objects he has made. Gallery owners are accustomed to being asked for suggestions for safe and effective display. These individuals are probably among the best to ask for the names of custom builders who can design and erect a display unit or armature for a particular piece.

Jack Lenor Larsen has solved conservation and display problems for his very large eclectic collection by housing many of the objects on shelves lining the rooms of his home. Sliding Japanese-style fabric-covered screens hide some of the shelves so that only a certain amount of the collection is on view at any time. The screens also protect what is not on view from airborne dirt and dust and from careless handling. Like many collectors, Larsen does all the rearranging, dusting and heavier cleaning of his collection himself.

Another method of achieving protection and visual excitement is to display glass or ceramic objects inside lighted glass-front display cabinets. Textiles, which in some cases may weaken and fade quickly when exposed to open air and daylight (and some fluorescent lights), can be protected by mounting them on stretchers and covering them with a special type of plexiglass that filters out harmful ultraviolet rays. To keep

fragile objects from being thoughtlessly knocked over, it's a good idea to secure the object to its base with wax or florist's clay. Exercising common sense about the placement of delicate objects is also important. Any room likely to be the scene of children's rough play is not appropriate for the display of breakable craft art.

When it comes to caring for art objects, collectors may find guidance from publications on conservation and from museum conservators and organizations dedicated to a particular medium. The American Association of State and Local History, for example, has published a number of technical bulletins designed to help local museums care for the articles in their possession. Though intended for museum personnel, the bulletins in many instances contain information that is very useful for collectors. Some examples include: "Care and Display of Glass Collections," "Conservation of Metals," "Leather: Its Understanding and Care," "Effects of the Environment on Paper: A Review of Recent Literature," "Care of Textiles and Costumes: Adaptive Techniques for Basic Maintenance," and "Storing Your Collections: Problems and Solutions." (Write AASLH, 172 2nd Ave. N., Nashville, TN 37201 for a publication catalogue.) The American Association of Museums has also prepared written materials on conservation. In addition, organizations such as Cooper-Hewitt Museum in New York and Winterthur Museum and Gardens in Winterthur, Del., may be able to provide guidance or suggest individuals who can undertake specific restoration work.

Since much of a collection of contemporary craft art will have been created by still-living artists, a collector can elect to ask the artist for guidance on care and help in restoration if an object becomes damaged.

In this piece by Sydney Cash, the protective glass box is part of the artwork. Constructed (cut and glued) triangular box with trifold interior form of slumped glass, 1986, 14 × 12 × 10 inches.

## LIGHTING

Lighting is quite obviously the single most important display variable in revealing and accenting the beauty of art objects, or in disguising or hiding that beauty. Because light produces heat and, in some cases, destructive ultraviolet rays, proper lighting is essential to maintain art in good condition.

Low-voltage systems are regarded as the greatest recent advance in lighting artwork, because they allow the use of smaller fixtures, generate less heat and consume less electricity. In addition, new fixtures and techniques are being developed rather rapidly, so those who install low-voltage systems will be able to benefit from new ideas as they come along. One such idea is the MR-16 bulb, which has been designed to function without emitting the ultraviolet rays that cause pigments to fade. Since low-voltage fixtures use 12 volts instead of the standard 120 volts, to make use of them it is necessary to purchase a transformer to convert the electric current. This transformer can be a separate box which converts the entire power supply in a particular system, or it can be an individual converter operating solely for a single light.

Low-voltage fixtures come in many configurations; they can be recessed, surface-mounted or clipped onto a track. Because of their small size, they are considerably less obtrusive than conventional fixtures regardless of how they are installed. Additionally, there are many choices of beam direction and width, and bulbs come in a variety of colors.

When considering lighting, collectors should be aware of the following points.

**Survey existing electrical system and wiring before doing anything.** A preliminary step is to investigate the existing power supply and wiring, exposing electrical hazards or situations that preclude one solution or another. In the absence of detailed architectural plans, a licensed electrician or a lighting consultant with the requisite technical and engineering background are excellent choices to make such a survey.

**There is more than one way to achieve the same or a similar effect.** It isn't necessary to install track lighting to light a collection properly. In some homes, for example, a more traditional type of fixture may be better employed. Having to work around technical limitations does not doom the collector to a poorly lit collection. However, the more limited the lighting options, the greater will be the need for technical consultation with a professional lighting expert.

**Don't attempt to solve all lighting needs with a single fixture or system.** A well-lit room usually has three different kinds of light. There is general illumination, which is also known as background or ambient light and includes the natural light entering through windows. There is foreground or task lighting, which provides specific pools of light for activities such as reading or desk work. And there is decorative or accent lighting, which supplies drama, illuminates the collection and creates an air of mystery or excitement. Examples of accent lighting include uplights such as floor cans that cast shadows on the ceiling at night and a chandelier over a dining table. Provide several different sources and systems of light to fulfill these three separate functions.

**Place all lights and systems on dimmers so that the level of light can be altered as**

**desired.** This provides the greatest flexibility and allows creation of a variety of effects. Sometimes you may wish to accent and emphasize your collection; at other times you may wish to diminish its importance in the room.

**Investigate colored bulbs.** Natural light has many different shadings and hues. The light on a hot, sunny day in the South is quite different from the cold winter's light in New England. Afternoon light differs from morning light; dappled shade produces colors different from the light found on a rainy day. Just as natural light offers varied possibilities, electric light also can accent or downplay a particular color. Bulbs are available that create a rosy, golden or hard blue light. Knowledgeable choices can accent the best in a particular object.

**To bring out the best in a collection, experiment.** Although science created the bulbs and fixtures, lighting is more an art than a science. Collectors can learn about and improve the lighting of their collections by experimenting.

You may find that different placements of lights produce different results. Grazing light shows off surface textures. Backlighting reveals a silhouette and calls attention to the shape of the object. To find out how lighting affects your objects, gather several portable lights and some helpers. Shine the brightest light on the front from above. Shine another light from one side, a third from behind. Move the lights around until you find the positions that create the greatest visual impact. Investigate the use of dispersion filters if the lighting appears to be too bright.

Lighting fixtures may look the same, but they provide a different shape and amount of light. One may produce a long, narrow beam while an identical-looking one produces a short, fat beam.

Sources for lighting information include lighting suppliers (particularly those who work with architects and designers), lighting designers and organizations of professional lighting consultants.

## DISPOSING OF OBJECTS

Building a fine collection sometimes means eliminating some objects, perhaps to buy others. Disposing of an art object by gift or sale completes the cycle that began with acquisition.

New tax laws adopted in 1986 affect collectors in several ways. The tax laws used to benefit individuals who held the art they bought for more than a year before selling at a profit by taxing the appreciated value at a lower capital gains rate. The new law eliminated preferential capital gains treatment, beginning in 1987. Any profits realized on the sale of artwork are now included in general income and taxed at the rate for your particular income bracket.

The new tax laws also make it more onerous to itemize, and charitable deductions can be taken only if the taxpayer does itemize. If you do itemize on your tax return, and elect to give an art object away to a museum, an heir or anyone else instead of selling it, you can deduct the fair market value of the object from your income tax at the time of the gift.

The IRS requires that anyone making a gift of an object worth $5,000 or more must attach a qualified appraisal to the tax return when the deduction is claimed. The appraiser must be a licensed authority in the field and cannot be the individual who sold you the object. The deduction could still be disputed by the Internal Revenue Service, which might decide you and the appraiser had valued the object too high.

The great appreciation in value of some art

Protect colorful textiles from fading by keeping them out of direct sunlight. Laura Foster Nicholson, *Emerald Box,* 1986. Brocaded tapestry wool with silk, 18½ × 20 inches.

objects has created a situation in which some individuals in high tax brackets have donated art to public institutions and obtained a tax deduction worth more to them than selling the item would be. However, because of a large number of questionable tax-shelter practices, valuation of artworks as gifts is being scrutinized by the IRS with considerable diligence. Doubtful appraisals and valuations are disallowed with some regularity and an advisory committee of experienced art experts has been created by the IRS.

Besides tax deductions for gifts to institutions, collectors may deduct expenses incurred in mak-

ing a loan or gift such as restoration, insurance and shipping. The deductions are taken as charitable contributions. If an object is on loan, deductions can be taken only for the period of time that it is actually on loan.

For some individuals, keeping a collection intact for heirs is an important consideration. One method of minimizing inheritance taxes is by an orderly divestiture, beginning in middle age. During his or her lifetime, an individual can make periodic gifts of up to $10,000 per recipient per year without incurring either a gift or inheritance tax. If it's a couple doing the giving, they are

Exercise a high standard of care to conserve functional craft art objects such as this stereo cabinet by Bruce Volz. *American Flyer #1*, 64½ inches tall. (Photo by Brian E. Gulick, courtesy Pritam & Eames Gallery, Easthampton, N.Y.)

exempted from paying such taxes on gifts worth up to $20,000 for each recipient in each year. Those planning to leave some or all of a collection to a public institution should make these plans known during their lifetime. Many institutions decline gifts because of the cost of housing them or when the acquisition does not fit the institution's plans.

When it comes to selling contemporary craft art objects, collectors are at a disadvantage due to the lack of development of a secondary market. This after-market includes auction houses, dealer specialists, collectors and museums seeking to fill in their own collections of an artist's work.

Those who want to sell a piece purchased originally from a gallery will probably first go back to the gallery, which may offer it for resale on consignment, charging a commission that typically runs from one-fifth to one-third of the sales price. With less of a market for old pieces, galleries may be less willing to take back work, even on consignment. If they do take it back, the collector may have a long wait for someone who wants to buy that particular piece. Other methods of disposing of work include advertising it or trading with another collector.

The real remedy is further development of the secondary market. Large auction houses especially can enhance the collectibility of a field in providing a marketplace for testing values. When prices rise, usually due to collector interest, auction houses follow through by scheduling more sales. An example of what can happen was observed in 1984 with a series of auctions of Judaica. During the year, prices for objects associated with Jewish history and culture more than quintupled in some instances, compared with prices in 1970, following a pattern established with other types of art in recent years, such

Norman Peterson's steel and canvas rocking chair should be able to survive anything movers can dish out. *Hard Rocker,* 1984. Steel tubing and canvas, 20 × 50 × 35 inches.

as Art Deco, 19th-century American painting and photographs.

The growth of collector interest in a field is not solely due to monetary appreciation. Other factors also operate. For example, with Judaica, there had been a rising interest in Jewish art, history and religion over some years, a growth of the market in general for art and antiquities as a hedge against inflation, and a widespread sense that the objects were going out of circulation as more collectors sought them. However, it took the auction to verify the market's growth. The enthusiasm of collectors thus helped alert dealers and perhaps museum curators that this field deserved more serious consideration.

Museum interest also gives a boost to value. For example, in 1984 the J. Paul Getty Museum acquired two major photography collections and at the same time hired away the photographic curator of the Metropolitan Museum of Art to run the Getty's newly established department.

"Practically everyone connected with photography seems to gain. Already gallery owners, private dealers and photographers are anticipating an upswing in public attention and collector's interest as a result of the museum's commitment [reported in the neighborhood of $20 million]," noted the *New York Times.*[4]

The addition of photography as one of seven areas of special concentration, and the only one

Adrian Saxe, *Antelope Jar,* 1982. Porcelain, 22 inches. (Photo courtesy Garth Clark Gallery, Los Angeles/New York.)

in the 20th-century art forms, was explained by museum director John Walsh. "We are only broadening if we can do something wonderful," said Walsh. So far, no major American museum has made a similar commitment to craft media, although some museums are expressing more interest in acquiring craft objects.

It takes widespread public interest to build the popularity of a particular art form. Some collectors vote with their donations of valuable pieces to museums. Other enthusiasts attend exhibitions, demonstrating their special interest in a new medium. Conceivably the museum stamp of approval must come last, since museums are usually reflectors of taste, not leaders.

## ARTISTS' RIGHTS

Many artists and art lovers endorse the idea that a collector should be willing to lend work for major exhibitions. The right of copyright is available to artists and their heirs for the lifetime of the artist plus fifty years. Under terms of the current copyright law, artists who omit copyright notice from their work have five years to correct their error and register the work.

Collectors who purchase a work do not, therefore, own the copyright. Nor do they need to do so to display or sell the work. But if they wish to reproduce the work, they must obtain permission from the owner.

Some segments of the art community feel that if a collector sells a work that has vastly appreciated in value, the artist should receive a royalty. In France, this right is part of a legal tradition, where it is known as *"droit de suite."* In the United States, California passed a law in 1976 that requires a seller to give an artist five percent of the resale price on paintings, drawings and sculptures sold at a profit, provided the seller resides in California or the sale occurs there.

A California law passed in 1979 prohibits mutilating, defacing or altering a work of fine art. In both instances, enforcement is left up to the artist.[5]

A number of states including California, New York, Maine, Illinois, Hawaii and Connecticut have passed legislation concerning buying and selling of art or of artists' rights in sales. In 1987, Senator Edward M. Kennedy of Massachusetts introduced a bill in the Senate that would expand the rights of visual artists to safeguard their work and to share in increases in value. As a matter of interest, collectors should follow developments as they occur by reading periodicals covering art.

## NOTES

1. For guidance on safe crating, see Stephen A. Horne, *Way to Go: Crating Artwork for Travel* (Hamilton, N.Y.: Gallery Association of New York State, 1985) 55 pages. This spiral-bound handbook can be ordered for $7.50 from GANYS, Box 345, Hamilton, NY 13346.

2. Carl E. Guthe, "Documenting Collections: Museum Registration and Records," American Association for State and Local History Technical Leaflet II, Nashville, Tenn.

3. For numerous pictorial examples of crafts integrated into the home setting, see Katherine Pearson, *American Crafts: A Sourcebook for the Home* (New York: Stewart, Tabori and Chang, 1983).

4. Andy Grundberg, "The Getty Shifts the Focus Westward, *New York Times,* June 17, 1984, Section 8, p. 1.

5. Lee Rosenbaum, *The Complete Guide to Collecting Art* (New York: Alfred A. Knopf, 1982) pp. 106-7. For a discussion of the issues in and state of artist's rights as of 1987, see Tad Crawford's *Legal Guide for the Visual Artist* (New York: Madison Square Press, 1987).

## FINE ARTS INSURANCE SPECIALISTS

### BROKERS

**Huntington Block Associates**
2101 L St.
Washington, DC 20037
202-223-0673 or 800 424-8830

**Republic Hogg Robinson**
355 Lexington Ave.
New York, NY 10017
212-682-7500

## UNDERWRITERS

**CIGNA Corp.**
127 John St.
New York, N Y 10038
212-440-4000

**Chubb & Son, Inc.**
15 Mountain View Rd.
Warren, NJ 07061
201-580-2000

**Fireman's Fund Insurance Cos.**
110 William St.
New York, NY 10038
212-962-6800

**Nordstern Service International (U.S.) Inc.**
116 John St.
New York, NY 10038
212-602-9300

**St. Paul Fire & Marine Insurance Co.**
160 Water St.
New York, NY 10038
212 248-2300

Interest in the figure is found in all craft media, as this piece by Dominique Caron illustrates. *Leather Mask*, 1986. Dyed and painted leather, 17 inches approximately. (Photo courtesy Elaine Potter Gallery, San Francisco.)

# CHAPTER SIX
# CRAFT ART MEDIA

Among hundreds of interviews conducted for this book, two comments helped pinpoint the motivations of those drawn to work in craft media. Potter Norman Schulman, who played a role in the early development of studio glass, explained why he dropped glass after only a few years. "I could see that there was a good future in glass, but it just wasn't my medium. I went back to pottery because I am a potter."

Jeweler Margaret Craver elaborated on this facet of a craftsman's mentality. "Do you want to know the difference between a craftsman and a painter? The craftsman is deeply involved with his material." A craftsman, continued Craver, explores life through the material—pushes it, pulls it, sees how far it will go. Ideas about relationships, events and life itself all are expressed in the work.

Deep involvement with a particular material is thus a common denominator of contemporary craft art. However, regardless of the material chosen, certain interests and attitudes cross media lines. Figuration, vessels and sculptural forms turn up in all the media, and whatever their medium, some craft artists choose to emphasize the tradi-

tion of which they are a part. Others deny that tradition. Individual examples of this denial include Garry Knox Bennett's furniture, which combines wood, metal and plastic in highly personal ways, and Richard Shaw's *trompe l'oeil* constructions. One of Bennett's signatures is an obvious blemish in an otherwise carefully constructed piece. Shaw uses clay both to imitate other materials and to create an obvious illusion. Some craft artists, such as Ed Rossbach, play both sides of the fence. Sometimes, Rossbach's baskets are within the traditional framework in use of material and technique, while at other times, he chooses to create baskets out of discarded commercial packaging. By contrast, Andrea Gill's figurative vessels are uniquely her own, but they are within the ceramic tradition.

Each medium has its independent history, organizations, galleries, periodicals and other reading matter. Yet there are similarities linking contemporary American ceramics, fiber, glass, metal and wood. An important mutual characteristic is that all developed in an academic setting characterized by sharing information.

Often, a few individuals served as catalysts. One would become fascinated with a little-known

Norman Schulman, *Thoughts of the Fertile Crescent,* 1986. Ceramic stele, 29 × 19 × 3½ inches. (Photos by artist.)

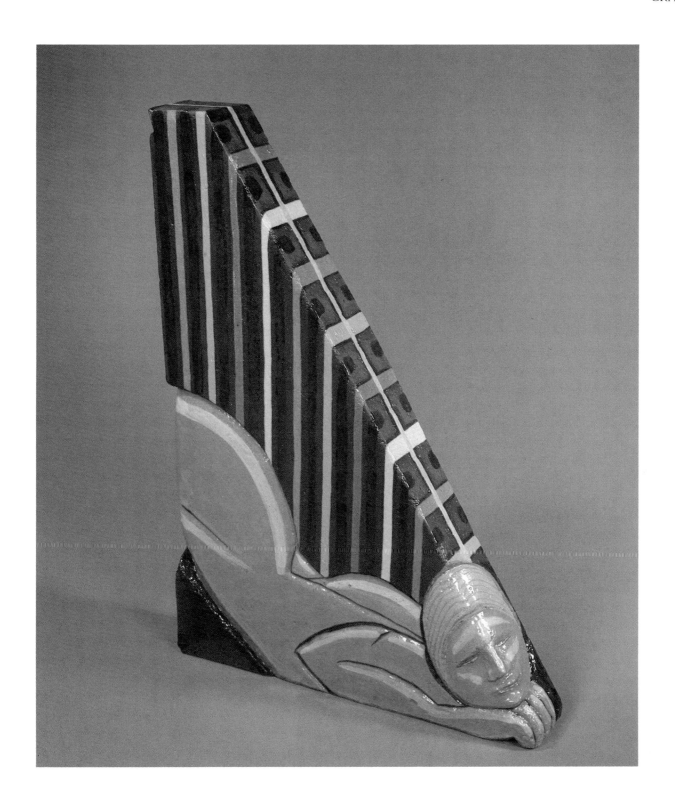

The intentional blemishes on the top of this table by Garry Knox Bennett deny the craft art tradition of preciousness. *Steel Table* (one of an edition of six), 1985-86. Steel, 94 × 36 × 30 inches. (Photo by Niocoli Zurek.)

technique or a particular way of handling a material. Then after intense experimentation, that person would teach others how to do it. In this way, a technique would become more widely disseminated, stimulating the interest of dealers, collectors, curators and critical writers.

A number of fields have been revitalized by the adaptation of industrial techniques to the service of art. Fiber artists transformed the power knitting machine into an artist's tool; ceramists have done the same with the air brush; furniture makers have turned plastic laminates into origi-

nal artworks. Improvements in lathes have led to more adventurous work by wood turners. Glass artists have made use of industrial grinding tools to produce artworks.

Recovery of ancient techniques within each medium appears to be complete. With these formative years of investigation behind us, it seems very likely that the future will hold many interesting explorations of ways to combine craft materials and to advance through new techniques. Nevertheless, knowledge of the present and past remains the best way for a collector to

Clay's chameleon-like qualities are emphasized in this *trompe l'oeil* work by Richard Shaw. *Camden Passage,* 1979. Porcelain with decal overglaze, 10½ × 13¼ inches. (Photo by James Dee, courtesy Braunstein/Quay Gallery, San Francisco, collection of Daniel Jacobs.)

understand the future.

If this book were being written five years from now, the traditional divisions by medium might no longer be serviceable. A current trend among craft artists is to ignore categorical divisions, and to work in either a different medium entirely or to combine media. For example, some of those who began by creating wearable art now make sculptures; individuals trained as goldsmiths now work in plastics; weavers make paper objects; glassmakers combine glass with metal and wood.

In this transitional period, division by medium still is meaningful and convenient for the sake of organization. But readers should be aware that new currents may soon make such distinctions academic and others, as yet unknown, more useful.

Andrea Gill, *Shadow Box Vase*,
1979. Terra cotta, 25¾ inches tall.
(Photo by Eric Shambroom, collection of Daniel Jacobs.)

Ed Rossbach's fascination with the nature of materials extends to finding uses for even society's throwaways. *Carton Basket,* 1987. Commercial packaging stapled together and sprayed with transparent lacquer.

Traditional divisions are breaking down as artists mix media to bring forth original and highly personal works, such as Augusta Talbot's haunting assemblage. *Guardian,* 1986. Wood, porcelain and rice paper, 63 inches tall. (Photos by Stanley Patz, courtesy Vanderwoude Tananbaum Gallery, New York.)

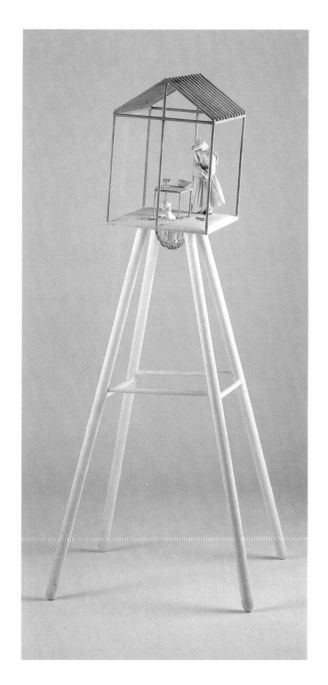

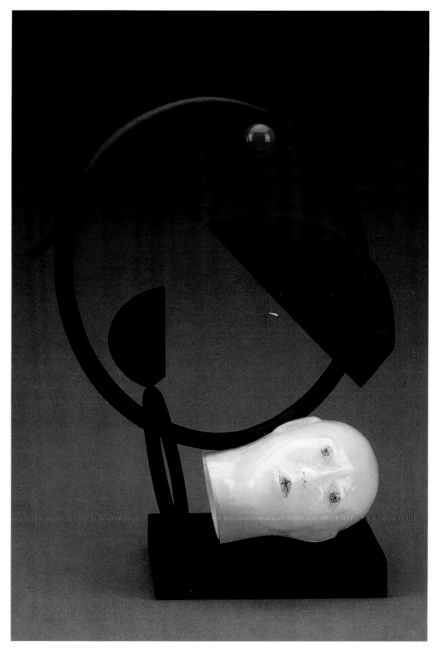

Joey Mace and Flora C. Kirkpatrick, *A Bridge of Blue Light*, 1986. Blown glass and painted wood, 25 × 20 × 11 inches. (Photo by Rob Vinnedge, courtesy Heller Gallery, New York.)

In this epic 10-foot-long work, ceramist Patti Warashina has fashioned the effigies of 72 Seattle visual artists. It was installed in the Seattle Opera House in 1986 as one of four artworks commissioned by the Seattle Arts Commission to inaugurate the Northwest Special Collection. *A Profession*, 1985-86. Earthenware, porcelain, wood and other media, 96 × 120 × 36 inches. (Photo by Roger Schreiber.)

# CERAMICS

Beverly Mayeri, *Stalking Cat*, 1984-85. Fired porcelain with acrylic painted surfaces, 24 × 9 × 6 inches. (Photo by M. Lee Fatherree, courtesy Garth Clark Gallery, Los Angeles/New York.)

There is so much clay in the world that scientists are continually trying to develop new uses for it. Rocket nose cones are made of ceramics and the future may bring forth a ceramic car engine more durable than metal ones because clay does not warp, even at high temperatures.

Clay also puts us in touch with the past. Anthropologists investigate ancient civilizations by analyzing their shards, and art historians study ceramics of past and recent eras, seeking in them clues to a culture's creative life.

As if these examples of the importance of clay were not enough, the English ceramics authority, Philip Rawson, offers another prime rationale for collecting ceramics. He notes the role of pottery in everyday life is a healing one. "Nowadays so much in our life says, 'don't touch me.' Pottery is interesting to touch."[1]

The way a pot or small ceramic sculpture feels when caressed is part of its great appeal. This is an important reason why collectors should make contact with the real object, rather than relying on photographs for first impressions. The growing dependence on slides when making collecting and exhibition decisions works against the tactility of this medium.

Because of the lengthy history of ceramics and the enormous number of options in shaping, glazing and firing clay, there is an obligation on the part of the collector to study both the great traditions and the nature of clay. While this knowledge is not a prerequisite for buying contemporary ceramics, it does help a collector evaluate what contemporary artists are doing. Deciding what type of work to collect, even what artists to include in a collection, is deeply personal. It may be based on the collector's (or his or her dealer's) educated opinion about those working in the field as well as on the financial resources at his or her command, but the importance of acquiring a solid background of information can hardly be overstressed as an antidote to confusion.

If a museum were to mount a large survey exhibition of ceramics, the hapless collector might leave with a figurative bellyache after sampling

The familiar can become strangely terrifying, as this figural work by Melissa Stern reveals. *The Bride,* 1985. Clay, paint, wood 24 × 14 × 5 inches.

a seemingly indigestible banquet. The display could range from functional plates, cups and bowls to abstract sculptures. Some pieces would announce their clayness, while others might fool viewers into believing they were looking at a pair of shoes or a pile of books.

Appreciation for the ceramic tradition would be evident in simple shapes that had been honed to express the very essence of the vessel form. But next to them could be irreverent mockeries of tradition, or bulbous shapes ludicrously colored or adorned with clashing encrustations of clay. The mundane experiences of every day, made larger than life and strangely terrifying, might compete for attention with mysterious columnar sculptures resembling prehistoric skeletons or piles of bones.

Working with ceramics today are production potters who produce in quantity primarily for the table, art potters engaging in limited production and artists who use their work to explore various aesthetic issues. This disparate group subscribes to no single philosophy. Some choose to examine properties of clay such as opacity and translucence, or to work with surface, texture or color. Others use clay to make personal statements about their own history, society or the human condition. Yet other artists employ it to imitate materials such as metal, rope, paper, leather and fiber. Contrasts abound. For example, Rudolf Staffel's light-gathering porcelain vessels are quite different from Patti Warashina's porcelain figures. Compare Ron Nagle's low-fired earthenware cups and Betty Woodman's earthenware pillow pitchers. The stoneware vessels of Peter Voulkos, gouged and pulled and subjected to the vagaries of the wood-fired kiln, bear little resemblance to Karen Karnes' controlled stoneware vessels, also fired in a wood-

Stephen De Staebler's tall figure leads the viewer to ponder the nature of the earth's clay and the clay of human beings. *Wedged Woman Standing,* 1985. Fired clay, 104 × 19 × 23 inches. (Photo by Scott McCue.)

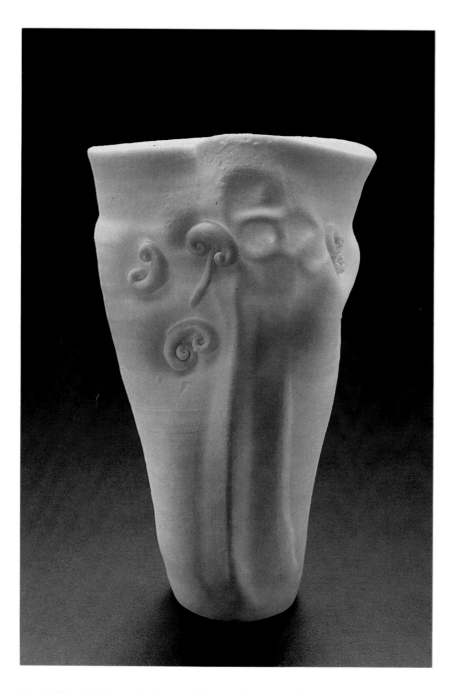

Rudolf Staffel's investigations of the translucency of porcelain have produced a series of ethereal vessels. *Light Gatherer,* 1983. Translucent porcelain, 7½ inches tall. (Photo by Thomas Brummett, courtesy Helen Drutt Gallery, Philadelphia.)

burning kiln.

The lesson is that clay is a chameleon. There is, in fact, not a single common clay but three types that differ from one another in chemical composition and to some extent in final appearance. They range in texture from a fine, dense material, as in porcelain and stoneware, to coarse-textured earthenware. Stoneware and porcelain are fired at high temperatures, earthenware at a lower temperature, which affects the kinds of glazes that can be employed.

A ceramist selects clay for the characteristics best suited to his or her needs. For fine detail work, porcelain functions best; for an earthier look, earthenware or stoneware. There are choices to be made at every step in the process from shaping through glazing to firing. Clay can be formed on a wheel, coiled and manipulated into shape, or rolled out into slabs to be assembled like a gingerbread house. It can be poured into a mold (called slipcasting) and allowed to drain and dry or pressed out mechanically. To harden it and render it vitreous (or waterproof), the clay can be fired in an electric or gas kiln, or the fuel might be wood or animal wastes. Additions to the kiln such as salt, sawdust, ash or chemicals all influence the appearance of the glaze. Wood shavings produce a runny glaze and rich texture; rock salt results in mottling. Some glazes are shiny and lustrous while others are dull; some are opaque, others translucent. Some go on thickly while others are so thin you can see the clay through them. There are crackle glazes and smooth, satiny glazes. As in firing, adding various chemicals to the clay body can create different effects—silicon carbide, for example, releases gas bubbles when the glaze melts and produces a crater-like texture. Raku, a Japanese process beloved by some, is achieved by pulling a piece from the kiln while it is red hot and placing it immediately in a combustible material such as leaves or sawdust. Smoke from this mix blackens the pot and leaves a surface in which hairline cracks (which do not hurt the piece) create a pattern of thin black lines.

Besides glazing, other methods of coloring or decorating clay include subjecting it to the air-brush or photo-reproduction techniques, or ornamenting it with decals. Clay can also be painted with china paints or acrylics. Each type of clay has its characteristic glazes and techniques. But artists often work against tradition to achieve a new look, to engage the material and, in art lingo, to have their own dialogue with it.

Given such a wide range of choices and so many diverse applications employed by individuals with different goals, it is not surprising that there is no single technical standard of quality for all ceramics. Ceramist Robert Sedestrom tells his students at SUNY New Paltz several tales to illustrate this point. In 1985 at the School of the Art Institute of Chicago an artist by the name of Kitty Ross demonstrated some of the properties of clay for students by making a plywood form and pouring into it several dry clays having various degrees of coarseness. Through compression, the clay became a compacted solid so that it stayed together after she took the plywood apart. Within ten days, however, the entire piece collapsed in upon itself, the victim of gravity and a few well-placed kicks from the students.

On another occasion, several tourists in Mexico bought some pottery from a roadside stand. They left it to soak clean overnight in a pail of water. The next morning the pieces were gone, but no thief was ever found. The pots hadn't been stolen; they had simply returned to their original liquid state when subjected to a prolonged water bath. The tourists didn't know that they

had purchased incompletely fired pottery that is not meant to be subjected to lengthy wetting.

In both instances the work was destroyed, but in the first, it met the standard of quality imposed upon it by its maker and audience. In the second case, the pottery met the maker's standards but didn't satisfy the expectations of the people who bought it and, from their point of view, can be considered a failure.

Standards are therefore related both to a maker's goals and the intended use. In throwing,

Ron Nagle's low-fired earthenware work is an abstraction of a cup. *Untitled Ceramic*, 1981, 5¾ × 5 × 5½ inches. (Photo courtesy Charles Cowles Gallery, New York, collection of Daniel Jacobs.)

Karen Karnes' wood-fired stoneware covered vessel (1986, 13 × 6 inches) conveys a powerful sense of controlled confinement. (Photo by Ralph Gabriner.)

it will be painfully obvious if the shape is wrong or if the bottom is too thick in relation to the sides, because the sides will dry first and the piece will crack. Marks of quality in wheel-throwing occur when a perfect spherical form is created (if desired). Certain constructions may pose a special problem of survival. Clay doesn't cantilever well: A top-heavy piece is liable to break. An immediate test of success or failure is whether a piece survives the fire. Paint on clay probably won't last as long as glaze, which in the kiln becomes an indissoluble part of a piece. Since clay doesn't take well to alternate wetting and freezing, using it in a situation where it will be exposed to these conditions may lead to failure. As these examples indicate, it is necessary to evaluate a piece to make sure it meets any requirements for use, but there is no single, universal quality guideline.

Porcelain is considered by many to be the best choice of material for dinnerware. Unglazed, its white or light gray color is interesting; it also takes glaze beautifully. It can be fashioned with a thinner edge than is possible with stoneware or earthenware. Since thinness is prized, dinnerware is often slipcast to produce thinner walls than are possible when clay is wheel-thrown or slab-formed. Porcelain is impervious to many stains and can be placed in the dishwasher.

Stoneware conveys an image of strength and timelessness, especially when thrown in simple forms and glazed in natural and muted colors. It is dishwasher and oven safe and retains heat well at the table.

Earthenware is fired at a lower temperature than the other clays and can be colored more brilliantly and more variously. However, it is not as durable as porcelain or stoneware and is more liable to chip.

A simple way of checking whether a piece is earthenware or stoneware is to ring it with your fingernail. Earthenware produces a low-pitched sound—a bong. High-fired porcelain and stoneware have a higher pitch when struck. If you place your tongue on porous earthenware, it will draw off the moisture. That won't happen with the other two.

For those who are buying objects to display, such distinctions will be of little interest. For them, aesthetic preferences are paramount, and these may change over time with growing knowledge. The changeability of taste is not surprising. Even makers resort to ad hoc judgments that are subject to change. Describing his own working process as an example, Sedestrom said that when his work is finished "I think it is wonderful. The next day I look at it and ask myself how could I make such a terrible thing, but there is just that little corner over there that I *do* like. Maybe I could do something with that. So the process of improvement begins . . . . When you are finished, maybe you have ten good pieces, but one of them is better; you make ten more and one of *them* is better; you are always following that upward path."[2]

Today's academically trained ceramists are well-educated in historic techniques, types of clay, methods of firing and glazes. Knowing history, they can pick and choose from the past, adding their own personal comments to the work. This vast storehouse of knowledge is responsible for the dominant feeling today that ideas are more important than the ceramic material itself.

As critic Suzanne Foley has written, "the rules of the game are open-ended . . . earthenwares, stonewares, and porcelains are used for varying effects. Forms are preconceived and arrived at by the method most appropriate to achieve them

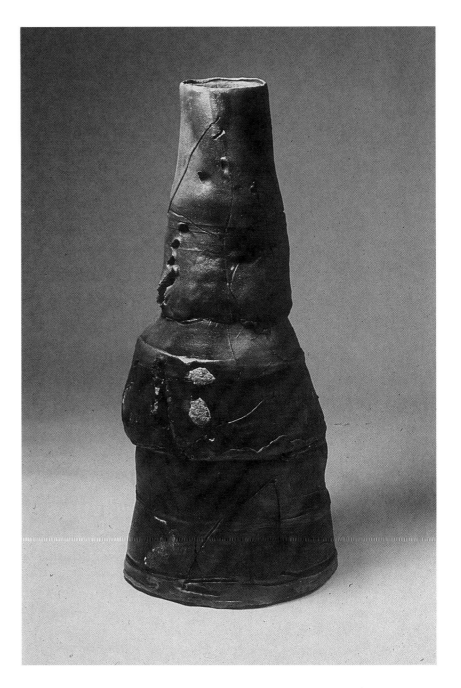

Peter Voulkos' 40-inch-tall wood-fired stoneware work, *Zarathustra,* bursts out of a rigid confinement. (Photo courtesy Exhibit A Gallery, Chicago.)

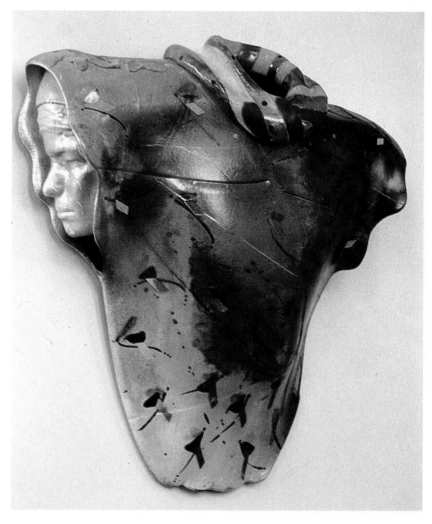

The white face within the left sleeve of Nancy Jurs' piece is balanced by a black face on the other side. The artist refers to the form as a blouse. *Adelpha VI*, 1985. Raku-fired wall piece, 26 × 24 × 7 inches. (Photo courtesy Elaine Potter Gallery, San Francisco.)

. . . decoration is equally wide open: low fired, intense color glazes, metallic lustres . . . ceramic decals . . . underglaze paints, china paints, celadon glaze and even acrylic paint on the surface after all firings . . . clay is often only one of the materials used to make the final object."[3]

The wealth of fascinating ceramic objects is almost certain to lead to confusion about how to shape a collection, and a diet of constant variety may eventually jade the palate. Some ways to narrow the choices include limiting oneself to a certain number of artists or a particular form such as vessels or figures, or perhaps collecting from a particular geographic area, within a specific time period or by technique, such as raku.

## BACKGROUND AND DEVELOPMENT

Ceramists working today owe something to foundations laid during the Arts and Crafts movement. This late 19th-century phenomenon introduced concepts such as the freedom of the artist to select any materials and methods desired, free access to technical information about clay formulas and glazes and a belief that an amateur working alone in the studio could advance to professionalism.

Before these reforms, the ceramics world consisted primarily of commercial firms producing wares for mass consumption. Ceramists found employment in commercial potteries. Formulas were closely held trade secrets and information was imparted according to the guidelines of the apprenticeship system. There was little or no connection between ceramics and art, and the art world was tightly bound by convention, which classified as art only painting, drawing and sculpture.

The Arts and Crafts movement helped ease these tight restrictions by encouraging amateurs to perfect artistic skills and by valuing objects made by hand above those made by machine. The names of many ceramists are honored for their role in the development of ceramics as a vibrant art form, and collectors will benefit by reading about the development.

Among early heroines of ceramics were Adelaide Alsop Robineau, Mary Louise McLaughlin and Maria Longworth Nichols.[4]

Carbon has penetrated the unglazed clay to produce the blackened rim of this vessel by Cynthia Bringle. Vessel, 1986. Raku-fired, 7 × 7½ inches. (Photo by Dan Bailey.)

McLaughlin was an originator of the type of work known as Cincinnati Faience, a form of underglaze painting on china, and her work was recognized at an international exhibition in Paris in 1879. Nichols established the hugely successful Rookwood Pottery in 1880. Robineau, a largely self-taught china painter at first, advanced knowledge of techniques and glazes through her publication, *Keramik Studio*, established with a colleague in 1899. Her work in porcelain was admired worldwide. All three women inspired and raised the standards of amateurs, while also elevating American ceramics. They were instrumental in gaining for women an early place

James Makins, *Beverage Service*, 1982-83. Unglazed oxided porcelain, 22 × 23 inches (tray), 10½ inches high, (pitcher). (Photo by Joshua Schreier, courtesy Exhibit A Gallery, Chicago.)

in ceramics. Today, of course, each woman's work (and examples from Longworth's Rookwood Pottery) are avidly collected.

Charles Binns, the first director of the New York College of Clayworking and Ceramics at Alfred University, shaped the concept of the studio potter as both artist and craftsman. He gave ceramics its academic start and left a major body of technical work on glazes and clay formulas, publishing the work as it was completed. He also trained may students, who went on to develop ceramics programs at other schools.

Glen Lukens established a place for ceramics in California after moving to the state in 1924. He was professor of ceramics at the University of California's School of Architecture for 30 years.

Besides his own magnificent work, his experiments with glazes were helpful to many others.

By 1940, ceramics programs were established not only at Alfred and the University of California but also at Ohio State, Cranbrook Academy, Syracuse University, the University of Southern California, San Jose State College, Scripps and Mills colleges and elsewhere. These academic departments were the superstructure that supported a rapid development of ceramics in response to a surge of interest in the field by students after World War II.

The 1950s was a period of spectacular growth. By 1958 (the year the National Council on Education for the Ceramic Arts was founded as an organization separate from the American

William Daley, *Toas Procession*, 1980. Stoneware, 28½ × 24 × 14½ inches. (Photo courtesy Garth Clark Gallery, Los Angeles/New York.)

Ceramic Society) there were 217 schools, colleges and art institutions offering ceramics programs and 39 master of fine arts ceramics programs. Approximately 7,000 students and 300 teachers were to be the first constituency of NCECA.[5]

But what were these students and teachers doing in all those ceramics studios? According to the English potter, Bernard Leach, who visited a number of the schools with Soetsu Yanagi and Shoji Hamada in 1953, American pottery was "second rate" and imitative because it was not based on indigenous traditions. Leach went so far as to say that Americans could never create great ceramics because there were no unified traditions within this nation of immigrants. This point was received with some resentment at the various schools where he lectured, although Hamada's demonstrations and Leach's discussion of Japanese Zen pottery met with positive reception. Later, Leach returned and so did a number of Japanese ceramists who were also given great attention.

The creation of a large number of Japanese teabowls and stoneware with dark, muddy glazes was one result of all these visits. But another was the increasing fascination and experimentation with Japanese techniques and Zen Buddhist aesthetic values. According to one interpreter of American ceramic history, the introduction of the oriental pottery aesthetic freed American potters from traditional European standards and provided "the aesthetic adze necessary to break

Low-fire earthenware takes colorful glazes well, as can be seen in this dimensional wall piece by Phil Schuster. *Self Portrait in Trailer*, 1983. Glazed earthenware, 20 × 21 × 6 inches. (Photo courtesy Elaine Potter Gallery, San Francisco.)

the bonds that had tied the American potter to Europe's stylistic mores for so long."[6]

Peter Voulkos, who would soon lead in the creation of a style that would serve a true American art movement, was influenced by Leach's thinking and by that aspect of the Japanese style that was most direct, natural and crude. Beginning in 1954, he and the group of talented students who collected about him at the Los Angeles County Art Museum School began to use these ideas and the new influence of current art and music to build a new edifice.

The large kiln that Voulkos built was soon going at a furious rate as he and his students turned out new objects that broke with the traditions of the past. This departure has been equated in importance with Abstract Expressionism in painting. Some of the students,

Adelaide Alsop Robineau, *Fox And Grapes,* 1922. Glazed porcelain, 7¼ inches high. (Photo courtesy Jordan-Volpe Gallery, New York.)

Maria Longworth
Nichols (Rook-
wood Pottery),
*Aladdin Vase,*
c. 1880-1884.
Ceramic, 30
inches tall.
(Photo courtesy
Jordan-Volpe
Gallery, New
York.)

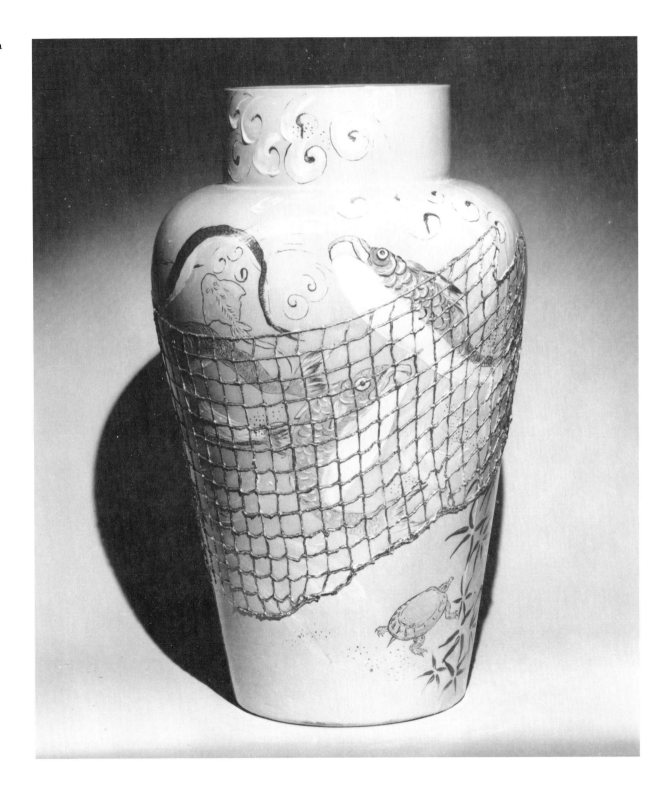

including Paul Soldner, Henry Takemoto, Jerry Rothman, Michael Frimkess, Malcolm McClain, Kenneth Price and John Mason, among others, went on to influence others as they established their own success as ceramists and teachers.

What the Voulkos group did was to divorce ceramics from the traditions it had embraced. They defied tradition, tore clay, colored it with acrylics and produced bulky sculptural forms that were "alive with tensions."[7] Ironically, this work at last produced what Leach said never could be—an American ceramics clearly reflecting those attitudes of iconoclasm, restless interest in change and refusal to bow to tradition that are part of the American character.

Whatever the eventual verdict of history of the meaning, importance and value of this early work, it was recognized as significant almost immediately.[8] The artists received shows at the Stuart Perls and Ferus Galleries in Los Angeles and at the Pasadena Museum of Art, and Voulkos' work was shown at the Museum of Modern Art in 1960.

The new work was christened "abstract expressionist" ceramics by influential critic John Coplans in a 1966 exhibition at the University of California at Irvine. This exhibit has been described as the most influential event in that period of ferment. The experimentation led to more departures. New work in other veins, much of it in California, began to appear.

Kenneth Price began working with low-fire glazes and earthenware, creating nonfunctional cups in bright colors. His work influenced a major development in low-fire ceramics. Robert Arneson, David Gilhooly and others in Northern California developed an irreverent pun-filled ceramics that was christened Funk and considered to be a western version of Pop Art. By 1961, Funk

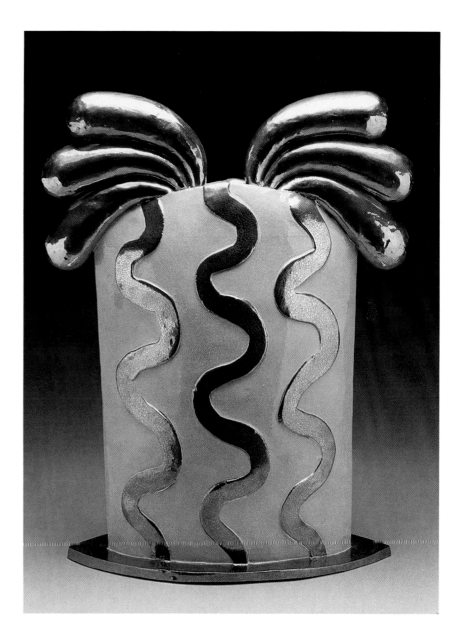

Howard Kottler's bright, almost garish, pot is an example of the exuberance of West-Coast ceramics of the 1960s and 1970s. *Lemon Punch Pot*, 1968, 19½ × 15 × 7 inches. (Photo by Eric Shambroom, collection of Daniel Jacobs.)

Richard T. Notkin's conceptual teapot is a metaphorical construction. Its bricks form an edifice of art. *Hexagonal Curbside Teapot* (Variation #9), Yixing Series, 1986. Stoneware, 4⅜ × 8 × 4⅛ inches. (Photo courtesy Garth Clark Gallery, Los Angeles/New York.)

was in full swing in California. As part of the debunking of middle-class life, it ridiculed not only the middle class but high art and intellectual pretensions.

These conceptual movements paid no allegiance to formal traditions and freed ceramists to make their own way. Naturally, many ceramists continued working within the vessel traditions of their field, especially in the more conservative South, Northeast and Midwest.

While the iconoclastic sculptural works of the 1950s and 1960s have perhaps imposed their own orthodoxy, they have also added substantially to the ceramics vocabulary. Today, ceramists can choose from among different traditions and make

a personal choice about what paths to follow.

Along with the new work came a series of major exhibitions, the catalogues from which are important reading for collectors. Some landmarks include a large retrospective survey in 1979, *A Century of Ceramics 1878-1978*, at the Everson Museum of Art in Syracuse, N.Y., curated by Garth Clark and Margie Hughto. The exhibition toured a number of cities and earned respectful treatment in art journals. The catalogue organized and made accessible to a wide public the development of American studio ceramics.[9] Then in 1981, the Whitney Museum of American Art conferred art world respectability on contemporary ceramics in its exhibition and catalogue,

*Ceramic Sculpture by Six Artists.* Updating that exhibition, in 1984 the Museum of Fine Arts in Boston mounted *Directions in Contemporary American Ceramics.* Then in 1987, the Everson Museum of Art resurrected its historic Ceramic National in an invitational juried exhibition.

As the 1980s continue to unfold, ceramics "has made its entrance (albeit awkward and dis-puted) into the art world. Its acceptance is by no means unanimous . . . but its place is secure because too many doors have been opened for the process to be reversed, too many collectors have been seduced by the magic of the medium, too many galleries have begun to appreciate the richness it brings to the art, and too many museums have begun to collect the work."[10]

## NOTES

1. Interview with author, 1987.

2. Interview with author, 1987.

3. Suzanne Foley, *A Decade of Ceramic Art 1962-1972 From the Collection of Prof. and Mrs. R. Joseph Monsen* (San Francisco: San Francisco Museum of Art, 1972) unpaged.

4. I have relied primarily on *A Century of Ceramics in the United States 1878-1978* (New York: E. P. Dutton, 1979) for historical information.

5. Statement by NCECA's first president, Ted Randall, *NCECA Bulletin,* 1984.

6. Garth Clark, *Who's Afraid of American Pottery?* (s'Hertogen-bosch, The Netherlands: Kruithuis, 1983) p. 11. This cata-logue of an exhibition in the Kruithuis Museum in Holland featured a number of essays on American ceramists, including the one cited.

7. Suzanne Foley, op cit.

8. Ibid.

9. A revised and updated new history by Garth Clark, *American Ceramics: 1876 to the Present,* will be published by Abbeville Press in 1988.

10. *Who's Afraid of American Pottery,* pp. 20-21.

## RESOURCES FOR CERAMICS COLLECTORS

### BOOKS

Jan Axel and Karen McCready, *Porcelain: Traditions and New Visions* (New York: Watson-Guptill Publications, 1981).

Tony Birks, *Art of the Modern Potter* (New York: Van Nostrand Reinhold, 1976).

Elizabeth Cameron and Philippa Lewis, *Potters on Pottery* (New York: St. Martins Press, 1976).

James E. Campbell, *Pottery & Ceramics: A Guide to Information Sources* (Detroit: Gale Research Co., 1978).

Garth Clark, *American Potters: The Work of Twenty Modern Masters* (New York: Watson-Guptill, 1981).

————, ed. *Ceramic Art: A Critical Anthology 1882-1977* (New York: E. P. Dutton, 1978). Useful anthology of important essays not readily available, such as John Coplans' influential "Abstract Expressionist Ceramics."

———— and Margie Hughto, *A Century of Ceramics in the United States 1878-1978* (New York: E. P. Dutton, 1978).

LaMar Harrington, *Ceramics in the Pacific Northwest, A History* (Seattle, Wash.: University of Washington Press, 1979).

Lloyd E. Herman, *American Porcelain: New Expressions in an Ancient Art* (Forest Grove, Ore.: Timber Press, 1980). Documents a traveling exhibition of por-celain clay.

Bernard Leach, *The Potter's Challenge* (New York: E. P. Dutton, 1975). A classic.

Glenn C. Nelson, *Ceramics,* 5th edition (New York: Holt Rine-hart Winston, 1978). A textbook.

Lee Nordness, *Jack Earl: The Genesis and Triumphant Survival of an Underground Ohio Artist* (Racine, Wis.: Perimeter Press, 1985).

Susan Peterson, *Shoji Hamada: His Way and Work* (New York: Kodansha International Press, 1974).

————, *Lucy M. Lewis, American Indian Potter* (New York: Kodansha, 1984).

————, *The Living Tradition of Maria Martinez* (New York: Kodansha, 1977).

Joanne Polster, *Bibliography: Clay* (New York: American Craft Council, 1979).

Tamara Préaud and Serge Gauthier, *Ceramics of the 20th Century* (New York: Rizzoli, 1982). A coffee-table book showing European as well as American ceramics.

Philip Rawson, *The Appreciation of the Arts: Ceramics* (New York: Oxford University Press, 1971). See also paperback reprint with introduction by Wayne Higby published by University of Pennsylvania Press in 1984.

Rose Slivka, *Peter Voulkos: A Dialogue In Clay* (Boston: New York Graphic Society, 1978).

Susan Wechsler, *Low-Fire Ceramics: A New Direction in American Clay* (New York: Watson-Guptill Publications, 1981).

## CATALOGUES

*American Ceramics Now: 27th Ceramic National Exhibition* (Syracuse, N.Y.: Everson Museum of Art, 1987).

*Directions in Contemporary American Ceramics* (Boston: Museum of Fine Arts, 1984).

*Who's Afraid of American Pottery* (s'Hertogenbosch, The Netherlands: Kruithuis, 1983).

*Historical References in Contemporary Ceramics* (Kansas City, Mo.: Nelson Atkins Museum of Art, 1983).

Ross Anderson and Barbara Perry, *The Diversions of Keramos: American Clay Sculpture 1925-1950* (Syracuse, N.Y.: Everson Museum of Art, 1983).

*Cranbrook Ceramics, 1950-1980* (Bloomfield Hills, Mich.: Cranbrook Academy of Art Museum, 1983).

Richard Marshall and Suzanne Foley, *Ceramic Sculpture: Six Artists* (New York: Whitney Museum of American Art, 1981).

*Funk* (Berkeley, Calif.: University of California Art Museum, 1967).

## PERIODICALS

**American Ceramics**
(quarterly)
15 W. 44th St.
New York, NY 10036

**Ceramics Monthly** (10T/year)
1609 Northwest Blvd.
Box 12448
Columbus, OH 43212

**Ceramic Review** (bimonthly)
Craftsmen Potters Association of
    Great Britain, Ltd.
21 Carnaby St.
London WIVIPH
England

**The Studio Potter**
(semi-annual)
Box 65
Goffstown, NH 03045

## ORGANIZATIONS

**Everson Museum of Art**
401 Harrison St.
Syracuse, NY 13202

The museum's Syracuse China Center for the Study of American Ceramics includes Ceramics National prize winners among 1,000 works in clay. Museum also houses a library and the largest public collection of Adelaide Alsop Robineau's ceramics.

**National Council on Education for the Ceramic Arts**
Regina Brown, Executive
    Secretary
Box 1677
Bandon, OR 97411

Annual meeting and journal; quarterly newsletter; also publishes "Survey of Ceramic Programs in Higher Education."

# FIBER

Katherine Westphal's paper kimono investigates color and pattern relations. Seizing well-known forms to convey a unique message (in this case the printed statements are about the natural history of life) is an important characteristic of fiber art. *Chutohanpa #2,* 1983. Dyed Hosho paper printed with messages, 36 × 50 inches.

There is an exceptional variety of fiber art—woven wall hangings and rugs, needlework, wearable art, quilts, masks, dolls, baskets and handmade paper, to name some examples. There are also works which derive from the fiber sensibility though they may be of leather, feathers, manufactured materials or found objects. The wide range of end products is a reflection of the varied ways in which fibrous materials can be handled. But it is also a result of a conscious search for a means of justifying the anachronism of handwoven fiber objects in an industrial society. We no longer *need* the hand-made baskets and brooms, the pieced quilts and woven rugs, the sweaters and caps that once were so essential to utility and comfort. Yet collectors appear to respond to fiber art on an almost primal level, appreciating it perhaps as an antidote to modern society.

In the field of fiber art, several construction techniques dominate. They are loom weaving, interlacing and surface decoration. Typically, weaving is used to create wall hangings, three-dimensional works and wearables. Interlacing, which is employed for baskets, wearables and sculpture, encompasses plaiting, knotting, crocheting, knitting and netting. Surface decoration includes painted or otherwise imprinted images on a fiber ground as well as the needlecraft

techniques used in wearables, quilts, embroidery and other products.[1]

Besides being fibrous in origin, many of the variations in materials and techniques have in common the goal of building up an object in an orderly layering. From this process comes a sensibility different, for example, from that involved in painting. For while paint can be applied anywhere and any way on a canvas, many textiles are worked in logical progressions and repetitions of rows, stitches and sections.

Many of the techniques employed in fiber works are so ancient that their origin cannot even be dated, and some methods of working are so labor-intensive that a full year may be required to complete a few works. Investment of inordinate time—so out of character with today's produc-

In an artist's hands, the loom becomes a tool for exploring abstract color relations, as in this wall piece by Adela Akers. *Tropical Night*, 1984. Sisal, linen and wool woven in strips and constructed, 46 × 66 × 5 inches. (Photo by Scott Hyde, courtesy Miller/Brown Gallery, San Francisco, and Patrick King Contemporary Art, Indianapolis.)

tion oriented values—imposes a rhythm which soothes and lulls the maker into a timeless world. Some fiber artists have spoken of a satisfying sense of connection with unknown craftsmen of the past who in their own time subjected natural fibers—grasses and plants—to the identical processes. Many of those working today prefer using the materials of nature, which have symbolic value. On the other hand, perhaps in reaction to what can become an overly precious identification, others have selected the most characteristic products of the present (commercial packaging, plastics, newspapers, for example) and used them artfully.

Collectors of fiber art often speak of the pleasure that they, too, derive from making contact with bygone eras through their acquisitions. But whether a piece refers to the past or present, collectors can better assure themselves that work will last into the future by finding out how to care for it. Reasonable questions when buying work concern the material used and cleaning and care instructions. Since most colored works should not be exposed to direct light and frequent exposure to unscreened sunlight can lead to fading, the collector should ascertain whether the dyes are colorfast and light-resistant. Display should also be discussed before purchase. Should the object be dis-

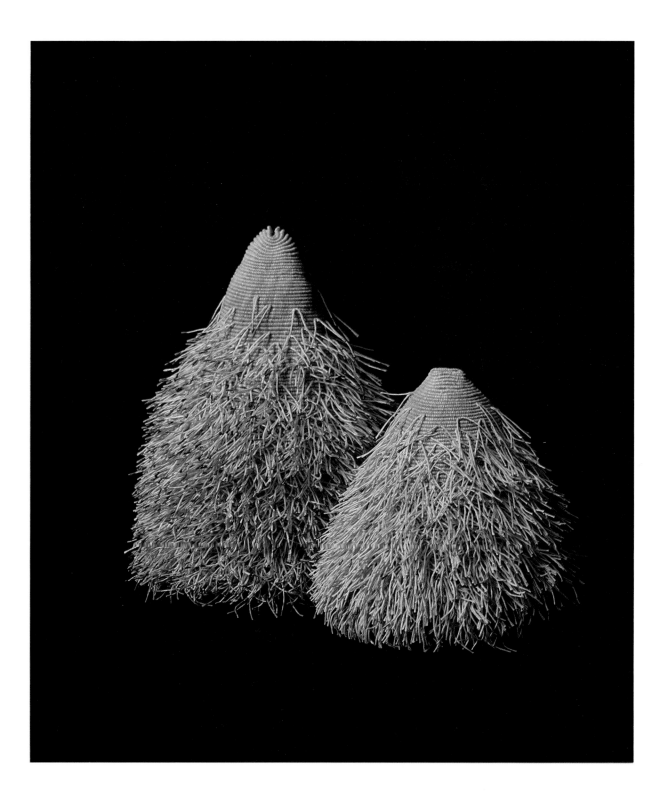

Jane Sauer's knotted linen and acrylic baskets bring associations with ancient ritualistic objects. *Reaching Thru The Past*, (8½ × 6½ inches) and *The Past*, (6 × 6 inches) 1986. (Photo by Pat Watson.)

Ordinary materials are transformed into an evocative object in this work by Dominic DiMare. *Domus #5/Harbor Lights,* 1983. Wood, Chinese horsehair, paint, glass and photograph, 43 × 14 × 5 inches open as shown. (Photo courtesy Braunstein/Quay Gallery, San Francisco.)

played under glass that screens out ultraviolet light? Placing a textile under glass prolongs its life but can hide the textural qualities of the work. Usually the gallery selling the work can recommend a framer with both technical and aesthetic

skills. Don't assume that works can be dry-cleaned or washed. (Some unwashable work can be vacuumed.) The artist should be consulted on fireproofing or application of stain repellers, since these processes can change the texture of some materials.

Evaluating a work's technical quality and suitability for its intended use is usually a matter of looking carefully and asking the right questions about display and care. But there is a point where technique and issues of aesthetic quality meet. Turning this corner places the viewer in a different neighborhood, an environment in which there are no universally correct answers. The gallery director cannot tell you whether the artist has selected the correct material and process to achieve the desired results. That's a question of judgment and the ability to unerringly make the right selection is a significant part of both the artist's technical skill and aesthetic sense. Each material has a different feel and different associations, and there are many techniques: Some weaves give a rough, coarse surface while others are more sensual. An art school class can give its students some clues. For example, weaver Lia Cook noted that "my students [at California College of Arts and Crafts] are learning how to employ technique to develop a personal art form. We cover issues in finishing techniques, for example, such as how to present work so that the finishing techniques don't get in the way of the art statement."

Just as the budding artist learns how to combine personal vision and technical facility, collectors, too, can seek a means of evaluating a work on both levels. As Cook says, "One thing I could suggest [to collectors] is to question whether the technique supports the artist's apparent goal or whether the technique is all that you see. Here is one that feels right and another that feels wrong; what is the difference? Many collectors want someone else to supply the answers but they should trust their own perceptions. The answers are often there if you look for them within yourself.

"There are people who have definite answers to these questions. Someone who was trained in the Bauhaus, for example, could tell you exactly what is a good fabric and what isn't. Many of us went through an education that was much more structured than now. The first question I ask is what is trying to be communicated?

"This doesn't mean there are no longer any standards. The question is: Has the artist selected methods that advance the goal? These then would be the standards. For example, if an artist wanted a sense of depth, we could talk about what techniques give a sense of depth. It might be choice of color or perspective." If the artist didn't want to convey a sense of depth, judging by these standards would be foolish.

## FIBER BACKGROUND AND DEVELOPMENT

From the vantage point of the present, weaving in the 1950s was remarkably uniform and lacking in spontaneity. Weaver Ed Rossbach recalled recently that anonymity was considered desirable for handweavers working in a machine society. Swatches from Gunta Stolzl or Anni Albers could easily be mistaken for others by Marianne Strengell, Trude Guermonprez or Azalea Thorpe, he said.[2] The same similarity from one weaver to another was found among traditional handweavers, too. However, locked within the fibers of uniformity in the 1950s were concepts that would produce the powerful and imaginative works that characterize today's fiber art.

Katherine Westphal named this piece when she noticed the tucked fabric's similarity to a window blind. *Levelor,* 1985. Tucked fabric handprinted with color Xerox images and patchwork applique, 90 × 50 inches.

Fascination with a primitive past is revealed in this work by James Bassler. *Skin Shield,* 1986. Painted silk warp, 54 × 60 inches. (Photo courtesy Miller/Brown Gallery, San Francisco.)

As we shall see, the 1950s were a bridge between the present and the first part of the century when, during the 1920s, '30s and '40s, a small number of individuals worked to revive handweaving. Having recovered these techniques, artists now range freely among them, adding new ideas and methods. In six decades, attitudes toward fiber techniques have progressed from no interest in handweaving to a belief that it is an antidote to a sterile, packaged civilization. Individuality, emotional freedom, playfulness and a sense of adventure are important elements in much of today's fiber art, as the output of artists such as Rossbach, Cook, Neda Al Hilali, Katherine Westphal and many, many others amply attests.

A preliminary look at the contemporary revival of handweaving, which in turn led to the birth of fiber art, reveals a history in which doctrinaire pronouncements were quite common. One may speculate that several reasons for the plethora of rules and regulations were related to the fact that the rebirth began as a means of helping the rural poor "better" themselves and of finding employment for women.

One of the first individuals to interest others in weaving was Mary Atwater, who began teaching and writing on the subject in 1919. She founded the Shuttle Craft Guild and published in monthly installments a course on handweaving. (An odd fact is that Atwater in World War I and Dorothy Liebes in World War II were both occupational therapists who taught wounded soldiers weaving as a means of speeding their recovery. Coincidentally, Margaret Craver played the same role in World War II, using jewelry making as the therapy.) Atwater, like Lucy Morgan, Penland's founder, organized classes in weaving to help impoverished communities earn a cash income. She crisscrossed the country giving workshops open to anyone interested in learning how to weave. Indications are that weaving and various forms of fiber work remained largely the province of do-gooders until after World War II, when the influence of the Bauhaus began to widen in this country and the concept of a collaboration between architects and weavers became accepted. Handweavers also designed for industry and for production by power loom.

An important center for these ideas was Cranbrook Academy, where Marianne Strengell took over the weaving department in 1942.[3] Cranbrook was one of few places where students could learn how to design for the power loom; fabric-printing techniques were also taught. Strengell herself had many industrial clients, including United Airlines and General Motors.

Strengell's classes, which Rossbach took as a postwar student, were "a blend of Scandinavian and Bauhaus modernism that became the 'good design' of the period," he recalled. "[M]any of us . . . were . . . content to work within a remarkably narrow range of weaving possibilities, untroubled by any awareness of what was possible and wonderful in weaving and untroubled too by the solemn restraints that somehow had been imposed upon us."[4]

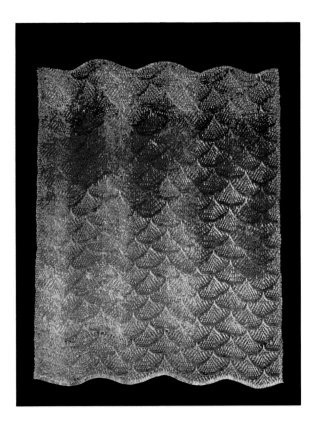

Lia Cook investigates pattern and subtle color gradations in this wall hanging. *Through the Curtain Looking Out,* 1985. Pressed, painted and dyed rayon, 59 × 44 inches. (Photo courtesy The Allrich Gallery, San Francisco.)

Meanwhile, however, Anni Albers' weavings and statements hinted at future dramatic changes. Though others spoke of handweaving in relation to utility, Albers (who agreed with them about the importance of designing for machine production) also wrote that handweaving had the potential of becoming a medium of personal expression.[5]

In 1949, Albers' work was shown at the Museum of Modern Art; the exhibition circulated to other cities for a period of three and a half years. This success as well as her Bauhaus history, her books, teaching and connection with the art world through her husband, Josef Albers, established her as a spokesman for fiber art.

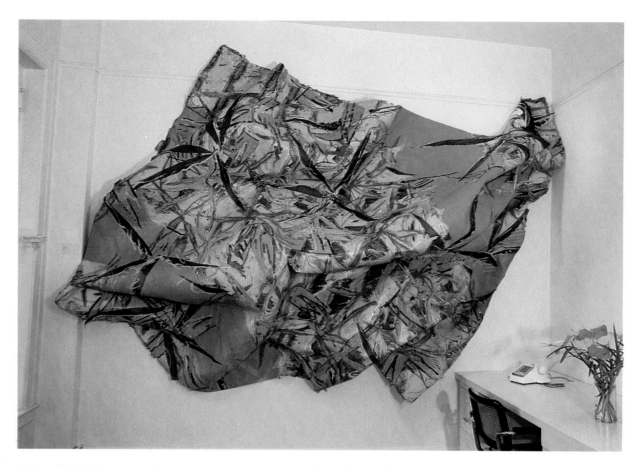

Neda Al Hilali's extraordinary enormous constructions have fire and passion. *Mangava,* 1983. Acrylic and paper collage on canvas, 132 × 144 inches. (Photo courtesy The Allrich Gallery, San Francisco.)

Through her words, Albers helped reclaim for contemporary society knowledge of the great fiber traditions of the past, especially Coptic and pre-Columbian Peruvian textiles. She essentially gave permission for intuitive expression in fiber.

If Albers verbalized the acceptability of intuitive creativity, it was the late Dorothy Liebes, a Californian whose career as a handweaver spanned the decades between the 1930s and 1950s, who provided the living example. Ross-

bach described her methods of working: "Liebes . . . would have a basket of bobbins prepared for her by one of her employees — bobbins of a variety of colors and textures that appealed to her. She then sat down at her loom, early in the morning, and started inserting yarns into a warp, watching what happened — without any sketch, only her own fresh emotional response."[6] In Liebes' weavings, concepts of what was suitable for warp and weft were trans-

Dorothy Liebes in her studio, New York City.
(Photo courtesy American Craft Council.)

The humble materials for this conceptual work by Norma Minkowitz include a commercial plastic container and plain white mercerized cotton. *Come Forth*, 1977. Crocheted mercerized cotton over plastic. (Photo by Bob Hansson, courtesy Julie: Artisans' Gallery, New York, collection of the Cortec Group.)

formed. "The repertory of weaving elements was expanded. Beads, ribbons, braids . . . scarcely practical or not practical at all. . . . This was . . . creating with material."[7] The excitement of a Liebes' textile comes "when it is poised most precariously over . . . what is regarded as bad taste. Challenging 'good design' and bland refinement, opposing the intellectual, the nonspontaneous, the restrictive and the dogmatic, Liebes emerges as an American force, really a

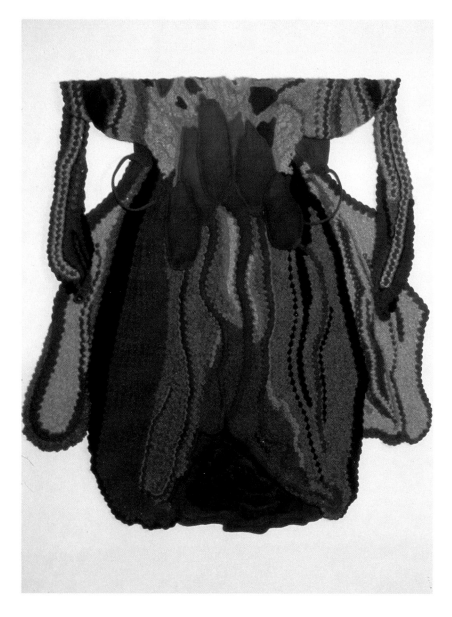

This work by Jean Williams Cacicedo is an example of the extraordinary level of craftsmanship and artfulness that gave birth to contemporary wearable art. *Tulip Kimono,* 1978. Wool jersey, mohair wool yarn, Dacron, crocheted, knitted, felted and hand-dyed. (Photo courtesy Julie: Artisans' Gallery, New York.)

California force—superabundant, brash, obvious and direct."[8]

Originality of expression soon became the goal of many working in fiber and, as the 1950s unfolded, the development of fiber art began to bristle with excitement. This was especially true on the West Coast, where the University of California at Berkeley offered a master of fine arts degree in weaving. Rossbach, who has been a consistent force for experimentation, joined the Berkeley faculty in 1952 and Trude Guermonprez was also active in California.

Meanwhile, activity was proceeding in other parts of the country. Lenore Tawney was weaving in Chicago. In New York, the Museum of Modern Art included a few art fabrics in its 1956 exhibition, Textiles USA. Then in 1962, Tawney was given a solo exhibition at the Staten Island Museum. The following year her work was included in Woven Forms, an exhibition at the Museum of Contemporary Crafts. Others in the show were Alice Adams, Sheila Hicks, Dorian Zachai and Claire Zeisler. Tawney's shaped weavings departed from the traditional rectangular format, pointing to a direction increasingly taken by those working in fiber. High-relief pieces became common as did three-dimensional works, which were now off the wall entirely and either self-supporting or on pedestals. Another trend was toward large, even monumental, pieces.

As the 1960s progressed, materials such as sisal rope, cord and loosely spun raw wool were used more and the declaration "own technique" or "off-loom technique" began to appear more frequently on labels at exhibitions. A weaving exhibition that traveled through the country, called Wallhangings, provided a review of a portion of the fiber arts in the 1960s. It ended at the Museum of Modern Art in 1969. The exhibition

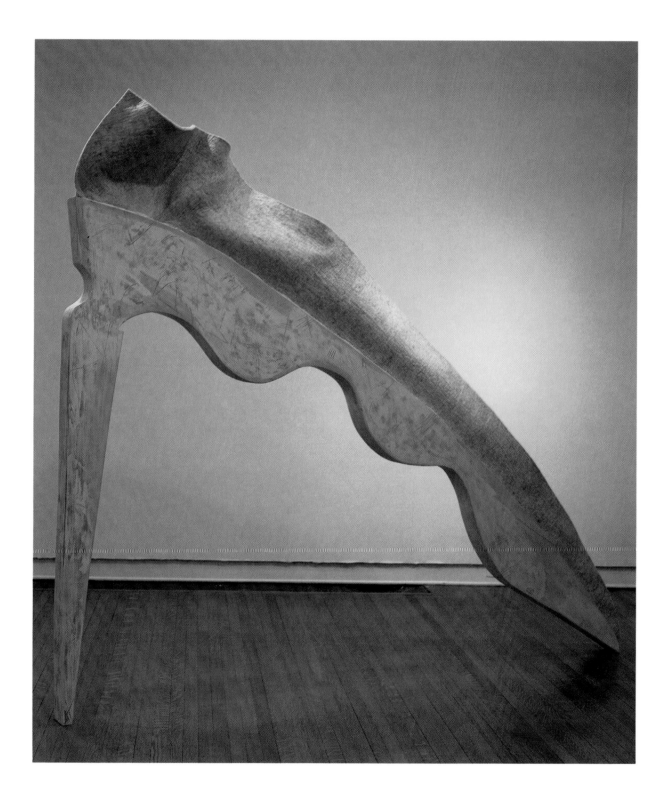

Joan Livingstone's massive sculpture suggests a fascination with prehistoric times. *Mantis*, 1985. Felt, wood and paint, 84 × 104 × 4 inches.

Ferne Jacobs, *Roots*, 1984-85. Coiled, twined thread and collage, 8 × 21½ × 6 inches in diameter. (Photo by J. Felgar.)

was organized by Mildred Constantine, a curator at the museum, and Jack Lenor Larsen. They commented in their book, *Beyond Craft: The Art Fabric*, that the title was a misnomer since many of the pieces weren't woven and they weren't wall hangings either.[9]

Experimentation continued in the 1970s. There was greater use of silk and cotton cloth as well as of unspun fibers. New interest in traditional resist-dye techniques such as batik led to a renaissance in skills which, while still known in Africa and the Orient, had been largely forgotten in western countries.

During the 1960s and 1970s, time-honored techniques such as knitting, crochet and macrame were investigated, with results that built on but did not imitate traditional work. A wide range

of decorative and surface techniques, such as embroidery and darning, was undertaken mostly by individuals trained as artists who became entranced with a particular methodology and followed their interest to the extreme. Stuffing added dimensionality to fabrics. Nonwovens such as felted wool, cellulose fiber, paper and leather were among the many materials treated to an intense scrutiny, out of which arose unique objects that are art in all but the most traditional definitions of that word.

Fabric itself was treated as an artist's material and appliqued and pieced cloth, leather, paper, plastic, film, rubber and vinyl were pressed into service. Many ways of working were tried, including pleating, tucking, plaiting, folding and dying. Some individuals, such as Arline Fisch, used silver and gold wire to weave objects that were somewhere between jewelry and clothing.

Baskets were also part of the experimentation, as traditional plaiting, twining and cording were employed in new ways by individuals such as Rossbach, John McQueen, Gary Trentham and Ferne Jacobs, among others. Rossbach considered what role baskets could play in the contemporary world in his books *Baskets as Textile Art*, published in 1973, and *The New Basketry*, published in 1976. He concluded that makers of new baskets did not consider themselves craftsmen or basketmakers in the traditional sense, but instead worked as artists, adapting various fiber techniques to make basketry a medium of art expression. This attitude was not entirely a new departure. It built on an appreciation of traditional Native American Indian baskets as art, which considerably predated the postwar period. Enthusiast George Wharton James, for example, wrote of Indian baskets as textile art in a magazine published around the turn of the century.[10]

During the 1960s and 1970s, a reexamination of clothing led some craftsmen to produce funky examples of embellished denim and others to make exquisite clothes that came to be known as wearable art. By the 1970s, funk seemed to fall by the wayside, or perhaps it was absorbed into the commercial fashion world. But the interest in surface embellishment that preoccupied those concerned with wearable art grew and even spread to the worlds of painting, architecture and ceramics.

As an example, when Pat Campbell and Elsa Sreenivasam planned the first Surface Design Conference in 1976 at the University of Kansas at Lawrence, they hoped for an attendance of 200.[11] The conference actually attracted more than 600 and a publication, *Surface Design*, which

at this writing continues, was begun. Since 1976 biannual conferences on surface design have been held.

Exhibitions in the 1970s documented many vibrant developments. In 1972, the influential Deliberate Entanglements show at UCLA was curated by Bernard Kester. It was the centerpiece in a number of concurrent events that included exhibitions at seven museums and a week-long colloquium to discuss and assess new work in fiber. By the 1970s, a number of California dealers were showing fiber art, including Margery Annenberg and Louise Allrich in San Francisco, Fiberworks and Kasuri Dye Works in Berkeley and Straw Into Gold in Oakland. In other areas

John McQueen's baskets are among the most imaginative on view today. *A Tree and its skin*, 1985. Wood and bark, 18 inches high. (Photo by Brian Oglesbee, courtesy Nina Freudenheim Gallery, Buffalo, N.Y.)

Lillian Elliott and Pat Hickman, *River Styx*, 1987. Mixed materials, 17 × 36 × 17 inches. (Photo by Pat Hickman, courtesy Miller/Brown Gallery, San Francisco.)

there were Hadler-Rodriguez and Florence Duhl in New York, the Contemporary Crafts Association in Portland, Ore., and Jacques Barruch in Chicago.

There was considerable cross-fertilization between the United States, Europe and countries such as Japan. Not only did artists travel back and forth, but exhibitions did, too. These exhibitions exerted an important influence on the artists who saw them. The year 1962, for example, ushered in the first *Biénnale Internationale de la Tapisserie* at Switzerland's *Musée Cantonal des Beaux Arts* in Lausanne. These important shows (which are still ongoing) have helped spread new ideas and introduced American fiber artists to the world. In 1974, the International Exhibition of Miniature Textiles at the British Crafts Center

in London is said to have led to a more widespread experimentation in small works of fiber. Later exhibitions in 1976 and 1978 followed and in 1979 the first American miniatures exhibition took place in Santa Fe, N.M.

This brief survey makes no attempt to consider the full range of shows, other than to note that the 1970s was a time of important traveling exhibitions which influenced the course of fiber development. Those interested in this aspect of fiber art should look at catalogues such as *Fiber Structures*, which documents a 1976 exhibition held in Pittsburgh in conjunction with the Convergence Conference of the Handweavers Guild of America, and *Fiberworks*, documenting a 1977 Cleveland Museum of Art show. The Dyer's Art exhibition (1976), curated by Jack Lenor Larsen,

Kiyomi Iwata,
*Red Stitched*,
1986. Fiber,
7 × 7 × 7 inches.
(Photo courtesy
Miller/Brown
Gallery, San
Francisco.)

By hand-painting cloth (usually silk) makers of wearable art like Julia Hill make it possible to wear a painting. *Storm Kimono, 1979.* Resist-painted silk. (Photo by Tohru Nakamura, courtesy Julie: Artisans' Gallery, New York.)

and a companion book, helped spread interest in this hitherto more or less neglected area. A recent important exhibition and catalogue is *Fiber R/Evolution*, which contains essays by a number of critics and fiber artists. It documents a 1986 exhibition at the Milwaukee Art Museum, which is expected to travel through 1987.

The preceding brief survey shows that a remarkable spirit of exploration and discovery have preoccupied fiber artists for the past three decades. Today's artists are the beneficiaries of this valuable heritage, which also extends to the papermaking, quilting and wearable art movements discussed below.

## HANDMADE PAPER

The medium of handmade paper was chosen for intense exploration by fiber artists beginning in

the late 1940s. Two concurrent exhibitions mounted by the American Craft Museum in the spring of 1982 revealed the creativity within the field and summarized the antecedents and recent history of paper as an art form.

In the joint-exhibition catalogue, *Papermaking USA: History, Process, Art* and *The Handmade Paper Book*, papermaker Winifred Lutz notes that there were two aspects to the revival. First, the almost lost craft of making paper by hand was revived in small papermaking studios. Second, artists began to explore paper as a medium by itself, separate from its traditional role as a surface to receive written and drawn images.

A factor encouraging experimentation is the large number of possibilities within this medium. Paper can vary from a silken to a leather-like tex-

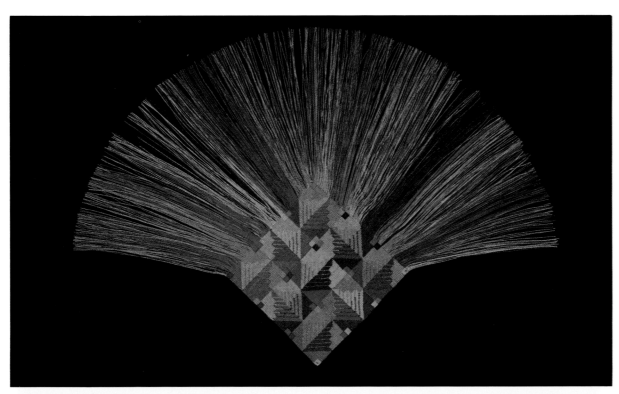

Diane Itter's miniature knotted constructions are marvelous explorations of color relations, flawlessly executed. *Leaf Game,* (top) 1987, 22 × 15 inches, and *Leaf Ledges,* 1986, 11 × 9 inches. Knotted linen. (Photos by David Keister.)

Despite its small size, D. R. Wagner's needlepoint on canvas conveys electric energy. *Get Out of My House,* 1987. Cotton threads, cotton canvas, 10 × 16 inches. (Photo by James Kline, courtesy The Allrich Gallery, San Francisco.)

Diane Burchard's colorful work is an example of assemblage, a common working style among fiber artists. *Huacas,* 1986. Hand-dyed paper, feathers, painted wood and linen, 7 × 12 × 12 inches each. (Photo by Marcus Lopez, courtesy Elaine Potter Gallery, San Francisco.)

ture, and dyes, pigments, sizing and other materials provide additional variation. Paper can also be stenciled, poured, layered, embossed, cast or manipulated freehand.

As with so many of the craft media, knowledge of papermaking by hand had largely disappeared from the scene by the 20th century. However, a few individuals, such as Dard Hunter, served as keepers of the flame. Hunter began his own paper mill in Lime Rock, Conn., in 1928. Though this was America's first hand-papermaking mill since the 19th century, it was not financially successful and he discontinued it

in 1931. Hunter also wrote *Papermaking: The History and Technique of an Ancient Craft,* a book still regarded as the most comprehensive on the subject. (The equipment he used in his mill and the photos, drawings and artifacts he collected from all over the world are now housed in the Dard Hunter Museum in Appleton, Wis.)

Beginning in the 1950s, Douglass Morse Howell continued the saga with experiments illustrating the immense variety of forms possible with handmade paper. Howell's contributions, included in an exhibition at the American Craft Museum while the Handmade Paper show was

Sylvia Seventy, *Tadpoles,* 1985. Paper, 4 × 13 inches in diameter. (Photo by Jacques Cressaty, courtesy The Allrich Gallery, San Francisco, collection of Mr. and Mrs. Sanford M. Besser.)

on, documented his interest in paper made of linen and flax without the usual chemicals. His fascination with the medium led him to try things without having any specific goal— simply to see what would happen. Coming as it did in the midst of the revival of American craft and of printmaking in the 1950s and 1960s, this procedure interested a number of other artists who have continued the explorations. Laurence Barker, who was Howell's student for a while, later became head of the print department at Cranbrook, where he established a papermaking facility.

Since approximately the early 1970s, mills to produce handmade paper have been established in the United States and in other countries. The revival is an international movement. Barker, for example, established a mill in Barcelona, Spain. Other locations include Australia, West Germany, Tanzania and Israel. Mills produce fine paper for use by artists or in handmade books, collaborate with artists on special projects and undertake original research on the nature of paper. Some printmaking studios also have papermaking equipment and individuals skilled in using it.

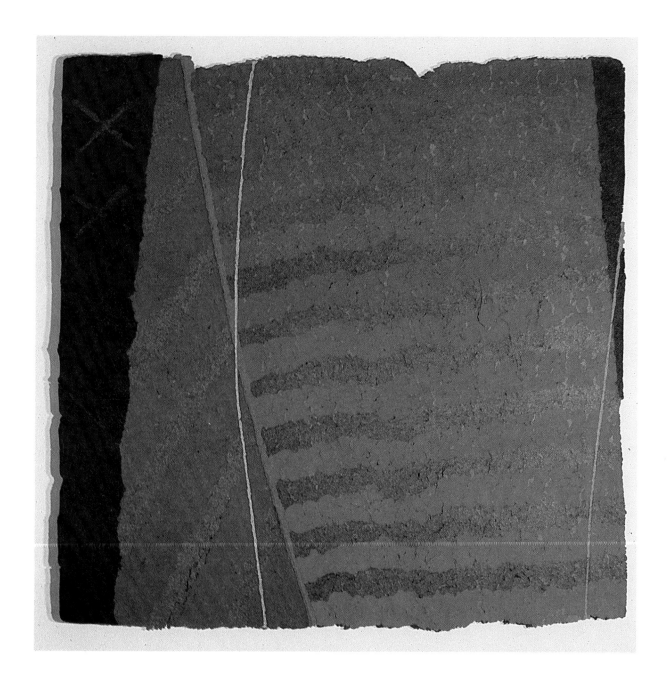

Handmade paper offers almost unlimited potential for art, as this work by John Babcock illustrates. *Blue Spirit Ladder*, 1987. Free-cast paper, 59 × 59 inches. (Photo courtesy Miller/Brown Gallery, San Francisco.)

Faith Ringgold's quilt trilogy eloquently summarizes the highlights of a couple's life: marriage, being lovers and, finally, death. *Quilt Trilogy,* 1986. Acrylic on canvas, tie-dyed, printed, pieced fabric. (Courtesy Bernice Steinbaum Gallery, New York, private collection.) *The Wedding: Lover's Quilt #1,* 77½ × 58 inches. *Sleeping: Lover's Quilt #2,* 79½ × 77 inches. *The Funeral: Lover's Quilt #3,* 58½ × 76½ inches.

## QUILTS

Unlike papermaking, quilting retained a loyal following, mostly among women needleworkers who pieced quilts for enjoyment once necessity no longer required the pastime. Both boys and girls were taught how to quilt as late as the early part of the 20th century, when both President Calvin Coolidge and Dwight D. Eisenhower were instructed in the skill.[12]

The 19th century was the heyday of quilting bees, and, after an early period in which artistry was not emphasized, quilters competed to create ever more dazzling geometric-patterned tops. Pictorial quilts were also popular, including album quilts with scenes of village life, animals or people, crazy quilts and autograph quilts.

The 20th century brought an influx of inexpensive blankets and bedcovers and quilting naturally declined. But there were periodic revivals of interest. For example, in the 1930s magazines and newspapers carried advertisements for quilting kits and bees, and interest grew in purchasing quilts made by experts. In May 1938, Macy's in New York advertised its "second annual show and sale of 115 superb hand-made American Patchwork quilts" at prices ranging from $19.98 to $64.54.[13]

During the 1960s, interest in quilts as decorative home furnishings again surfaced. By the late 1960s, small coops such as the Freedom Quilt-

Therese May, *Anthurium,* 1986. Stitched fabric, acrylic paint, 41 × 45 inches. (Photo by Curtis Fukuda.)

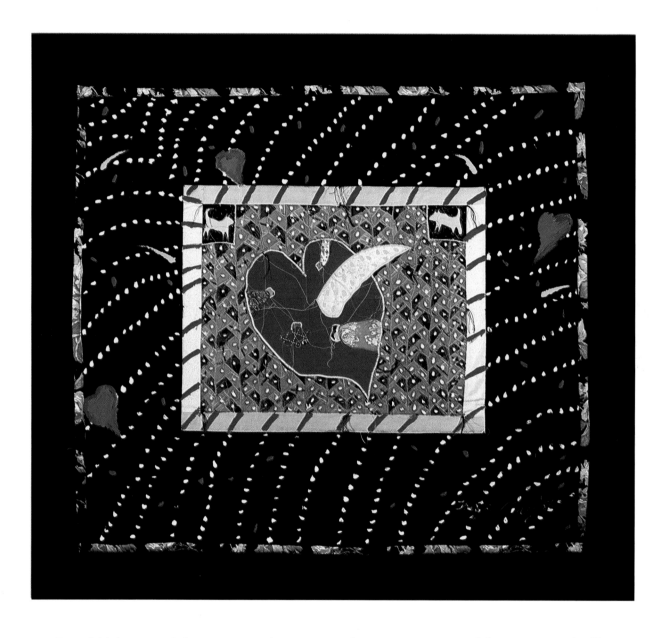

ing Bee of Alabama and the Mountain Artisans Cooperative of West Virginia were selling their wares in department stores like Bloomingdale's.

Several important exhibitions of antique quilts raised the status of quilting, as did the gathering strength of feminism. Among museums having important exhibitions were the Denver Art Museum (1963), The Newark (N.J.) Art Museum (1965) and the Chicago Art Institute (1966). In 1971, the Whitney Museum of American Art put old quilts on the art map in an exhibition of quilts in the collection of Jonathan

Holstein and Gail van der Hoof. This touring show was sent to Paris. The exhibition and an accompanying catalogue by Holstein led to a major revival of interest in quilts as examples of folk art.[14]

As the 1970s unfolded and Bicentennial fever hit, both old and new quilts were exhibited all over the country. An exhibition called Quilt National in 1979 was an important milestone since the examples shown were selected from a competition for innovative contemporary quilts. The exhibition at The Dairy Barn Art Center in Athens, Ohio, was repeated in 1981, 1983, 1985 and 1987. The 1983 exhibition was shown at the American Craft Museum and became one of the museum's best-attended shows. In 1986, *The Art Quilt*, documenting a traveling exhibition sponsored by The Art Museum Association of America, was published.

Quilting has figured in several interesting collaborative projects. These include Judy Chicago's "The Dinner Party," an art happening which involved the efforts of 400 women. Working for more than five years under Chicago's direction, they created a quilted artwork which has been exhibited around the country, opening at the San Francisco Museum of Art in 1979.[15]

Another joint effort paired excellent quilters and well-known women artists. The artists designed and the quilters made 20 quilts that were shown in an exhibition which opened at the McNay Art Institute in San Antonio, Tex., in 1983 and then traveled around the country.[16]

A number of contemporary quilters have veered far off the beaten path of patterned quilts to travel their own private roads. They use the quilt as a canvas on which to create original visual images, which they bring to life through the medium of fabric. They may employ traditional

In their unique art quilts, Gayle Fraas and Duncan Slade use fabric as a canvas which to paint and otherwise embellish. *Palermo Pencils,* 1987. Machine- and hand-stitched cotton painted with fiber-reactive dyes and pencils, 44 × 44 inches. (Photo by Dennis Griggs, collection of the Palermo School.)

patterns, which they modify, or invent original images, shapes and sizes.

## WEARABLE ART

Unique clothing resembling costumes more than everyday apparel began to appear on the scene in the 1960s. The clothes were produced with extraordinary technical skill and often took a

K. Lee Manuel, *Conflicts/Contrasts,* 1982. Painted feathers glued onto painted leather, 41 × 55 inches. (Photo by David Reese, courtesy Elaine Potter Gallery, San Francisco.)

great deal of time to construct. A part of the protest movement of the 1960s, the makers of these clothes rejected expedience, shoddy materials and poor workmanship.

So powerful was the appeal of the clothing that several galleries began to show and sell it as art. Though wearable art is plainly part of the fiber arts, this category does appear to have fewer collectors and there have been fewer exhibitions than of other types of fiber art. Two institutions which have supported this work with shows are the Kohler Art Institute in Wisconsin and the American Craft Museum.

Recent trends have included the potential of displaying as well as wearing the work, for much of it is really not wearable. Other ideas gaining currency are to mix media, combining traditional and industrial materials and techniques such as photography with traditional sewing techniques.

## NOTES

1. See Irene Emery's book, *The Primary Structure of Fabric* (Washington, D.C.: The Textile Museum, 1966, revised 1980) for definitions and descriptions of the various techniques.

2. *American Craft,* April/May 1984, p. 10.

3. *Design in America: The Cranbrook Vision 1925-1950* (New York: Harry N. Abrams, Inc., 1983) pp. 196-97.

4. *American Craft,* April/May 1984, p. 10.

5. *American Craft,* December 1983/January 1984, p. 11

6. *American Craft,* December 1983/January 1984, p. 10.

7. *American Craft,* December 1982/January 1983, p. 12.

8. *American Craft,* December 1982/January 1983, p. 12.

9. Jack Lenor Larsen's and Mildred Constantine's books, *Beyond Craft: The Art Fabric* and *The Art Fabric: Mainstream* (see Resources section), remain important for the history and insights they offer on fiber art. I have relied on these books extensively for my account of the development of fiber arts in the 1950s, '60s and '70s.

10. The magazine had a bizarre title: *Journal of the Basket Fraternity of Lovers of Indian Baskets and Other Good Things.* The title suggests the existence of a coterie of Indian basket lovers.

11. *The Art Fabric: Mainstream,* p. 96.

12. Patsy and Myron Orlofsky, *Quilts in America* (New York: McGraw Hill Book Co., 1974).

13. Ibid., p. 64.

14. *Quilter's Newsletter,* 25th anniversary issue, 1984, p. 26.

15. For an account of this project, see Judy Chicago, *The Dinner Party* (Garden City, N.Y.: Anchor Press/Doubleday, 1980).

16. Charlotte Robinson, editor, *The Artist and The Quilt* (New York: Alfred A. Knopf, 1983).

# RESOURCES FOR FIBER COLLECTORS

## BOOKS

Anni Albers, *On Weaving* (Middletown, Conn.: Wesleyan University Press, 1965).

Virginia Bath, *Needlework in America* (New York: Viking Press, 1979).

Peter Beagle, *American Denim* (New York: Harry N. Abrams, Inc., 1975).

Pattie Chase, *The Contemporary Quilt* (New York: E. P. Dutton, 1978).

Judy Chicago, *Judy Chicago, The Dinner Party A Symbol of Our Heritage* (Garden City, N.Y.: Anchor Press/Doubleday, 1979).

Mildred Constantine and Jack Lenor Larsen, *Beyond Craft: The Art Fabric* (New York: Van Nostrand Reinhold, 1973). Reprinted by Kodansha International, 1986.

————, *The Art Fabric: Mainstream* (New York: Van Nostrand Reinhold, 1981). Reprinted by Kodansha International, 1986.

Leslie Cook, *The Craftsman in Textiles* (New York: Praeger, 1968).

J. D. Crawford, *5,000 Years of Fibers and Fabrics* (New York: Brooklyn Museum, 1946).

Julie Schafler Dale, *Art To Wear* (New York: Abbeville Press, 1986).

*Fiberarts Design Book II* (Asheville, N.C.: Lark Books, 1983).

Jonathan Holstein, *American Pieced Quilts* (New York: Viking Press, 1972).

————, *The Pieced Quilt* (Boston: The New York Graphic Arts Society, 1973).

Dard Hunter, *Papermaking: The History and Technique of An Ancient Craft* (New York: Dover Publications, 1978). An unabridged republication of the second edition of the book originally published by Alfred A. Knopf in 1947.

Alexandra Jacopetti, *Native Funk & Flash, An Emerging Folk Art* (San Francisco: Scrimshaw Press, 1974).

Jack Lenor Larsen, *The Dyer's Art: Ikat, Plangi, Batik* (New York: Van Nostrand Reinhold, 1976).

Jack Lenor Larsen with Betty Freudenheim, *Interlacing The Elemental Fabric* (New York: Kodansha International, 1986).

Colleen Lahan Makowski, *Quilting 1915-1983: An Annotated Bibliography* (Metuchen, N.J.: Scarecrow Press, 1985). Includes books, catalogues, articles, non-print media, and periodicals.

Penny McMorris and Michael Kile, *The Art Quilt* (San Francisco: The Quilt Digest Press, 1986).

Dona Z. Meilach, *Soft Sculpture* (New York: Crown Publishers, 1984).

Patsy and Myron Orlofsky, *Quilts in America* (New York: McGraw Hill Book Co., 1974).

Joanne Polster, *Bibliographies: Fiber: Knotting, Stitchery and Surface Design* (New York: American Craft Council, 1979).

————, *Fiber: Weaving & Off-loom Weaving* (New York: American Craft Council, 1979).

Charlotte Robinson, ed., *The Artist & The Quilt* (New York: Alfred A. Knopf, 1983).

Ed Rossbach, *Baskets as Textile Art* (New York: Van Nostrand Reinhold, 1973).

————, *The New Basketry* (New York: Van Nostrand Reinhold, 1976).

Elyse Sommer, *Textile Collector's Guide: Valuables, Usables, Reusables* (New York: Sovereign Press, Simon & Schuster, 1978).

*Textile Collections of the World*, 3 vols. (vol.1 United States and Canada, vol.2 United Kingdom and Ireland, vol.3 France) (New York: Van Nostrand Reinhold, 1977).

Michael Thomas, et al, *Textile Art* (New York: Skira Rizzoli, 1985).

Irene Waller, *Textile Sculptures* (New York: Taplinger Publishing Co., 1977).

## CATALOGUES

*Convergence '86* (Chiloquin, Ore.: American Tapestry Alliance, 1986). Catalogue documenting exhibition at biennial conference of the Handweavers Guild of America.

*Fiber R/Evolution* (Milwaukee, Wis.: Milwaukee Art Museum, 1986).

*The Woven and Graphic Art of Anni Albers* (Washington, D.C.: Smithsonian Institution Press, 1985).

*Quilt National* (exhibition catalogues published in 1985, 1983, 1981 and 1979 by The Dairy Barn Art Center, Athens, Ohio).

*Papermaking USA: History, Process, Art* and *The Handmade Paper Book* (New York: American Craft Council, 1982). Two catalogues published in one volume.

*Maximum Coverage* (Sheboygan, Wis.: John Michael Kohler Arts Center, 1980).

*Deliberate Entanglements* (Los Angeles: University of California, 1971).

*Dorothy Liebes: Retrospective Exhibition* (New York: Museum of Contemporary Crafts, 1970).

*Perspectief in Textiel* (Amsterdam, Holland: Stedelijk Museum, 1969).

## PERIODICALS

***Fiberarts*** (bimonthly)
50 College St.
Asheville, NC 28801

***Shuttle Spindle and Dyepot***
(quarterly)
(see Handweavers Guild of America)

***Surface Design Quarterly***
(see Surface Design Association)

***Textile Museum Journal***
(annual)
(see The Textile Museum)

***Threads Magazine*** (bimonthly)
63 S. Main St.
Box 355
Newtown, CT 06470

## ORGANIZATIONS

**Center for Book Arts**
15 Bleecker St.
New York, NY 10012

Founded in 1974 for artists working in the book format and bibliophile-collectors to foster book arts. Holds courses in papermaking and other skills, sponsors exhibitions, has small reference library and publishes *Book Arts Review* quarterly.

**Fiberworks Center for the Textile Arts**
1940A Bonita Avenue
Berkeley, CA 94704
415-548-6030

Holds exhibitions, classes and promotes fiber art.

**Handweavers Guild of America**
65 LaSalle Rd.
West Hartford, CT 06107

Founded in 1969 for persons, weaving guilds, schools, teachers and suppliers who wish to promote interest in and practice of handweaving and textile arts. Publishes *Shuttle Spindle and Dyepot* and holds biennial convention, usually in June.

**Surface Design Association**
311 E. Washington
Fayetteville, TN 37334

Founded in 1976 for individuals interested in promoting art fabrics emphasizing surface design. Holds conferences and workshops and publishes *Surface Design Journal.*

**The Textile Museum**
2320 S St., NW
Washington, D.C. 20008

Exhibitions, research library and annual journal.

# GLASS

I n a contemporary history that extends back only 25 years, American glassmakers "have blown, cast, slumped, cut and sandblasted their way through 2,000 years of glass forms, adding personal flourishes along the way."[1] The resulting smorgasbord poses interesting questions about how to organize a meaningful collection. Many collectors want one of everything, but there are other possible strategies. For example, you could follow the development of one or a few artists, collecting their work in depth. You might choose a particular methodology such as cast or mold-blown glass, constructed sculptural pieces or those made by working glass over a torch (called lampworking). Other ideas include collecting work by women, who are prominent in this field, or of a particular geographic area, such as the work of those active at the Pilchuck School in Seattle or in and around Penland, N.C., where Harvey Littleton, Mark Peiser and many younger glassmakers live and work.

Making sense of the great variety of techniques in use today takes a considerable amount of looking and learning. One way to classify these techniques is to think in terms of hot glass, cold glass and warm glass. Hot-glass techniques include blowing and casting; cold techniques include cutting, grinding, polishing, sandblasting and etching. Another option employed by studio

Mary Van Cline uses the medium of glass to investigate psychological realities. *The Healing Series Part I,* 1987. Photosensitive glass, painted wood, 42 × 18 × 15 inches.

glassmakers is to warm glass in a furnace or over a flame until it is malleable enough to bend and then to fuse, slump or lampwork it into new forms. Some glassmakers employ more than one technique in the same piece. They may create a form by using traditional blowing techniques and then go on to embellish it through one of the warm or cold techniques. Others (and this is a growing trend) employ glass as only one of a num-

*The Healing Series Part 2*, 1987, photosensitive glass, neon, wood. (Photos by Rob Vinnedge.)

today by going beyond method can be an interesting intellectual exercise, though a difficult one, given the extraordinarily wide range of forms. One can make a start by realizing that some glassmakers prefer to work with figures, others with vessels and others with abstract sculptural shapes. Several themes that cut across technique include a concern with the beauty and character of glass (work by Harvey Littleton, Dale Chihuly, Karla Trinkley and Jay Musler, for example); interest in fantasy forms (Ginny Ruffner and Amy Roberts, William Morris' glass "stones," Stephen Dee Edwards' sea forms); the use of glass to express social comments or psychological insights (Mary Van Cline, Dan Dailey, Hank Murta Adams); and architectural concerns (displayed by David Huchthausen, William Carlson and Michael Pavlik, among others).

Glass is an extremely difficult material to work. Mastering the necessary techniques takes many years of study and devotion. Consequently, it is natural that this art form is very deeply about the material's nature and physical characteristics. Some issues glassmakers have investigated include glass's translucency and opaqueness, its ability to simultaneously hold color and be translucent, its layered quality and the variability of its form under different temperatures. Some artists purposely obscure the obvious attributes of glass, whether out of perversity or communication is for each viewer to decide.

While collectors undoubtedly appreciate the great skill behind the craftsman's artistry, many are not overly concerned with methodology. However, investing time and energy in learning about the glassmaking process does have value, since understanding the reason why a particular object is (or is not) a tour de force requires knowl-

ber of materials, such as metal, wood or stone. A number of glassmakers have developed unique methodologies. For example, Michael Glancy blows, incises and then electroplates glass, Tom Patti fuses sheets of glass and then subjects them to further processing and Steven Weinberg employs casting and other techniques in his work.

Attempting to classify the variety of work

With the botanically exact paperweights for which he is known, Paul Stankard has expanded the art of traditional paperweight making. *Botanical,* 1985. Lampworked colored glass encased in clear glass, ground and polished, 5 × 2¾ inches. (Photo courtesy Heller Gallery, New York.)

Mark Peiser, *House Plans*, 1985. Cast glass, cut, ground and polished, 12 × 4½ × 3 inches. (Photo by artist, courtesy Heller Gallery, New York, collection of University of Iowa Hospital System.)

edge of the problem the maker was attempting to solve. Glassmakers seem to be a playful lot who, it may be imagined, often do some of their most interesting work by saying to themselves: "I wonder what will happen if I do that."

Evaluating individual examples requires weighing both aesthetic and technical issues. Patti says that the aesthetic issues are the same in all sculptural forms. "You consider form and material, then color, texture, surface quality. Glass is unique because of its ability to use light. The first impression of the object is often related to its form, but then look at it more closely. Taking time to look and study and to make yourself vulnerable to the object is part of the process of looking at art."

It is often helpful to know something of the artist's body of work before drawing conclusions about the success of a piece under study. Perceived flaws could come from several causes. Perhaps the maker's technique was not sufficient to execute the piece in the best way, or perhaps he or she did not have access to the required equipment. But it is always possible that a perceived flaw, such as hazy or impure glass, is precisely the effect the artist wanted.

Speaking of his own work, Patti points out that his output over the years shows an evolution of form and technical development. "Some of my early works don't reach the level of technical perfection of more recent work, but reveal an exciting part of my growth. Often a younger person approaches things with an energy, freedom and searching exploration. He pushes the material even though there may be technical problems. If you were to clean up the object later on, it would lose this sense of energy."

These thoughts indicate that imposing doctrinaire technical standards can remove from

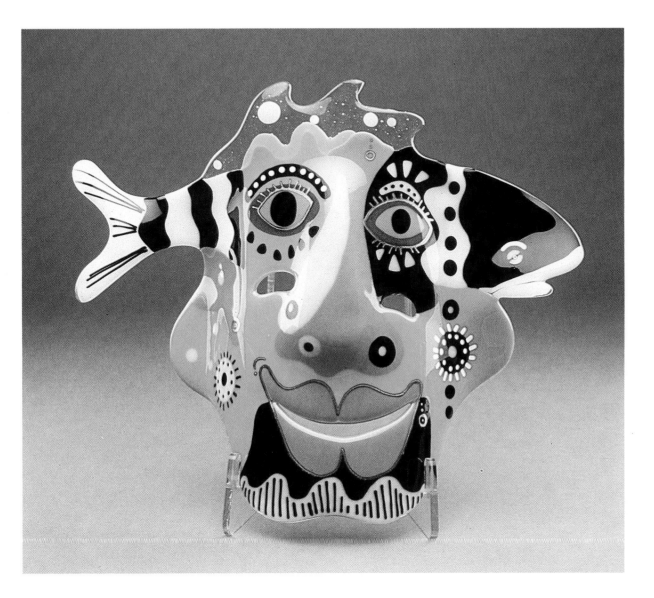

For part of its inspiration Ruth Brockmann's figural work calls on the creative spirit of Northwestern coastal Indian culture. *Shaman with Whale Spirit,* 1985. Fused and slumped glass, 14 × 16 × 5 inches. (Photo by Roger Schreiber.)

consideration the most interesting work. On the other hand, there are some flaws that most glassmakers consider unacceptable. A crack, for example, may signify incompatibility of material or improper annealing, which is the process of controlled cooling. Proper annealing gives the glass stability and incorrectly annealed glass can shatter. To see if the glass is stable, it has to be examined under a polariscope, a method which does not, however, work with opaque glass. Other flaws include laminations with visible vestiges of adhesive or discolored epoxy. The right adhesive has to be used in laminating or a piece may not hold together. If work fails after it has been purchased, a gallery with integrity will take it back and an artist will fix it. However, an attitude that

Karla Trinkley, *Green Arrow*, 1986. Cast glass (*pate de verre* technique), 12½ × 11½ inches. (Photo by Tom Weigand, courtesy Heller Gallery, New York.)

breakdowns are somebody else's responsibility also exists.

"I would worry about cracks, even very small ones that may not be obvious. It is ludicrous to imagine carrying around a polariscope, but it would be appropriate. Some glass made in the early 1960s shows technical problems, although if a piece hasn't broken within a few years, it should be okay," said Patti.

Glass has no grain and stress follows the path of least resistance, so even a tiny crack weakens the structure. If the piece were left on a windowsill on a sunny day and then placed in very cold water, conceivably it could break along the crack. Likewise, pieces constructed with several types of glass having different expansion and contraction rates could break under some circumstances.

Since tiny surface cracks, even severe

scratches on the exterior of an object, can lead to bigger problems, when making a selection examine the work under a good light, turning the piece or walking around it slowly. Look at thin edges to see that there are no chips. Once an object is brought home, install it in a safe place and avoid mishandling it.

## CONTEMPORARY GLASS DEVELOPMENTS

The contemporary American studio glass movement can be traced back to 1962, when two glass-blowing workshops were organized and led by Harvey Littleton on the grounds of the Toledo Museum of Art. Studio craftsmen worked in glass before 1962 by employing techniques such as cutting and fabrication, melting glass and then reforming it, painting on glass or working in the stained-glass tradition. But the blown-glass movement was the one that attracted the larger number of practitioners and collectors. Littleton, the leader of the movement, has explained his fascination with glass as perhaps an inevitable result of growing up in Corning, N.Y., where his father was director of research for Corning Glass. He rejected a career in glass for one in art,[2] but although he became a potter, he never lost interest in glass as a potential material. In 1957 and 1958, Littleton traveled to Italy, where he visited small glass factories in Naples and on the island of Murano. There he observed working situations in which only two men labored together at a small demonstration furnace. This experience convinced him that an artist could have a glass facility in the studio.

Returning to the United States, he began to experiment by melting small batches of glass in his studio, using one of his own stoneware bowls set inside an old ceramic kiln. He described these

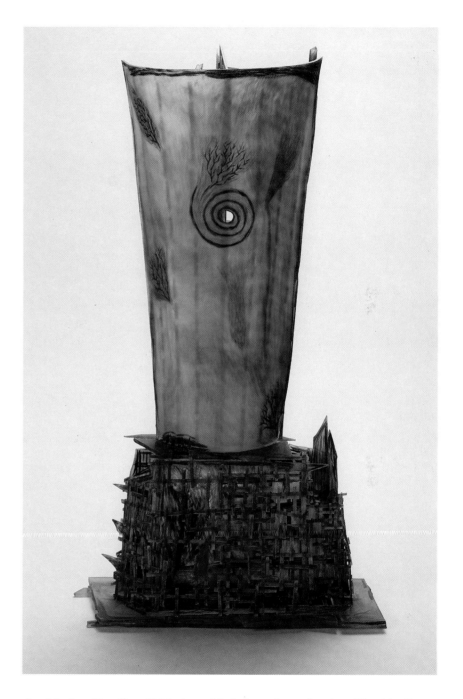

Jay Musler, *Derelict,* 1984. Assembled plate glass, oil paint, 27 × 14 × 7 inches. (Photo courtesy Heller Gallery, New York.)

Hank Murta
Adams, *Prig*,
1986. Cast glass
and copper,
20 × 20 × 12
inches. (Photo
courtesy Heller
Gallery, New
York.)

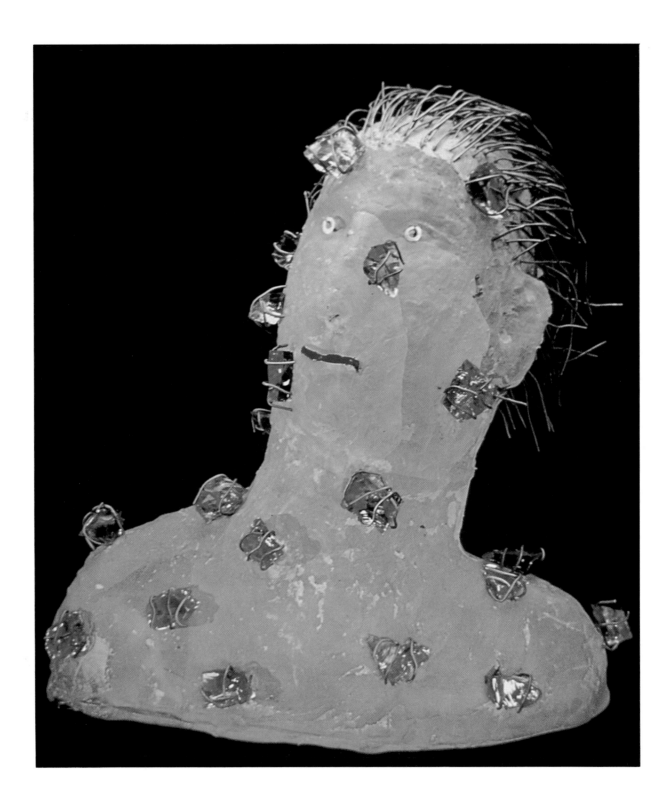

Dan Dailey loves puns. His mastery of the art of caricature in the glass form is evident in this delightful portrait. *Fat Cat*, 1984. Vitrolite, plate glass, gold-plated brass, 18 × 20 inches. (Photo by Susi Cushner.)

experiments in 1959 at the American Craft Council's third national conference at Lake George, N.Y. He amplified the information at the fourth conference in 1961, where he also displayed several glass objects he had produced by melting glass in the studio and afterward cutting and polishing the lumps into faceted sculptures.

Littleton sought financial support for further experiments and the Toledo Museum obliged by providing an outbuilding for a week-long workshop to explore hot glass. In March of 1962, Littleton, the late Dominick Labino, (director of research for Johns-Manville Fiber Glass Corp.), Norman Schulman (a pottery instructor at the Toledo Museum School of Art), and a few craftsmen gathered to melt glass in a small pot furnace

Littleton had built. Labino provided the low-melting glass formula and also redesigned the furnace, which didn't work on the first try.

A second workshop at the same location was held in June with larger participation from a wider geographic area, aided by a travel grant from Just Lunning, president of Georg Jensen in New York. The two-week workshop included demonstrations by Littleton, Labino, Schulman and Harvey Leafgreen, a Corning technician. There were also gallery talks on glass by members of the curatorial staff of the museum.

By the summer of 1962, the only pottery Littleton was making consisted of stoneware crucibles in which to melt #475 glass marbles. That fall, he opened his own glass studio one day a

Surprisingly, Tom Patti's monumental works in glass are only inches tall. *Compacted Horizontal Solarized Blue,* 1986-87. Laminated, expanded glass, 3 inches high.

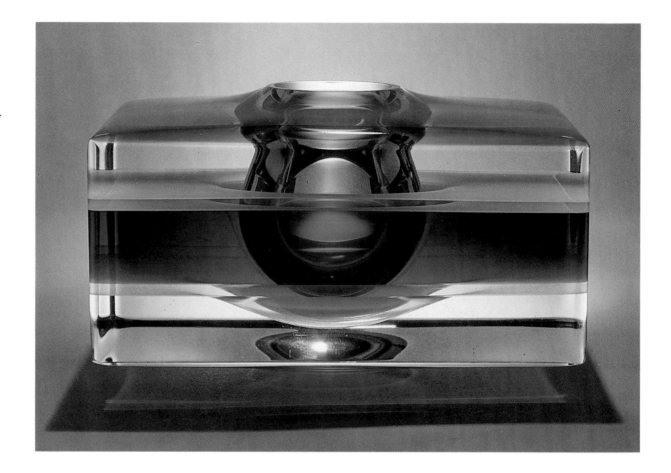

week to six students of ceramics. Among them was Marvin Lipofsky, who would eventually establish a glass program at Berkeley and later head a thriving glass department at the California College of Arts and Crafts. By the fall of 1963, Littleton had secured university funding to rent and equip an off-campus space in Madison for a studio, and the first university-level hot-glass program in this country opened at the University of Wisconsin. Littleton also began an extensive series of lectures at art schools, colleges and before craftsmen's groups in the Midwest and Northeast, recounting his struggles to develop tools and techniques with an openness that con-

trasted sharply with the tradition of secrecy in the glass industry.

In 1964, he took the story of his experiments in hot glass to the first meeting of the World Crafts Congress at Columbia University in New York, demonstrating the technique by melting a tankful of glass marbles. From this point on developments came faster. Lipofsky introduced glass to the University of California at Berkeley in 1964. Other glass programs initiated as a result of the Columbia demonstration included those at Haystack Mountain School of Crafts in Maine and at San Jose State College in California.[3] In 1967, Dale Chihuly and Fritz Dreisbach

This early work by Tom Patti reveals a fascination with the nature of glass and with architectural form. *Banded Clear*, 1977. Laminated, expanded glass, 4¼ inches high.

Marvin Lipofsky, a historic figure in the post-war studio glass movement, has helped forge international ties through his collaborative work at European glass facilities. *Serie Fratelli Toso,* 1977-78. Blown glass form made at the Fratelli Toso Factory, in Milan, finished at artist's California studio. (Photo by M. Lee Fatherree.)

graduated from the University of Wisconsin's glass program. Chihuly went on to further develop the glass department at the Rhode Island School of Design, which Schulman had established in 1965, and to found the Pilchuck School. Dreisbach would build the glass program at the Toledo Museum Art School and at Penland.

On October 3, 1969, when Objects USA opened at the Smithsonian's National Collection of Fine Arts, the work of 18 glassblowers was included. By 1971, there were 69 schools offering glass programs, 15 of them in California. In the early 1970s, a growing number of galleries and collectors became interested in the new work.

In 1979, only 15 years after the Columbia University demonstrations, a landmark exhibition was mounted by the Corning Museum. This follow-up to the museum's 1959 exhibition of contemporary glass revealed the changes: Fewer than 200 glassmakers had submitted work for the 1959 exhibition. The 1979 submissions amounted to nine studio pieces for every one made by industry. There were 1,000 individual entrants.[4]

Considering that the technical ability to work hot glass in the studio was achieved only in 1962, American glassmakers have made startling progress in their mastery of this medium.

## FLAT GLASS

Swept along by the fascination with hot glass, other types of glass art have recently engendered interest. One of these is flat glass. Stained- and leaded-glass windows and panels are being used by some individuals as a medium for personal expression.

In the United States, before the present, the greatest era for flat glass (whose venerable history and traditions go back to the Middle Ages) occurred during the late-19th-century Aesthetic period. The most notable examples of stained glass windows and panels from this period were by Louis Comfort Tiffany and John LaFarge.

Although flat glass work continued in the 20th century in hundreds of studios where ecclesiastical and commercial windows were made of colored and leaded glass, aesthetic advances were little publicized or noted. But beginning in California about two decades ago, a number of individuals with art training and interests began to work with flat glass. Especially in California, museum and gallery exhibitions documented the new approaches to this pictorial art form, which treated the glass as a canvas on which to record images. Some individuals, such as Narcissus Quagliata, emphasize expressionism while others such as Albinus Elskus, Paul Marioni and Robert Kehlmann have employed more abstract images in some of their recent work.

A renewed demand for architectural orna-ment and interest in building restoration are among the factors leading to a rebirth of interest in flat glass. But large scale architectural instal-lations of flat glass are usually permanently fixed, which makes it unrealistic to collect them in quantity. As a rule, a collector will acquire a single powerful piece in a permanent installation for a residence or office building. Often, however, a

Amy Roberts' dreamlike fantasy piece suggests a carnival at night. Though it is bright and gay, there is an undertone of vulnerability in the precarious attachments. *Voyage Into the Flatlands,* 1986. Painted wood, blown vessel and broken glass shards, painted metal, 66 × 52 × 18 inches. (Photo by Kevin La Tona.)

Making a joke in glass appears to be the point of this piece by Doug Anderson. *Mail Fish*, 1983. Cast glass (*pate de verre* technique) 5½ × 7 × 2 inches. (Photo courtesy Heller Gallery, New York.)

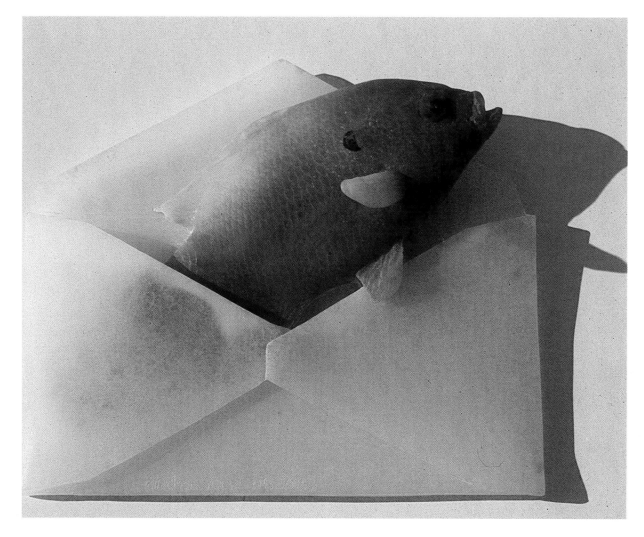

maker will be able to suggest a means of making a work removable and portable. For example, Quagliata has developed a method of framing stained-glass screens and panels. The frame (which is designed as part of the piece) conceals wiring for lighting and is a stable mount so that the piece can stand on its own.

Since flat glass is not a typical college art concentration, those who work in the medium usually have come from somewhere else. A few examples of training include architecture, graphic art or fine art and engineering. Contemporary stained glass is rarely hung in museums so to find individuals whose work appeals, attend shows in untraditional places. Look for examples in churches and public buildings and ask gallery directors.

When commissioning work, it is sensible to be concerned with the technical proficiency of the maker. Contact previous clients, ask the gallery and artist to provide information on training, installations and so on. The larger the proj-

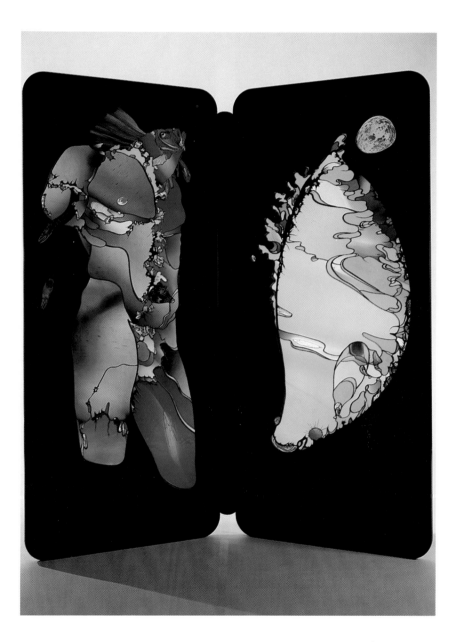

Wendy Maruyama's lamp employs neon tubes and paint to voice her concern on a possible nuclear disaster. *It Was Only A Test,* 1986. Neon, medium-density fiberboard, basswood, acrylics, 72 inches high. (Photo by Cary Okazaki.)

A wood frame makes it possible to display stained glass panels in a freestanding unit against natural light or in front of a lighted surface, as in this work by Narcissus Quagliata. *Treasures in the Mediterranean,* 1986. Stained glass and wood, 76 × 111 inches. (Photo by M. Lee Fatherree, collection of Anne and Ronald Abramson.)

Kathie Stackpole Bunnell, *Grandmother*, 1983. Stained-glass panel, 25⅞ × 24½ inches. (Photo by artist.)

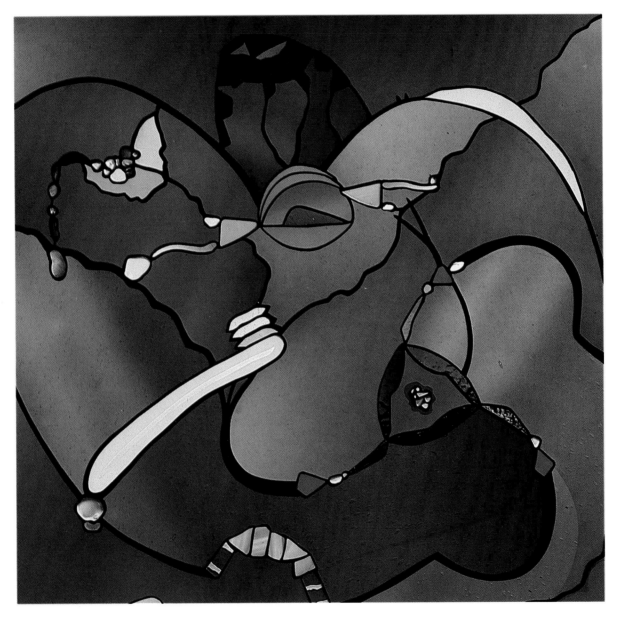

ect, the more technical expertise is required, since glass is heavy and requires proper structural supports.

Besides the techniques of leading, others in use today include beveling, sandblasting, etching, fusing, laminating, gilding, mosaic, painting and relief.

Another format that can be used to make art combines glass tubes with neon and other gases. Though more than 150 colors can be achieved by combining different gases and phosphors, those most commonly used are orange-red neon and lavender argon. Recently, after a long period of eclipse, the brightly colored glass tubes that

John Nygren, *Crested Lizard On A Rock*, 1986, blown glass. (Photo by Smith/Weiler, courtesy Heller Gallery, New York.)

can be bent into many different shapes have once again been employed by artists. Among glass-makers who have worked with neon are Dale Chihuly and James Carpenter, who in the early 1970s created a series of glass and neon environ-ments at the Rhode Island School of Design. Currently, glassmaker Paul Seide (who studied with Chihuly at RISD) is working in this medium and in 1987, Wendy Maruyama employed neon in furniture.

## NOTES

1. Essay by Paul Hollister in *New American Glass: Focus 2 West Virginia* (Huntington, W.Va.: Huntington Galleries, 1986).

2. Joan Falconer Byrd, *Harvey K. Littleton: A Retrospective Exhibition* (Atlanta Ga.: High Museum of Art, 1984). I have relied on Byrd's account of the Toledo workshops and other early events, augmented by conversations with Littleton and Norman Schulman in April 1985.

3. Schulman recalls he built the kiln which was designed by Dominick Labino for the demonstration at Columbia. The kiln was later given to Haystack, where it was used in the first glass summer program. The class was taught by Michael Boylen.

4. *New Glass: A Worldwide Survey* (Corning, N.Y.: Corning Museum of Glass, 1979) p. 25.

## RESOURCES FOR GLASS COLLECTORS

### BOOKS

Paul V. Gardner, *Frederick Carder: Portrait of a Glassmaker* (Corning, N.Y.: Corning Museum of Glass, 1986).

*Chihuly: Color, Glass & Form* (New York: Kodansha International, 1986).

*Glass Collections in Museums in the United States and Canada* (Corning, N.Y.: Corning Museum of Glass, 1983).

Ferdinand Hampson, *Insight: A Collector's Guide to Contemporary American Glass* (Huntington Woods, Mich.: Elliot Johnston Publishers, 1985). One hundred four glass artists describe their creative process. Available from Habatat Galleries, Lathrup Village, MI 48075.

———, *25 Years: Glass as an Art Medium* (Lathrup, Mich: Habatat Galleries, 1987).

Robert Hill, et al, *Stained Glass: Music for the Eye* (San Francisco: Scrimshaw Press, 1979).

Lawrence Lee, et al, *Stained Glass* (New York: Crown Publishers, 1976).

Harvey K. Littleton, *Glassblowing: A Search for Form* (New York: Van Nostrand Reinhold, 1971).

*New Glass Review* 8 (Corning, N.Y.: Corning Museum of Glass, 1987). Annual publication showing 100 glass objects judged best in 1986; nos. 3 and 7 are also available.

Joanne Polster, *Bibliography: Glass* (New York: American Craft Council, 1978).

Narcissus Quagliata, *Stained Glass from Mind to Light: An Inquiry into the Nature of the Medium* (San Francisco: Mattole Press, 1976).

William Warmus, *Emile Gallé: Dreams into Glass* (Corning, N.Y.: Corning Museum of Glass, 1984).

Michael Webb, *The Magic of Neon* (Layton, Utah: Gibbs M. Smith, Inc., 1986).

H. Weber Wilson, *Great Glass in American Architecture: Decorative Windows and Doors Before 1920* (New York: E.P. Dutton, 1986).

### CATALOGUES

*New American Glass: Focus 2 West Virginia* (Huntington, W. Va.: Huntington Galleries, 1986). Includes overview of developments in the past ten years.

*World Glass Now '85* (Tokyo: Kinokuniya Co., Ltd., 1985). Available from Kinokuniya Co., Export Division, 1707, Shinjuki 3-chome, Shinjuki-ku, Tokyo 60-91, Japan.

*Harvey K. Littleton: A Retrospective Exhibition* (Atlanta, Ga.: High Museum of Art, 1984).

*Americans in Glass* (Wausau, Wisc.: Leigh Yawkey Woodson Art Museum, 1978, 1981 and 1984), three separate catalogues.

*New Glass: A Worldwide Survey* (Corning, N.Y.: Corning Museum of Glass, 1979). An important catalogue to own; still in print.

### TECHNICAL LEAFLET

*The Care and Display of Glass Collections* (Nashville, Tenn.: American Association for State and Local History, no date). Technical Leaflet #127.

## PERIODICALS

### Neues Glas/New Glass
(quarterly)
Verlagsanstat Handwerk Aufm
Tetelberg 7
D 4000 Dusseldorf, W. Germany

The major periodical in the field
(in German and English). Since
1985, the annual *New Glass
Review* has been bound into the
spring issue.

### Stained Glass (quarterly)
The Stained Glass Association
   of America
1125 Wilmington Ave.
St. Louis, MO 63111

## ORGANIZATIONS

### Bay Area Studio Art Glass
   (BASAG)
c/o Julia Peters Maslach
44 Industrial Way
Greenbrae, CA 94904

Organization of studio glassmakers formed in 1979, who
cooperate in joint open-studio
exhibitions each May and
December.

### Corning Museum of Glass
Corning, N.Y. 14831
607-937-5371
Susanne Frantz, Curator 20th
   Century Glass
Museum, library, publications,
research department, exhibition
program

### Creative Glass Center of
   America
Glasstown Rd., Box 646
Millville, NJ 08332
609-825-6800
Karl Hensel, Director
Museum, artists-in-residence
   fellowships, symposia

### Glass Art Society
Box 1364
c/o Corning Museum of Glass
Corning, NY 14830
607-937-5371

Annual conference, proceedings
of which are available in published form.

### New York Experimental Glass
   Workshop
142 Mulberry St.
212-966-1808
New York, NY 10013

Courses; working space for
artists, gallery, publishes *New
Work* quarterly

### The Penland School of Crafts
Penland, NC 28765-0037
Verne Stanford, Director
704-765-2359

Besides classes in glassmaking,
Penland serves an an information center for glassmakers in
the area. Collector groups may
arrange special tours of studios
of area glassmakers, normally
closed to the public.

### The Pilchuck School
107 S. Main St.
Seattle, WA 98104
Alice Rooney, Director
206-621-8422
June-July: Stanwood, WA 98292
206-445-3111

Summer classes and open house
for serious amateurs and
collectors

## COLLECTOR GROUPS

Largely informal groups of
collectors have been organized
in a number of areas. Typically
members meet in one another's
homes to hear guest speakers,
take trips to artists' studios and
provide mutual guidance on
issues of interest to collectors.
As a rule, officers change from
year to year, but the following
individuals should be able to
provide information on their
groups.

### Collectors Group of Chicago
c/o Ron Isaacson
Mindscape Gallery
1521 Sherman Ave.
Evanston, IL 60201
312-864-2660

### Delaware Valley Glass
   Collectors Group
(Philadelphia-South Jersey area)
Suzanne Hildebrandt, president
One Rittenhouse Square, 135 S.
   18th St.
Philadelphia, PA 19103
215-564-3773

### Detroit Area Contemporary
   Glass Group
c/o Ferdinand Hampson
Habatat Gallery
28235 Southfield Rd.
Lathrup Village, MI 48076
313-552-0515

### Metropolitan Contemporary
   Glass Group
(New York-New Jersey area)
c/o Heller Gallery
71 Greene Street
New York, NY 10012
212-966-5948

This piece by Deborah Aguado is an unobtrusive demonstration of technical proficiency and inspired use of mixed materials. *Idol's Eye*, 1986. Sterling silver and 18-karat gold with phenomenal-cut golden citrine, 3 × 2 × ⅜ inches. (Photo by Bob Hansson, courtesy Elaine Potter Gallery, San Francisco.)

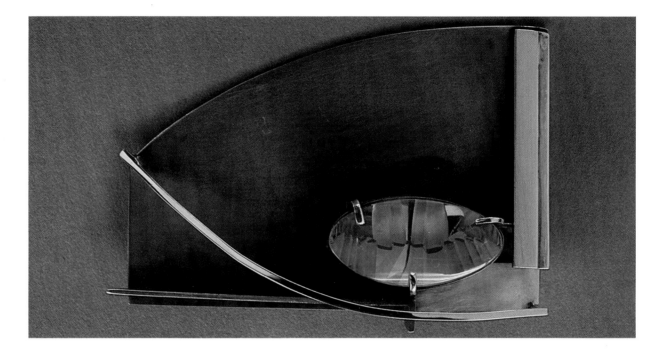

These brooches by Eugene Pijanowski and Hiroko Sato Pijanowski are an example of the general trend in art jewelry of using nonprecious materials. *OH! Am I Precious?* 1987. Dried fish skin, paper, colored pencil, Mizuhiki (Japanese paper cord), glue and lacquer spray, 11½ × 3½ × ¼ inches (largest).

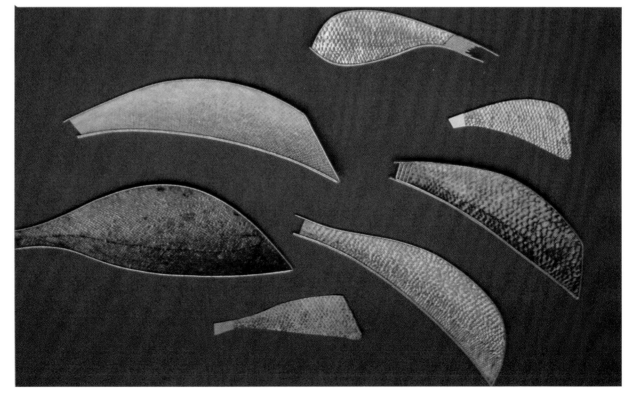

# JEWELRY AND METALWORK

Anne K. Graham's bracelet cuff combines color and size to create the presence once found only in pieces lavishly embellished with precious materials. *Quetzal,* 1986. Anodized aluminum and sterling silver, 4½ × 3½ × 3½ inches. (Photo by artist, courtesy Elaine Potter Gallery, San Francisco.)

There will always be those for whom a jewel must be made of precious metals and gemstones. But the play of imagination and greater freedom to select from among all of the world's materials are enriching the contemporary art jewelry field. Briefly summarized, trends in jewelry today include using nonprecious materials, employing graphic images with a social, political or emotional message and enlarging the range of forms.

Today, old ideas of what a brooch, necklace or earrings should look like have been substantially expanded. A contemporary "jewel" may be made of aluminum, plastic, wood, found objects, safety pins or any other material that intrigues the maker. In addition, a number of artists working in a jewelry format are not particularly concerned with wearability. Some objects are made both to display and wear. Others, nominally wearable, would be extremely uncomfortable. Some makers have abandoned wearability altogether in favor of work that is purely sculptural or decorative.

Invention for its own sake has always been a feature of modern jewelry, but nowadays, a goal of many artists is to assimilate technique so that it is unobtrusive, even unnoticed. Virtuoso demonstrations of technique and displays of color (in anodized aluminum and titanium, for exam-

ple) are still as seductive as when first introduced in the 1970s, but some jewelers are asking more of themselves by showing greater concern for the overall piece, rather than problems of construction.

An interest in combining jewelry and technology that became evident in the 1960s continues to be important. In addition, some jewelers have begun to look outside their own traditions to fields such as ceramics for useful ideas. "There is more communication with those in other fields and a jeweler is not necessarily so isolated as in the past," notes jeweler Eleanor Moty.

Although outside influences are invigorating

These earrings made by Ivy Ross in 1987 employ Color-core Formica, a plastic laminate, and 24-karat gold plate.

some work, the segmentation overtaking other fields is also present in jewelry. In place of the lively experimentation of the 1960s and 1970s, when individual artists tried new ideas with abandon, today jewelers are more likely to choose either to specialize in fashion jewelry or to remove themselves from the issues of wearability entirely and concentrate on conceptual and sculptural works. While a small group of collectors has responded with enthusiasm to revolutionary pieces, the majority is more interested in classic jewelry in precious materials bearing the names of well-known makers. This mismatch of intentions may eventually lead to more adventurous collectors or to less venturesome jewelry. One pos-

sibility is that jewelers interested in experimentation will put their efforts into new fields such as performance art. Or they may enter the arena of pure sculpture, pitting their talents against those who practice in the sculpture mainstream. But in today's atmosphere where a work's power is often equated with its large size, the intimacy of jewelry can be a decided disadvantage.

Clearly, how a piece is evaluated must be guided by the use to which it will be put. Conceptual works, which will be displayed rather than worn, need not conform to the same standards of comfort as jewelry purchased for adornment. Pieces worn only on special occasions perhaps need not be as wearable as a watch or a wedding

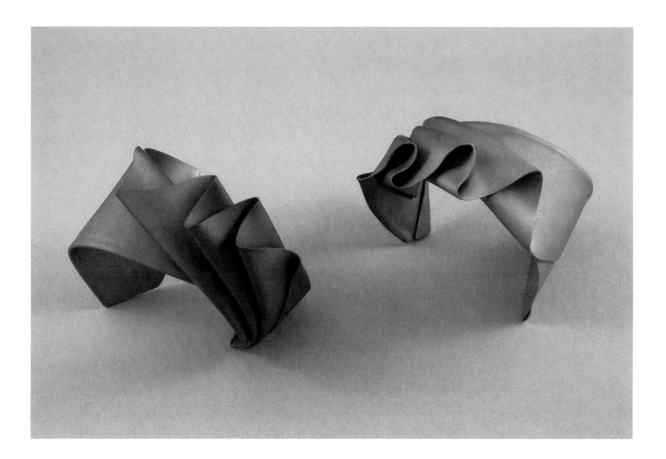

Gerhard Herbst's anodized aluminum bracelets are like frozen waves of color. They are part of a series begun in 1983.

ring. For example, Robert Ebendorf's large bracelets were created to be worn as "performance pieces. You can't put a coat on and you can't do the dishes when you are wearing them. Some collectors enjoy the sense of occasion, even notoriety, when wearing this type of jewelry," he said.

If a collector intends to wear art jewelry, the issue of wearability naturally is important. Making informed decisions about the wearability of a piece is considerably easier if one is cognizant of jewelry construction. "To understand if the mechanics are well executed, a collector has to know the craft. Go to Haystack and take a basic jewelry class and you will know if a hinge is

properly done, if the solder is good, if the mechanism is likely to last," said Ebendorf, who is head of the metals department at the State University of New York at New Paltz. This sensible though time-consuming solution to the problem of increasing knowledge and judgment has other advantages as well, since learning the difficulties of mastery firsthand helps a collector to recognize and appreciate it.

A few obvious issues to consider when purchasing jewelry for wear include comfort, the difficulty of putting it on and the effect it will have on clothing. Earrings may be so large or heavy that they weigh down the ear or fall off. Rings may not fit under gloves. A necklace may be too

Even the humble safety pin has been successfully transformed into a material for jewelry in Tina Fung Holder's necklace (1986) of crocheted cotton yarn, safety pins and glass beads. (Photo by Jeff Bayne.)

bulky to wear with a coat. To attach some pieces may require a second set of hands. The pin stem of a brooch may be too close to the back to be serviceable on heavy fabric or a brooch may be so heavy it tears a sheer blouse. If care has been taken in the method of manufacture, the jewelry should stand up. Careful workmanship and attention to detail such as the attachment of earring posts or screw backs are marks of concern for the wearer. Reputable galleries will not sell poor-quality pieces, or if the work breaks down in use, they will see that it is repaired.

Beyond issues of wearability, understanding the history of the medium is a good way to hone an appreciation of contemporary work. A general background can be developed by looking at the great jewelry of the past which is on display at large art museums across the country. It is a tough test, but contemporary jewelry does have to compete with the Islamic, Egyptian, medieval and Art Deco jewelry collectors can see in museums and buy at auction and in antiques shops.

Despite the fact that today's work could hardly better the outstanding workmanship, preciousness of materials and objective beauty of the best old pieces, contemporary studio jewelry measures up and surpasses in interest the work of the past for many collectors because it reflects the interests and values of the present.

## BACKGROUND AND DEVELOPMENT

As any schoolchild knows, Paul Revere was not only an American Revolutionary War hero, he was also a great silversmith. Boston, Philadelphia, New York and other colonial cities were metal-working centers and 17th- and 18th-century American silver and pewter are rare and cherished collectibles—a testament to the early development of American metalsmithing skill. Jewelry, however, does not appear to have been accorded much attention in the early days of the Republic.

Even as late as the early part of the 19th century, comparatively little jewelry was produced in this country and wealthy Americans purchased their jewels from Europe, especially France.[1] The development of mass-production techniques in holloware and flatware effectively eliminated the master craftsmen from competition. By the end of the century, a thriving commercial jewelry, holloware and flatware industry that relied little on hand craftsmanship had developed. As the century drew to a close, however, the ideas of the Arts and Crafts movement stimulated interest in the metal arts, and a number of individuals set up small workshops and began to execute and sell handcrafted silver, copper and art jewelry. In jewelry (as in other crafts) an important goal was to simplify the florid, over-ornamented work of the past, using forms and motifs drawn from nature, and to demonstrate the value of hand craftsmanship.

A number of American Arts and Crafts workshops and craftsmen achieved national, even international, reputations. They included the Kalo Shop in Chicago and the Handicraft Shop in Boston. Some well-known metalsmiths were socialites Madeline Yale Wynne and Florence D. Koehler, as well as Dirk Van Erp, Harry Dixon,

Josephine Hartwell Shaw and Janet Payne Boles, to name only a few.[2] The Americans were well aware of their European counterparts. They knew about C. R. Ashbee's Guild of Handicrafts, established in 1887 in London; Josef Hoffmann's *Wiener Werkstatte*, organized in Vienna in 1903; Joseph Olbrich's artists' colony in Darmstadt after 1901; and Georg Jensen's workshop in Copenhagen, established in 1904.

The international ties within today's metal-working world mirror the cross-Atlantic ties that existed at the turn of the century, when there were numerous comings and goings between America and Europe. Just as today, this was not merely a one-way street running from east to west. For example, Siegfried (Samuel) Bing commissioned and sold Tiffany glass and mosaics in his Paris shop, *Art Nouveau*, and William Randolph

Donald Friedlich has employed a ceramic tile as a brooch material. *Erosion Series*, 1985. Ceramic tile, 18-karat gold, 1⅜ × 2 × ⅜ inches. (Photo by James Beards, courtesy Elaine Potter Gallery.)

**Marjorie Schick changes the concept of jewelry in this necklace of painted wood, 1985, 26 × 28 × 20 inches. (Photo by Gary Pollmiller, courtesy Helen Drutt Gallery, Philadelphia.)**

Hearst purchased most of the work exhibited by Georg Jensen at the Panama-Pacific International Exhibition in San Francisco in 1915.[3]

Jewelry is inextricably linked to the social and cultural milieu in which it is created and worn. It is therefore not surprising that the rise of the middle class and the slow attrition of royalty and its trappings should have led worldwide to affordable pieces crafted in a great variety of nonprecious materials. As the 20th century progressed, the roles of women in the jewelry-wearing classes changed into more active ones, and the kind of jewelry offered began to change, too. Styles became far less fussy and more wearable. The design ideas of the era were worked out in pieces that had sweeping curves and bold, straight lines, and in which form became more dominant than ornament. In addition to Art Deco, another important source of new ideas was the Bauhaus, whose aesthetic also emphasized form and lack of ornament.

Weimar, Germany, was the birthplace of the Bauhaus in 1919, but it was the Paris (the birthplace of Art Deco in the *Exposition des Arts Decoratifs* in 1925) of the 1920s where many of today's attitudes and ideas about jewelry were first put into practice. There "the great artist-jewelers of the 1920s . . . used materials, precious or otherwise, not for their intrinsic value but solely for their suitability and effectiveness in expressing the design concepts that were typical of their work and epoch . . . they were sensitive to people's need for jewelry that was more than mere ornamentation or symbol of status and wealth."[4]

As vital as these ideas were, the world that produced them was soon to disappear, a casualty of a worldwide depression which struck earlier in Europe than in the United States and then

Robert Ebendorf, *Cuff Bracelet*, 1987. Metal, wood, Colorcore Formica, 8 inches in diameter. (Photo by Alex Casler.)

This necklace (1984) by Eugene Pijanowski and Hiroko Sato Pijanowski demonstrates the *mokume-gane* technique, which imitates wood graining on non-ferrous metals. In this case, the metal is copper and alloys.

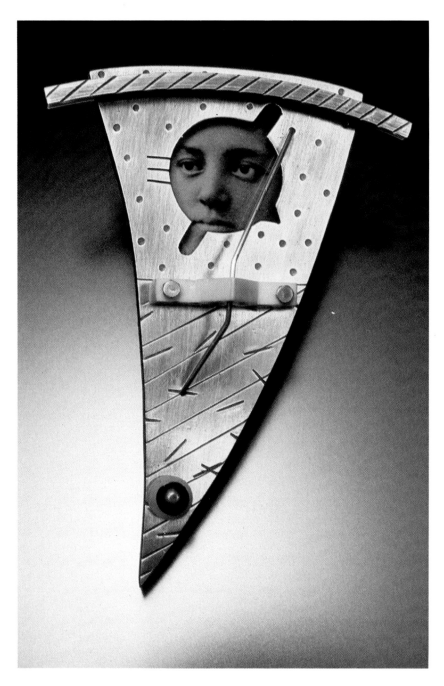

Thomas Mann's pin displays a contemporary sensibility of the concept of beauty. *Art Collage Brooch,* 1986. Brass, silver, Micarta and antique photo, 3 × 1¾ inches. (Photo by Ralph Gabriner, courtesy Elaine Potter Gallery, San Francisco.)

of World War II, which effectively put an end for almost a decade to the making and selling of contemporary jewelry. As these cataclysms approached, it is interesting to note that Margaret Craver, the American jeweler and teacher who would contribute significantly to the development of the contemporary American studio jewelry movement, was in Sweden studying metalsmithing. She returned to the United States in 1938 and became a teacher at the Wichita (Kan.) Art Museum.

After the war ended, a revival of interest in metal techniques occurred as part of an overall interest in crafts. One important vehicle for increasing knowledge of metalsmithing occurred in 1947, when the first of a series of five annual metalsmithing workshops helped start the contemporary process of development.

Sponsored by Handy & Harman, metal refiners and dealers in precious metals, the conferences were planned by Craver and held first at the Rhode Island School of Design and later at Rochester Institute of Technology's School for American Craftsmen.[5] Craver, who had previously developed a rehabilitation therapy program for wounded war veterans, using metalcraft techniques under the auspices of Handy & Harman,[6] had to recruit European metalsmiths to provide training that was unavailable here.

Each of the five month-long seminars trained about a dozen students, who were selected competitively. All were teachers with backgrounds in design. Of the 60 or so students are a number who have substantially contributed to the development of the studio metal movement. Among them Craver recalled recently were John Paul Miller and Fred Miller, Alma Eikerman, Robert Von Neumann, Ruth Pennington and Earl Pardon.

Stanley Lechtzin, *Torque #20F*, 1985. Electroformed silver gilt, quartz crystal, pearls, 8 × 9 × 1¾ inches.

During the 1960s, interest in puns and sexual innuendo reached its zenith, as this brooch by Robert Ebendorf indicates. *Man and His Pet Bee,* 1968. Copper, old photo tintype, silver and found parts, 5 × 3½ inches.

Also during the late 1940s and early 1950s, metal programs were organized at a number of schools. For example, Richard Thomas was put in charge of the metals program at Cranbrook Academy while John Prip established a department at the School for American Craftsmen.[7] Prip, who was trained in Scandinavia, in 1954 invited Hans Christensen of Denmark to teach at the school.

Thomas, Christensen, Prip and others who embraced the Scandinavian tradition had an enormous influence on contemporary American silversmithing. Like the Scandinavian woodworkers who came here at about the same time, these craftsmen valued self-discipline and a thorough knowledge of materials and techniques. American students benefited from the rigor that characterized Scandinavian and all European craft education.

The 1950s was a time for development of schools, dissemination of information about metal and exhibitions that brought the new, mostly Scandinavian-style, work to the attention of the art public. In 1952, for example, the Minnesota Museum of Art (then known as the St. Paul Gallery and School of Art) began a series of biennial craft competitions in metal, fiber and clay. Each one culminated in an exhibit which circulated to other cities and, in two instances, abroad. Other institutions showing an interest in goldsmithing and silversmithing included the Wichita Art Association and the Cleveland Museum of Art. By 1958, a sense of excitement had penetrated to the world of commerce and the Sterling Silversmiths Guild, representing American manufacturers of holloware and flatware, instituted a student competition known as "Statements in Sterling." This competition, which ran for many years, encouraged students

Arline Fisch has employed fiber techniques to expand the vocabulary of jewelry. *Collar* (back view, 1985. Machine-knit coated copper with fine silver accents, separate front pin/clasp, 6½ × 9½ inches in diameter. (Photo by William Gullette.)

Eleanor Moty, *Fan Brooch,* 1981. Photo-etched silver with abalone shell and silk thread, 4 × 3 × ½ inches.

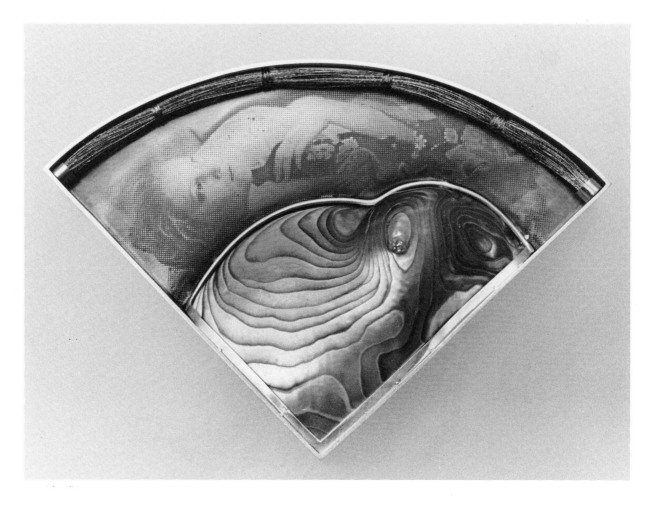

to explore the creative potential of silver and publicized contemporary forms.

A great expansion of technical knowledge and experimentation characterized the decades of the 1960s and 1970s, as metalsmiths tried their hand at jewelry, holloware, architectural metal and eating utensils. Individuals who carried one discipline forward, such as architectural metal, were often distinguished in another, such as jewelry. The elimination of boundaries between goldsmithing, vessel making and architectural metal that occurred in the 1960s and 1970s represented a challenge to convention and a desire to extend boundaries that was typical of the era, according to Stanley Lechtzin, who participated in the movement. Lechtzin and others experimented with coating objects with metal in a process known as electroforming. Heikki Seppä and others experimented with reticulation, a surface enrichment that creates a raised surface. Olaf Skoogfors and others employed casting, which widened the possible forms of a metal object. Other traditional techniques that were updated and presented at conferences and workshops included repoussé work and a variety of enameling techniques. In all cases, the artists did not

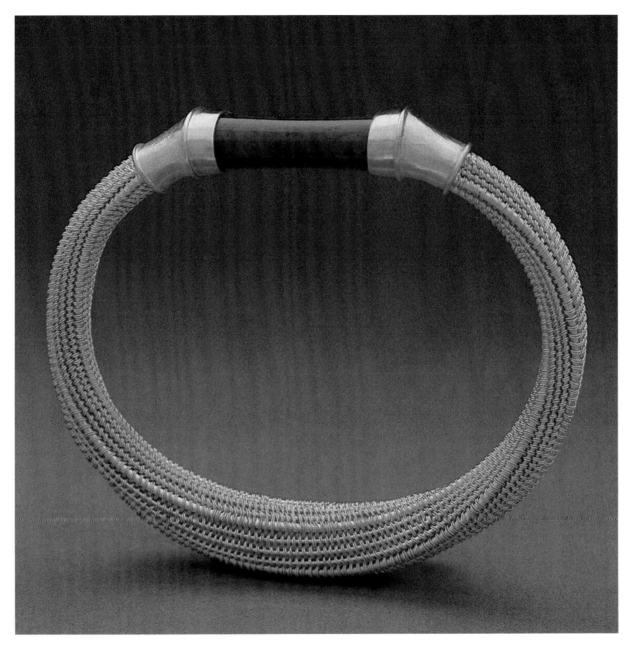

Mary Lee Hu, *Bracelet #37*, 1986. Lapis and 18- and 22-karat gold. (Photo by Richard Nicol.)

simply reinstate old techniques, but built on them. In the best tradition of the studio craft movement, the research was made public so that others could employ it and expand on it.

Examples abound of craft artists sharing their experiments. In 1964, Lechtzin addressed the first World Crafts Congress in New York and described electroforming, illustrating his talk with 30 objects fashioned by himself and other metalsmiths at a workshop he organized at Tyler Art

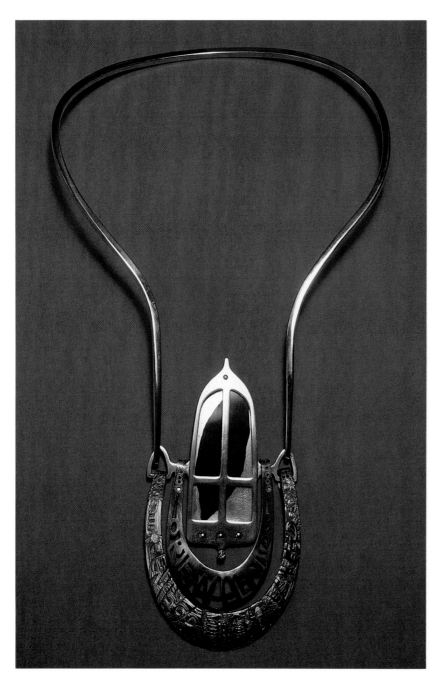

Mary Ann Scherr is among contemporary metalsmiths who often combine precious and nonprecious materials in jewelry. *Bay Leaf Necklace, 1983.* Gold, silver, diamond and acrylic-encased bay leaf. (Collection of Mr. and Mrs. Anthony Scoville.)

School in Philadelphia, where he was teaching.

Eugene Pijanowski and Hiroko Sato Pijanowski introduced to the United States the traditional Japanese nonferrous-metal technique known as *mokume gane*, which is translated as 'wood grain in metal,' as well as the Japanese method of inlaying metal into metal without heat or solder. They shared their knowledge of the techniques in writing and through workshops held all over the country.

Pijanowski, now associate dean of the art school at the University of Michigan, recalls that during the 1960s, 1970s and even early 1980s, recovery of forgotten techniques was an important part of the studio craft movement. Recently, Lechtzin said that "the importance of electroforming and other new ideas, such as the use of plastics in jewelry, is that they proved that current technical processes and new materials can be used in an expressive and personal manner to generate new forms."[8]

Technical innovations aside, the jewelry world was prey to fashion that laid emphasis on one type of work over another. J. Fred Woell, who is known for the political content of his work, recalled recently that it required considerable effort to remain outside the quiet, understated Scandinavian sensibility that prevailed in the 1960s. Woell was one of the first to use found objects in jewelry to make serious and humorous comments, working in a vein similar to the Funk movement in ceramics and Pop Art in painting. (Others were Barry Merritt and Robert Ebendorf.) Recalling a pivotal moment in his development,[9] Woell recounted the time ceramist Peter Voulkos and another, but unremembered, luminary came to Minnesota in the early 1960s to jury and ostensibly make awards for the best work. But they refused to award a jewelry prize.

"Instead, they made a piece they called 'First Prize' out of a sheriff's badge and a bone and awarded it to themselves. I thought this was wonderful and gave myself permission to finally just let go. I made a piece called 'Lincoln For President,' [probably in 1964] from a silver watch case, a picture of Lincoln I made out of junk and a metal campaign badge."

Woell had accumulated drawers full of oddments, and soon, despite his inability to find a gallery to carry this work, he started "making things out of hardcore junk. I made an effort not to put anything precious in them at all. These things came very fast and people seemed to like them. They started giving me old stuff to put in my jewelry. Instead of getting rid of junk, I was accumulating it."

He sent off some slides of the work to Paul Smith at the Museum of Contemporary Crafts and in 1967 it was shown by the museum. The following year, *Craft Horizons* wrote about it and, in 1969, the work was included in the Objects USA show.

Woell is one of a small number still working in this idiom. "I have strong feelings about how people treat each other and the environment. The throwaways call attention to the need not to throw away things. Sermonizing turns people off, so I use humor," he said.

As the 1960s progressed, more metalworking students graduated with fine arts degrees, expanding the field and looking for opportunities to show their work in galleries. The enlargement of the field made possible the formation of the Society of North American Goldsmiths in 1969. The organization, known as SNAG, has been important for the creative development of metal-

In June Schwarcz's enameled vessels, the convoluted forms seem to be roadmaps to the secret life of minerals, if only the viewer could penetrate their mysteries. The bowl (1984) is 10⅜ × 5½ × 5¼ inches. The vessel (1986) is 9 inches tall. (Photos by M. Lee Fatherree.)

Helen Shirk,
*Ring Around
the Rosy*, 1986.
Copper, brass,
patina, 17 × 5
inches. (Photo by
Alan Watson.)

working through its annual meetings and its publication, now called *Metalsmith*.

The program of SNAG's first meeting gives the tenor of the times. Papers given at that conference in St. Paul were: silversmithing by Hans Christensen; body jewelry by Arline Fisch; electroforming by Stanley Lechtzin; photo-fabrication by Eleanor Moty; jewelry mechanisms by Albert Paley; reticulation by Heikki Seppä; and casting by Olaf Skoogfors. Presentations such as these helped spread the word about techniques and most likely accelerated the use of new methods and materials. Also during the 1960s, the foundation for an invigorated architectural metals

discipline was laid. This development is discussed separately below.

While SNAG's founding demonstrated the growth of metalsmithing in this country, the internationalism of the studio jewelry movement was advanced by the opening of a new museum in Pforzheim, Germany, which has been a center of jewelry making since the middle ages. The *Schmuckmuseum*, which is entirely devoted to jewelry, has what is said to be the best and most extensive collection of antique and modern jewelry in the world. Its trend shows, publications and international competitions have helped keep communications open among art jewelers

As this vessel by Randy Long shows, free-form holloware displays great vitality. *Vessel For A Magician*, 1983. Sterling silver and nickel silver, 6 × 6½ × 6 inches. (Photo by artist.)

and enthusiasts.

Jewelry is portable, can be made inexpensively when precious materials are eliminated, and makes an immediate statement about the wearer. These characteristics help to explain why the hippie movement of the 1960s so greatly influenced the development of the field. The flower children who went traveling to the world's most remote outposts brought back with them and wore the ornaments they found on their voyages of discovery. The result was a flowering of interest in ethnic jewelry, which was imported to the United States in great quantity. Some of the hippies also began making and selling their own versions of ethnic jewelry and the designs expanded the horizons for both jewelers and collectors. Many of these ethnic originals and copies were exact opposites to the precious and carefully made jewelry that had dominated the contemporary art jewelry movement up to the 1960s. The ethnic work was primitive, rough-finished and enormously engaging. These qualities effectively demolished the idea that jewelry must be precious. They have entered the mainstream as one possible aesthetic a jeweler can adopt.

During the 1970s, experimentation continued unabated. Arline Fisch and Mary Lee Hu separately adapted textile weaving techniques to

William Baran-Mickle, *Canyon Song*, 1987. Bronze, sterling, copper, nickel silver and patinas, hollow-constructed. (Photo by Jamey Stillings, courtesy Elaine Potter Gallery, San Francisco.)

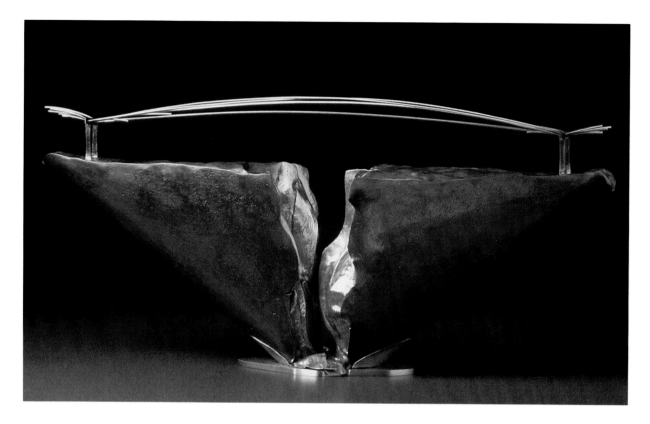

jewelry. In 1972, Mary Ann Scherr made a bracelet that monitored the heart rate of the wearer and registered significant changes in heart beat with an electronic alarm. Eleanor Moty continued her experiments with photofabrication. (The technique combines photoetching and electroforming.)

Exhibitions now occurred with more frequency. Among noteworthy ones were The Goldsmith, mounted by the Renwick Gallery and the Minnesota Museum of Art in 1974, and American Metalsmiths, held the same year at the DeCordova Museum in Lincoln, Mass. Forms in Metal: 275 Years of Metalsmithing in America was a joint exhibit of historic and contemporary work held by Finch College and the Museum of Contemporary Crafts. Silver in American Life at Yale

University in 1979 educated the public about the venerable history and interesting present of silver. When they can be found, the accompanying exhibition catalogues make interesting reading.

The 1980s have continued developments in jewelry manifested in the preceding decades, as artists search for new methods and materials with which to express themselves. Two exhibitions which show the state of the art include Good As Gold: Alternative Materials in American Jewelry at the Renwick Gallery in 1981 and Jewelry USA at the American Craft Museum in 1984.

The same loosening that marked jewelry has also occurred in holloware. Whereas in the 1960s, the Scandinavian traditions embodied in the pure silver work of individuals such as Christensen and Prip were ascendant, metalsmiths now frequently work in copper and copper alloys, steel, aluminum and pewter. In general, holloware today displays a playfulness, wit and inventiveness that is a departure from the past. Instead of dwelling within the orthodoxy of traditional techniques of vessel raising, some artists are casting, bending and developing other methods of making vessels.

A national exhibition of holloware by 38 metalsmiths at the State University of New York at Brockport in 1987 demonstrated some current concerns. Besides the shift away from silver to nonprecious materials, these pieces emphasize surface texture and rich patina, often revealing contrasting surface treatments. Some artists employ paint to deny the metallic surface; others work in mixed media, including wood, plastics, epoxy and various other materials.[10] Comparing the work in the exhibition with the first holloware exhibition in 1971, Thomas R. Markusen, curator of both shows, noted that the range of work is more diversified and functional objects less dominant, but technical excellence still prevails.

The vibrancy of past developments in the metal arts lends credence to the thought that new forms are on the horizon. Hazarding an opinion on the future, Stanley Lechtzin said that: "After an intense period of rapid development in the 1960s and 1970s, the 1980s have been a time of consolidation." He believes the future can hold an opportunity for artists to make a new synthesis with science. "I think that it is impossible for any discipline today to ignore the impact of the computer. It is a tool without limits and the artist who learns to use it with facility and advantage will make a contribution."

Claire Sanford, *Fin*, 1986. Copper, cupric nitrate, patina, 21 × 6 × 6 inches.

The abstract design in Carrie Adell's three-way necklace was taken from a printed computer-generated image. *Solar Wind,* 1983. Sterling silver, copper, 23-karat gold, chased and repousséd, 8½ × 8 × 4½ inches. (Photo by Sharon Deveaux, courtesy Elaine Potter Gallery, San Francisco.)

## ARCHITECTURAL METAL

Weathervanes, window grilles, fireplace implements, garden gates and fences, door handles and other architectural embellishments of metal are of ancient origin and obvious current utility. However, despite the great success enjoyed by Samuel Yellin, a blacksmith who in the early 1900s had as many as 300 workers producing architectural metal at his Philadelphia forge, by 1964 the number of forges in the United States had dwindled to almost nil. This did not deter L. Brent Kington, who decided that year to become a blacksmith.

Kington (who had been Lechtzin's fellow student at Cranbrook Academy in Richard Thomas's metals program) was in New York to attend the 1964 World Crafts Congress. While in the city, he visited the Metropolitan Museum of Art, where he was so intrigued with the museum's armor collection that he decided to look into blacksmithing when he returned to his teaching position at Southern Illinois University at Carbondale.[11]

By 1970, Kington had organized the first contemporary blacksmithing conference and workshop at SIU. He invited Alex Bealer, author of a practical how-to book, *The Art of Blacksmithing*, to demonstrate and instruct a group of metalsmiths who included Lechtzin, Ronald Pearson, Fred Fenster, J. Fred Woell, Richard Mawdsley and Robert Ebendorf.

This conference proved to be the spark that led to a blacksmithing renaissance in the United States. By March of 1973, the Artist Blacksmiths' Association of North America was established with Alex Bealer as president and 27 members. A publication, *The Anvil's Ring*, was soon initiated.

Then in 1976, another means of education

L. Brent Kington, *Gaberal*, weather vane, 1970. Mild steel, 84 × 48 × 6 inches.

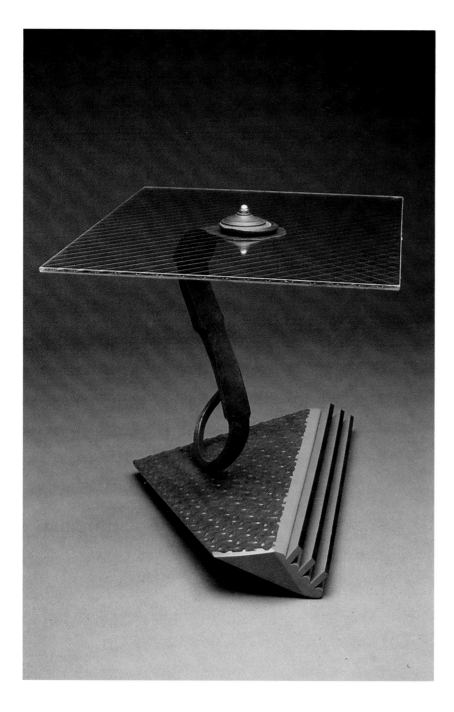

Dennis Luedeman, *End Table,* 1987. Steel, glass, paint, 18 × 24 × 36 inches. (Photo courtesy National Ornamental Metal Museum, Memphis, Tenn.)

and promotion was developed with the incorporation of the National Ornamental Metal Museum. The museum, located on several acres overlooking the Mississippi River in Memphis, Tenn., opened its doors to the public in 1978. Since then, founding director James Wallace and others have worked to build a public for fine decorative and architectural metalwork. The museum sponsors a variety of exhibitions and other events and is located in an area with a strong history of ornamental iron. Memphis used to be a manufacturing center for large-scale architectural iron which was shipped to all parts of the country.

An event of interest is the museum's annual weekend repair day held in October. It provides an opportunity for collectors to meet as many as 30 metalsmiths at a time. They are there to fix free of charge the bent and broken metal objects the public is invited to bring.

The museum also houses a library on the history and development of forged metals and operates a referral service for collectors and others with a specific project in mind. A working forge and metalworking studio, the scene of workshops and classes, are open to the public.

Recently, the scope of architectural metal has expanded to include (besides cast and forged iron), cast and fabricated bronze, stainless steel, aluminum and other metals. Regional styles have begun to appear, which Wallace characterizes as traditional in the northeast, gothic in the southwest and relating to the Arts and Crafts movement in the northwest. Many different design themes are being pursued. Work encompasses everything from the historical to contemporary forms and, according to Wallace, new assembly techniques and electric welding are making this costly and labor- and time-intensive craft more accessible.

Jonathan Bonner, *Weathervane #115*, 1987. Copper, granite base, 51 × 106 × 6 inches. (Photo by Andrew Dean Powell.)

Albert Paley, *Window Grille,* 1985-86. Forged and fabricated mild steel and brass, approximately 48 × 72 inches. (Photo by Bruce Miller, courtesy Fendrick Gallery, Washington, D.C., private collection.)

## NOTES

1. Barbara Cartlidge, *Twentieth-Century Jewelry* (New York: Harry N. Abrams, Inc., 1985) p. 12.

2. See *The Art that is Life: The Arts & Crafts Movement in America, 1875-1920* (Boston: Museum of Fine Arts, 1987) pp. 264-285 for information on metalworkers and jewelers of the Arts and Crafts movement.

3. Cartlidge, op cit, p. 11. See also Gabriel R. Weisberg, *Art Nouveau Bing: Paris Style 1900* (New York: Harry N. Abrams, Inc., 1986). Note 1, p. 268, explains how Siegfried Bing came to be known erroneously as Samuel.

4. Ibid., p. 42.

5. Interview with Margaret Craver.

6. Ibid, p. 75.

7. Robert Cardinale, "A Decade of Metalsmithing in the United States: 1970-1980," *Metalsmith,* Fall 1980, pp. 22-33.

8. Interview with author.

9. Interview with author.

10. *Holloware '87* (Brockport, N.Y.: Tower Fine Arts Gallery, SUNY College at Brockport, 1987) unpaged.

11. Robert Cardinale, op cit, pp. 26-27.

# RESOURCES FOR JEWELRY AND METALWORK COLLECTORS

## BOOKS

Barbara Cartlidge, *Twentieth-Century Jewelry* (New York: Harry N. Abrams, Inc., 1985).

Peter Dormer and Ralph Turner, *The New Jewelry Trends + Traditions* (New York: Thames & Hudson, 1985).

Dona Z. Meilach, *Decorative and Sculptural Ironwork: Tools, Techniques and Inspiration* (New York: Crown Publishers, 1977).

Philip Morton, *Contemporary Jewelry* (New York: Holt Rinehart & Winston, rev. ed. 1976).

Joanne Polster, *Bibliography: Metal* (New York: American Craft Council, 1978).

————, *Bibliography: Enamel* (New York: American Craft Council, 1978).

Oppi Untrecht, *Jewelry Concepts and Technology* (Garden City, N.Y.: Doubleday & Co., Inc. 1982).

## CATALOGUES

*Holloware '87* (Brockport, N.Y.: Tower Fine Arts Gallery, SUNY College at Brockport, 1987).

*Jewelry USA* (New York: American Craft Museum, 1984).

*Electronic Jewelry* (San Bernardino, Calif.: California State College Art Gallery, 1983).

*Good as Gold: Alternative Materials in American Jewelry* (Washington, D.C.: Smithsonian Institution, 1981).

*Copper Two* (Tucson: University of Arizona, 1979).

*Silver in American Life* (New York: American Federation of Arts, 1979).

*Iron Solid/Wrought USA* (Carbondale, Ill.: Southern Illinois University, 1976).

*Forms in Metal: 275 Years of Metalsmithing in America* (New York: Museum of Contemporary Crafts and Finch College, 1975).

*The Goldsmith* (St. Paul, Minn. and Washington, D.C.: Minnesota Museum of Art and Renwick Gallery, 1974).

*The Art of Enamels* (New Paltz, N.Y.: SUNY New Paltz Art Gallery, 1973).

*Goldsmith '70* (St. Paul, Minn.: Minnesota Museum of Art, 1970). First exhibition sponsored by SNAG.

*Made of Iron* (Houston, Tex.; University of St. Thomas, 1966).

## PERIODICALS

**Metalsmith** (quarterly) (see Society of North American Goldsmiths)

**Ornament Magazine** (quarterly) 1221 S. LaCienaga Los Angeles, CA 90035

**The Anvil's Ring** (quarterly) (see Artist Blacksmiths' Association of North America)

## ORGANIZATIONS

**Artist Blacksmiths' Association of North America** Box 303 Cedarburg, WI 53012

**National Ornamental Metal Museum** 374 W. California Memphis, TN 38106 James Wallace, Director

Has "Friends" group including collectors.

**Society of North American Goldsmiths (SNAG)** 6707 N. Santa Monica Blvd. Milwaukee, WI 53217

Founded in 1970 for metalsmiths, collectors and others interested in metal arts. Holds annual meeting and convention, publishes bimonthly newsletter in addition to *Metalsmith*. Sponsors exhibitions especially in conjunction with annual meetings.

**Samuel Yellin Metalworkers Museum** 5510 Arch St. Philadelphia, PA 10139 215-472-3122

Open by appointment only; contains examples of work of early 20th-century metalsmiths.

James Krenov, pearwood cabinet, 1986. (Photo by Jon Reed, courtesy Pritam & Eames Gallery, Easthampton, N.Y.)

# ART FURNITURE AND OTHER FORMS IN WOOD

Craft art in wood includes furniture and furniture-like forms, wood turnings and sculptural works. Most craft artists working in wood make furniture or objects that come out of a furniture tradition. Today's art furniture landscape is a forest of conflicting aesthetic and philosophical attitudes. At one end of the spectrum are individuals who revere wood and whose work displays virtuosity in handling it. At the other end are those who conform to no construction or material constraints. The majority subscribe to some rules about craftsmanship but their interests lead them to emphasize one or the other of these two divergent attitudes.

Beginning in the early 1950s, the first contemporary school of thought adopted a traditional truth-to-materials aesthetic. It had strong ties to the Scandinavian tradition of unornamented surfaces, fine joinery and craftsmanship, and naturally finished wood. Tage Frid and James Krenov are examples of makers who work in this style.

Another branch of this group stresses organic forms and reveres wood for its philosophical associations. You can recognize this aesthetic when some or all of the following are present in a piece: surfaces that include the tree's bark; rounded shapes that appear to take direction from nature; furniture worked with great attention to

Judy Kensley McKie, *Coyote Chest*, 1986. Limewood, carved and painted, 14 × 28 × 16 inches. (Photo by David Caras, courtesy Pritam & Eames Gallery, Easthampton, N.Y.)

the wood grain; and natural finishes. Workers in this school also owe a debt to Japanese craft attitudes. The furniture of George Nakashima is a good illustration of these characteristics and reading his autobiographical book, *The Soul of a Tree*, is an excellent introduction to this school of thought. Besides Nakashima, other practitioners include the late Wharton Esherick, Sam Maloof, Arthur Espenet Carpenter and Jere Osgood.

Many of the younger furniture makers, most of whom have been trained by members of the first two groups, have a complex attitude toward their craft. Though they may pay homage to the past in carefully constructed pieces that conform

Mitch Ryerson, *Comb Mirror*, 1987. Maple, oil paint, 30 × 16 × 5 inches. (Photo by Andrew Dean Powell.)

to tradition and employ historical techniques, they produce work that could not have been made in the past because it combines attributes of more than one era in a single piece.

A branch that has christened its approach "high style" works with the most expensive materials and delights in executing beautiful, tasteful, classical furniture inspired by traditional forms and the great names of the past, such as Thomas Chippendale and Jacques-Emile Ruhlmann. A few examples of individuals include Richard Newman, Tim Philbrick, John Dunnigan, Wendy Stayman and Kristina Madsen. Wendell Castle, who has since moved on to other issues, has worked spectacularly in this idiom.

Other furniture makers, such as Mitch Ryerson and Tommy Simpson, also use traditional techniques and images to reflect on the past, but combine disparate elements that would not in common sense ever be used together in furniture. Their work may comment ironically or humorously on their relationship to furniture making or on our society and its past and present and how (or if) they fit together. Simpson's 19th-century toy wagon is a useful coffee table, but also is a joke. A wagon in a middle-class, late 20th-century household is as much a toy as it would have been to a 19th-century child. In both instances, the reality of hard physical labor symbolized by the wagon is remote. Rosanne Somerson also uses a variety of designs from different periods in one piece. "When I saw some of the same decorative patterns occur in Japanese, Egyptian, African and Art Deco furniture, I got excited." She communicates this information in furniture that combines some of these disparate elements and says she finds it rewarding when viewers notice these details and respond to them.

Another large group of makers uses furniture as

John Dunnigan, three floor lamps, 1986. Cherry and ebonized cherry, faux pear, hand-blown glass shades, 71 inches high. (Photo by Roger Birn, courtesy Pritam & Eames Gallery, Easthampton, N.Y.)

Tommy Simpson, toy wagon coffee table, 1986. Mixed woods and wrought iron, approximately 40 × 22 × 18 inches. (Photo by William Bennett Seitz.)

metaphor. If a member of this anything-for-art school could address the public directly, he or she might say: "I will employ any material, any technique or historical reference to get my point across. Nothing is out of bounds, and I will push furniture to the limits to see how far I can go and still call it furniture." Some practitioners are Wendell Castle, Garry Knox Bennett, Wendy Maruyama and Tom Loeser. Illustrating the impossibility of placing each individual in a particular school, some art furniture makers go to great lengths to create pieces of superb technical quality while others devote minimal attention to this aspect of their work.

While it is always thrilling to experiment with

new forms, newness creates a problem for those who try to comprehend and describe it. This is made more difficult because within the art furniture world there is no well-established national organization with its own publication to discuss the aesthetic issues germane to furniture. The bimonthly *Fine Woodworking* does cover this subject from time to time and a professional group, the Society of Furniture Artists, was recently organized.

Guidelines for evaluating art furniture can profitably begin with how well it functions, since this is a prerequisite for use. With this criterion satisfied, one can consider whether the furniture is successful as sculpture or as a conceptual object.

Rosanne Somerson, *Upholstered Bench*, 1986. Pearwood, bleached curly maple, leather, 23 × 22½ × 58 inches. (Photo by Andrew Dean Powell, collection of Museum of Fine Arts, Boston.)

This kind of evaluation hinges on issues such as form, proportion, composition, materials use and scale. Tactility, which in furniture relates both to aesthetics and craftsmanship, may also be important. A surface cannot be smooth if it hasn't been properly finished. If it is not smooth, is that because of poor workmanship or because the maker consciously chose to leave it rough?

Stephen Whittlesey, whose pieces are often made of recycled wood on which the existing (usually faded) surface is retained, raises an interesting quality issue. He does on purpose just the kind of thing that in second-hand furniture stores would be considered a serious defect, and sold "as-is" to be repainted. He says that "To me

quality is putting in your best in the direction in which you are going. Some people equate it with classical methods but to me the highest quality for my work is the most interesting woods, as much freedom as possible, as much function as possible, as touchable as possible." Sometimes people emphasize pure form and surround themselves with things that can't be touched, he said, citing for example house furniture that is so valuable it becomes unusable.

To develop connoisseurship requires thinking about these issues but it takes looking more than anything else. For maximum growth, don't simply turn away from work you do not like or understand. Instead, analyze what it is that dis-

Garry Knox Bennett, *Aluminum Bench*, 1986. Aluminum, wood, paint. (Photo by Schopplein Studio.)

turbs you. What, for example, can one make of the illustrated chairs by Jay Stanger? Stanger pushes all the limits and the color and shape of these chairs (part of a group of six commissioned by collectors Anne and Ronald Abramson) stand in opposition to many conventions. They use a highly unorthodox and idiosyncratic mix of materials. One might react by finding them delightful, vulgar, frightening, humorous or mysterious, to name a few possible responses. Regardless of the reaction, the chairs can expand a viewer's understanding and response to form, and stretch his or her ability to see.

Several artists point out that a difficulty in experimental and new work is that the pieces could function poorly or break down; often later versions are technically better than the earlier pieces. While many makers see an obligation to correct earlier pieces, this is by no means true of all. "If I were a collector, there are some popular pieces that I wouldn't trust to last under daily use, although of course the maker may not have intended such use," said Somerson.

Of the issues of technical quality in furniture, connections (joinery) are undoubtedly the most important, as they are under the greatest stress

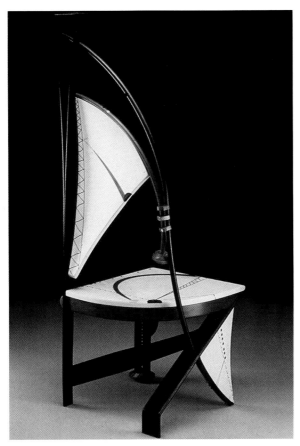
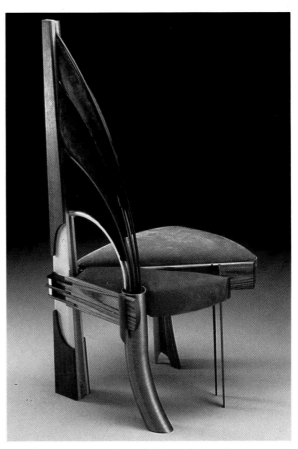

Jay Stanger's dining chairs (1983) are part of a set of six. *Casual Communications* (left), curly maple, epoxy paint, anodized aluminum, purpleheart wood, approximately 55 inches tall. *Monolith With Dancers,* mixed woods, anodized aluminum, pigskin, approximately 55 inches tall. (Photos by Andrew Dean Powell, courtesy The Gallery at Workbench, New York, collection of Anne and Ronald Abramson.)

regardless of whether hardware, traditional joints or dowels have been used. With education, you come to know what to look for in terms of appropriate construction and strength. A few other details, not so important as joinery, may indicate a positive attitude toward quality on the part of the maker. For example, if a leg is not flat against the floor but has been relieved by a small chamfer, its form will not become distorted, scratched or chipped as the piece wears.

If a piece includes drawers, they ought to open smoothly with one hand. On expensive pieces, the bottom face of the drawer should be as nicely finished as the visible top. A plywood drawer is a good sign since plywood is stable and won't expand or contract; the plywood should be veneered on the showing surfaces. Another good solution is "floating" a solid wood drawer bottom so that it can move slightly from side to side as it expands and contracts with seasonal changes in moisture content. Under no circumstances should a drawer bottom be glued tightly

Lee A. Schuette and Linda Schiwall-Gallo, *Beach Ball Table*, 1986. Painted aluminum, cast bronze, wood and glass, 18 × 51½ × 30½ inches. (Photo by Malcolm Varon, courtesy Alexander F. Milliken, Inc., New York.)

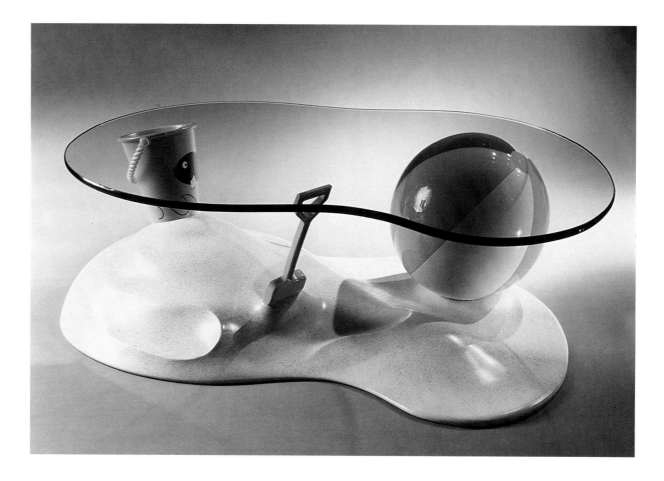

into the sides because it could crack as it loses and gains moisture.

Since furniture can break or wear under use, an important practical consideration is whether a piece can be repaired and refurbished. "When I first began making painted pieces, I custom-mixed paint and didn't save any samples," said Somerson. "Now I save some paint." But if the paint or other finish simply wears (as opposed to becoming chipped) a collector might find the resulting patina beautiful. Reasonable questions to ask before purchase concern the durability and repairability of the finish and how it should be cleaned. If the piece includes upholstery, can the fabric be easily removed and replaced? If there is a fragile part, such as a glass or marble insert, is it replaceable? "If the maker has made it possible to remove parts that might break or need cleaning or to repair the piece, that suggests that the maker is concerned with longevity. I feel that whatever your medium, you should be making things to last as long as you are capable of and as long as is appropriate to the idea," said Somerson.

A collector also needs to find out what kind of restrictions there are in using the piece. If it is a table, can you put a hot plate on its top? Can the top be refinished? Is the table's shape so odd that finding a tablecloth will be impossible?

A special issue for furniture is the way the body interacts with a piece. The importance of comfort depends on whether a piece has been purchased primarily for use. Because some furniture makers think of their work as art that happens to be in the form of furniture, they aren't concerned with chair comfort or table height or how the two relate in a dining-room set.

Somerson sees comfort as a two-part issue. There is the question of whether the furniture is physically accommodating and there is what might be called aesthetic comfort. Makers of contemporary art furniture see objects as a chance to be expressive. A collector may have to give up some physical comfort in order to enjoy living with some art furniture. (Of course, this is true with some of the classics of manufactured modern furniture design, too.) "I am drawn to things that look great even if they are uncomfortable. If I am making dining chairs, I will design a chair that is ergonomically comfortable because it is part of the problem. But if I am designing chairs to be placed along a wall as a sculptural form, I may take more liberties. I won't be as concerned with getting all the angles perfect."

She also points out that an item of furniture is functional in some situations, but not in others. A chair seat that is 13 inches off the ground is not comfortable in the living room, but in a bedroom as a place to sit on briefly to tie your shoes, it might be. As an example, she refers to Alphonse Mattia's valet chairs, which "are designed for dressing and are comfortable if you put them to the use for which they are intended."

Somerson summarizes, "Furniture makers

Stephen Whittlesey, *Pine Cupboard*, 1985. Salvaged wood, 73 × 36 × 14 inches. (Photo courtesy The Gallery at Workbench, New York.)

Tom Loeser, three blanket chests, 1987. Mixed hardwoods, milk paint, patinated copper, glass, 37 × 35 × 14 tallest. (Photo by Andrew Dean Powell.)

today put so much time and effort and care into these pieces, they are eager, even happy, to talk about them. I think collectors should ask questions in order to better understand if a piece is intended to last or only to look good in 1987."

## THE COLLECTOR'S POINT OF VIEW

Warren Rubin, president of The Workbench, a commercial furniture chain, and founder of The Gallery at Workbench, where art furniture is sold, has been buying furniture for his stores for more than 30 years. He says that "a craftsman working alone can produce better furniture than the most modern shop with the best equipment."

The pieces Rubin and his wife, Bernice Wollman, collect for their own home are held to the same standards they would require in the best commercial furniture. "When I look at a piece of furniture, I consider the design and construction. If it isn't well crafted, we don't want it."

To Wollman "A knowledgeable collector in this medium by definition understands the technical aspect. Part of the appeal and the specialness of the piece is the way it has been made. The obligation of the enthusiast is to be knowledgeable about the craft. That is true of whatever medium a collector may select. If you didn't care about the finish and the joinery and the selection of wood and loving details of construction, why are you doing it?"

## CONTEMPORARY DEVELOPMENTS IN WOOD

The first two decades of the postwar rebirth of studio woodworking were primarily devoted to achieving technical mastery over the materials. Today, with an impressive growth of training institutions, the superstructure has been put in place to support new departures in woodworking. Whereas in the 1940s only the School for American Craftsmen offered special training in wood, by the early 1980s, 150 institutions were providing courses in furniture making at the college level and 11 schools granted degrees.[1]

In addition to this organized learning, resources for self-taught woodworkers have also increased substantially. Besides a large number of books, magazines and even videotapes, adult

Rosanne Somerson, *Earring Cabinet,* 1986. Glazed and painted hardwood, padouk, handmade paper, 27 × 22 × 7 inches. (Photo by Andrew Dean Powell, collection of Anne and Ronald Abramson.)

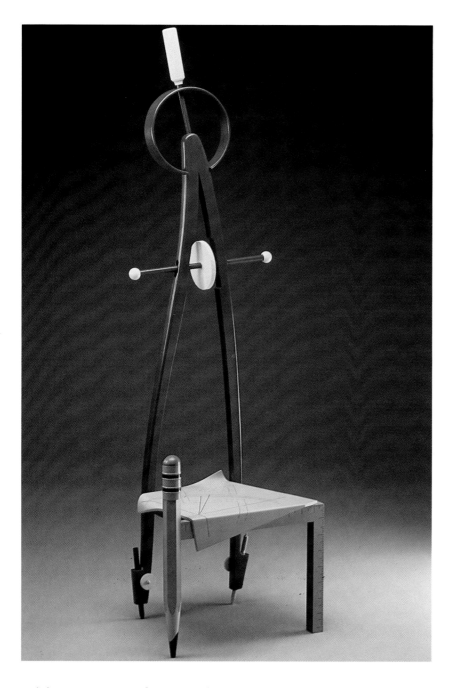

Alphonse Mattia, *Architect's Valet*, 1985. Painted wood, 76 × 22 × 18 inches. (Photo by Andrew Dean Powell, collection of Anne and Ronald Abramson.)

education courses are widespread. Tools for woodworkers are sold through the mail and hobby shops; home centers offer instruction through workshops. Though amateur efforts, no matter how skilled, cannot be compared to the breadth of training, experience and commitment of professionals, the amateurs are part of the public for art furniture and possibly for the growing number of galleries showing it.

Resources for collectors include Pritam & Eames in Easthampton, N.Y., the Gallery at Workbench in New York City, and the Snyderman Gallery in Philadelphia. Other New York galleries that show art furniture include the Alexander F. Milliken Gallery (Wendell Castle and the Wendell Castle School), Gallery Henoch, Max Protech Gallery, Holly Solomon Gallery, Inc., White Columns and Gracie Mansion Gallery. Each year, the Leeds Design Workshop, in Northampton, Mass., holds an annual show. The Western States Invitational Wood Show is held annually at Gallery Fair in Mendocino, Calif. Recently the show featured 90 woodworkers from the Pacific and mountain states. The Northwest Gallery of Fine Woodworking in Seattle, in existence since 1979, is a cooperative of 30 Puget Sound area woodworkers.

While the attitudes of professionals today go beyond it, the historical Arts and Crafts movement has been particularly important within this medium. At the turn of the century, Gustav Stickley, whose furniture is highly collectible today, and others achieved considerable artistic success and in a sense developed the workshops and clientele that have provided a model for today's woodworkers.

Frank Lloyd Wright and other architects advanced the concept of furniture as an integral feature of domestic architecture. This conception,

Judy Kensley McKie, *Grinning Beast Table* (detail), 1986. Carved maple, bleached, 30 × 60 × 60 inches. (Photo by David Caras, courtesy Pritam & Eames Gallery, Easthampton, N.Y.)

which led to built-in furniture, stands apart from today's emphasis on the individual unique piece. (It is ironic that Wright's furniture designs, which were carefully integrated with their surroundings, are now being removed from their places of origin to be sold.)

In the United States during the early and middle part of the 20th century, Wharton Esherick, a sculptor who eventually concentrated on making furniture, was a model for postwar furniture makers. Esherick, who was born in 1887, studied at the Pennsylvania Academy of Fine

Arts. He began working in wood in the 1920s and died in 1970 after a highly productive career. His methods of working and his concerns provide an early example of the attitudes of studio woodworkers.

Esherick enjoyed the play between his idea of an object and the natural variations he found in the wood used to make it. "A crack might be sanded to emphasize its shape, a knot might be left higher than the surrounding surface to become a point of tactile interest, the very conception of his design could be directed by the flow

Jere Osgood, *Ash desk,* 1987, 72 × 26 × 32 inches. (Photo by Andrew Dean Powell, courtesy Pritam & Eames Gallery, Easthampton, N.Y.)

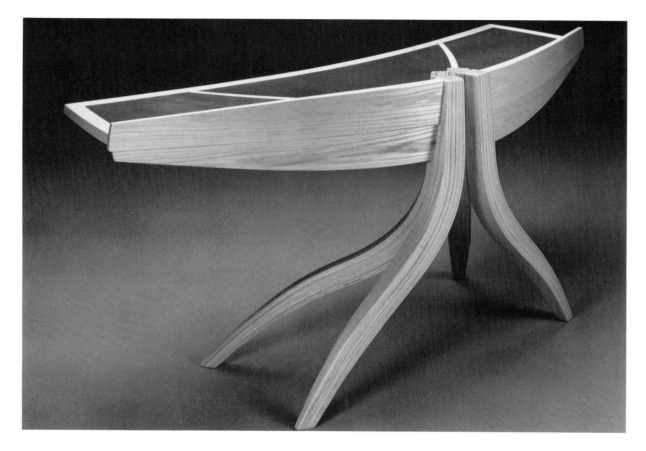

of grain in a piece of wood."[2]

So great was the demand for his work that eventually he established a workshop, employing a number of helpers to whom he left much of the joinery and finishing. He reserved to himself the original design of furniture and interiors. Esherick's work and ideas can be seen today by visiting the house and studio he built for himself in Paoli, Pa., a suburb of Philadelphia. The Wharton Esherick Foundation administers the small museum, which is open by appointment.

Beginning just after World War II, George Nakashima in Pennsylvania and Sam Maloof in California established independent furniture workshops where, working either alone or with helpers, they have continued the traditions that

Esherick began. More recently, Wendell Castle has set up a workshop and school near Rochester, N.Y.

Another important group within this field have been its teachers. Tage Frid, James Krenov, Jere Osgood and Alphonse Mattia, to name a few of the important teachers, have influenced scores of other woodworkers. Krenov's four books, especially *A Cabinetmaker's Notebook,* published in 1976, have exposed many to his precepts about the importance of careful detailing and fine workmanship.

Danish-born and trained Frid recently retired as professor emeritus at the Rhode Island School of Design after a career spanning more than 40 years of teaching in this country. His insistence

Hap Sakwa, *Against That Which All Else Is Measured*, 1985. Turned and constructed poplar, maple, acrylic lacquer, violin neck, 18 × 16 × 14 inches. (Photo by Ralph Gabriner.)

David Ellsworth, *Inversion Bowl,* 1986. Redwood lace burl, 18 × 18 inches in diameter. (Photo by artist, collection of Sam Rosenfeld.)

that basic skills be perfected, as director of the wood program at the School for American Craftsmen and later at RISD, has influenced many of today's best-known woodworkers.

The role of Osgood and Mattia in shaping the wood program at Boston University's Program in Artisanry (now at the Swain School of Design in New Bedford, Mass.) has been pivotal in the careers of furniture makers such as Wendy Maruyama, Tom Hucker, Tom Loeser, Tim Philbrick, Mitch Ryerson, James Schriber, Jay Stanger and others.

## WOOD TURNING

Wood turning has had a largely utilitarian past, which in this country reached its zenith in the 19th-century turnings of the Shakers. Their mastery was directed toward a wide range of practical objects, such as tiny bobbins, pegs and furniture.[3] Turnings were the distinctive decorative elements in gingerbread architecture in the latter part of the 19th and early 20th centuries.

By the late 1930s, James Prestini was turning thin-walled but practical wooden bowls. His work was shown in 1949 at the Museum of Mod-

Melvin Lindquist, *Red Maple Burl Vase*, 1982, 11 × 11½ inches in diameter. (Photo by Paul Avis.)

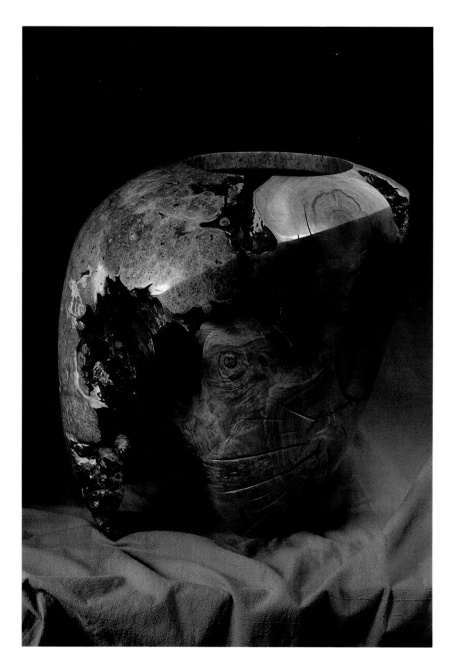

Stoney Lamar, *Winged Vessel,* 1987. Red maple burl, 16 × 12 × 14 inches. (Photo by Richard Brown.)

ern Art. But despite this early recognition for the man who has been called the father of contemporary wood turning, little additional acknowledgment occurred until the late 1970s. Others who began working with the craft as early as the 1940s include Bob Stocksdale, Melvin Lindquist, Rude Osolnik and Ed Moulthrop.

At first, platters, salt and pepper shakers and other examples of functional wares were found at craft fairs. "But up to the late 1960s, you could hardly give wood turnings away," recalled Mark Lindquist, who was an early exhibitor at fairs. Nevertheless, the early innovators were increasing their technical facility and developing new attitudes and methods that would lead to growth of interest in the field during the next decade.

As interest focused on communicating the beauty they saw in the material, turners began developing techniques to work half-rotted wood (the correct term is spalted wood) and wood burls. These formerly discarded waste products were changed into carefully worked vessels that are a distinct departure from the utilitarian. Other recently developed techniques permit the production of vessels of enormous size with thin walls and beautifully finished surfaces, while innovations in lathe design make it possible to add rough, textured surfaces to the wood turner's vocabulary.

Several events occurred in the 1970s that resulted in growth of the field. In 1976, Albert and Alan LeCoff in Philadelphia initiated a series of ten wood turning workshops, which were given from time to time between 1976 and 1982 at the George School outside Philadelphia. The craft of wood turning was made known to an even larger audience in three books written by Dale Nish in

Mark Lindquist, *Silent Witness*, 1983. Walnut, pecan, elm, 96 inches high. (Photo by Paul Avis, collection of Margaret A. Pennington.)

the same period. The books, *Creative Wood Turning, Artistic Wood Turning* and *Master Wood Turning,* were published by Brigham Young University Press.

Beginning in 1977 at the Renwick Gallery, a series of exhibitions exposed the work of such adepts as Bob Stocksdale, Ed Moulthrop, Melvin Lindquist and Mark Lindquist. Other shows include one organized by Albert LeCoff in Philadelphia in 1981 at The Works, which later toured five museums around the country. In 1983, Paul Smith curated an exhibition at the American Craft Museum of both historic and contemporary turnings.

A milestone in October 1985 was a conference and exhibition at Arrowmont, "Wood Turning: Vision and Concept." At that conference, the American Association of Woodturners was organized. The group now has 2,000 members and a quarterly journal, according to David Ellsworth, president.

Edward Jacobsen of Phoenix, Ariz., an early collector, has written a book (see p. 77) documenting the growth of the field. It is a companion to an exhibition of his collection shown at Arizona State University Museum in Tempe in 1985 and at the Renwick Gallery in 1986. In September of 1988, a survey of current work will be on view in an international exhibition which will open at the Port of History Museum in Philadelphia in connection with the annual symposium of the American Association of Woodturners.

---

## NOTES

1. "Woodworking Education," *Fine Woodworking* #26, 1981, p. 92.

2. *Woodenworks,* exhibition catalogue (Washington, D.C.: Renwick Gallery, 1972) p. 24.

3. *The Art of Woodturning* (New York: American Craft Council 1983) p. 10

## RESOURCES FOR COLLECTORS

### BOOKS

Sharon Darling, *Chicago Furniture Art Craft and Industry: 1833-1983* (Chicago: Chicago Historical Society, 1984).

*Design Book Three* (Newtown, Conn.: The Taunton Press, 1983). Primarily a picture book of black and white photos of contemporary work organized geographically.

Denise Domergue, *Artists Design Furniture* (New York: Harry N. Abrams, 1984).

Jonathan L. Fairbanks and Elizabeth Bidwell Bates, *American Furniture, 1620 to the Present* (New York: Richard Marek Publishers, 1981).

Tage Frid, *Tage Frid Teaches Woodworking: Furnituremaking* (Newtown, Conn.: The Taunton Press, 1985). Frid has also written extensively on his methods of working in books of interest mainly to hobbyists.

David A. Hanks, *Innovative Furniture in America from 1880 to the Present* (New York: Horizon Press, 1981).

Helena Hayward, ed., *World Furniture: An Illustrated History* (London and New York: Hamlyn Publishing Group Ltd., 1965).

R. Bruce Hoadley, *Understanding Wood, A Craftsman's Guide to Wood Technology* (Newtown, Conn.: The Taunton Press, 1980). For those wishing to expand their knowledge of wood construction.

James Krenov, *A Cabinetmaker's Notebook* (New York: Van Nostrand Reinhold, 1976).

———. *James Krenov: Worker in Wood,* 1981.

Both books describe Krenov's life and philosophy and picture his work. He has also written books of interest to hobbyists.

Mark Lindquist, *Sculpting Wood Contemporary Tools & Techniques* (Worcester, Mass.: Davis Publications, 1986). Technical information on wood turning; profusely illustrated.

Sam Maloof, *Sam Maloof Woodworker* (New York: Kodansha International, 1983).

Dona Z. Meilach, *Woodworking: The New Wave* (New York: Crown Publishers, 1981). Though dated, the section on how woodworkers organize their studio life is interesting.

George Nakashima, *The Soul of a Tree* (New York: Kodansha International, 1981).

Nicholas Roukes, *Masters of Wood Sculpture* (New York: Watson-Guptill Publications, 1980).

Michael Stone, *Contemporary American Woodworkers* (Layton, Utah: Gibbs M. Smith, Inc., 1986).

## CATALOGUES

*Material Evidence: New Color Techniques in Handmade Furniture* (Washington, D.C.: Smithsonian Institution Traveling Exhibition Services, 1985).

*The Art of Wood Turning* (New York: American Craft Council, 1983).

*The Fine Art of the Furniture Maker: Conversations with Wendell Castle, Artist, and Penelope Hunter-Stiebel, Curator, About Selected Works from the Metropolitan Museum of Art* (Rochester, N.Y.: Memorial Art Gallery, University of Rochester, 1981).

*Woodenworks* (Washington D.C. and Minneapolis, Minn.: Renwick Gallery and Minnesota Museum of Art, 1972).

## PERIODICALS

### Fine Woodworking
(bimonthly)
Newtown, CT 06470

Though geared to hobbyists and professional woodworkers, there are also articles on wooden art objects and exhibitions.

## ORGANIZATIONS

### American Association of Woodturners
Box 982
San Marcos, TX 78667
512-396-8689

A quarterly journal is a benefit of membership.

### College of the Redwoods
542 N. Main St.
Fort Bragg, CA 94537
James Krenov, Director of Wood Program

### Mendocino Woodworkers Association
Box 95
Caspar, CA 93420

Enclose a stamped, self-addressed envelope and information on galleries and woodworkers clustered in Mendocino and Northern California will be provided.

### National Wood Carvers Association
7424 Miami Avenue
Cincinnati, OH 45243
513-561-9051

### Rochester Institute of Technology
School for American Craftsmen
Douglas Sigler, Woodworking Program Director
One Lomb Memorial Dr.
Rochester, NY 14623

### Society of Furniture Artists
Box 416 Kendall Square
Cambridge, MA 02142
Alphonse Mattia, president

### Swain School of Design
388 County St.
New Bedford, MA 02740

### Wendell Castle Workshop
18 Maple St.
Scottsville, NY 14546

### Wharton Esherick Museum
Box 595
Paoli, PA 19301

Now a museum, Esherick's house and studio is open by appointment.

### Woodworking Association of North America
Box 706, Route 3
Plymouth, NH 03264
615-433-6804

# INDEX